(Re)reading Ruth

(Re)reading Ruth

William A. Tooman
with Marian Kelsey

CASCADE *Books* · Eugene, Oregon

(RE)READING RUTH

Copyright © 2022 William A. Tooman. All rights reserved. Except for brief quotations in critical publications or reviews, no part of this book may be reproduced in any manner without prior written permission from the publisher. Write: Permissions, Wipf and Stock Publishers, 199 W. 8th Ave., Suite 3, Eugene, OR 97401.

Cascade Books
An Imprint of Wipf and Stock Publishers
199 W. 8th Ave., Suite 3
Eugene, OR 97401

www.wipfandstock.com

PAPERBACK ISBN: 978-1-7252-6271-3
HARDCOVER ISBN: 978-1-7252-6270-6
EBOOK ISBN: 978-1-7252-6272-0

Cataloguing-in-Publication data:

Names: Tooman, William A. [author]. | Kelsey, Marian [author]

Title: (Re)reading Ruth / William Tooman, with Marian Kelsey.

Description: Eugene, OR: Cascade Books, 2022 | Includes bibliographical references and index.

Identifiers: ISBN 978-1-7252-6271-3 (paperback) | ISBN 978-1-7252-6270-6 (hardcover) | ISBN 978-1-7252-6272-0 (ebook)

Subjects: LCSH: Bible—Ruth—Criticism, interpretation, etc. | Ruth (Biblical figure) | Bible—Ruth—Commentaries

Classification: BS1315.52 T66 2022 (print) | BS1315.52 (ebook)

02/28/22

for Liam & Cole

Contents

Acknowledgements | ix

Abbreviations and Symbols | xi

Introduction | xv
    What This Book Does and How It Does It | xv
    What This Book Does Not Do and Why | xvii
    God, Scripture, and Hebrew | xxi

1. Reading Ruth | 1
    Three Distinctives of Biblical Hebrew Narrative | 2
    Structure | 9

2. Act 1 ~ Ruth 1:1–22 | 21
    Prologue (1:1–5): From Israel to Moab; from Life to Death | 22
    Excursus 1. The significance of names | 26
    Act 1. Naomi's Ill-fortune (1:6–22) | 30
    Excursus 2: Ḥesed | 33
    Excursus 3. Did Ruth Convert? | 45
    Excursus 4. Naomi and Job | 51

3. Act 2 ~ Ruth 2:1–23 | 56
    Excursus 5. Ruth and Hannah | 63
    Excursus 6. Ruth and Judas | 69
    Excursus 7. Boaz and the Levite | 71
    Excursus 8. Ruth at the Well | 81

4. Act 3 ~ **Ruth 3:1–18** | 90
    Excursus 9. Ruth, Lot, and Lot's Daughters | 97
    Excursus 10. Boaz, Judah, and Tamar | 102
    Excursus 11. Ruth & Boaz, the Strong Woman & Strong Man | 109
    Excursus 12. Act 2 ∥ Act 3 | 117

5. Act 4 ~ **Ruth 4:1–22** | 120
    Epilogue (4:18–22): From Death to Life, from Poverty to Glory | 129
    Excursus 13. Levirate Law & Land Redemption | 131
    Excursus 14. Act 1 ∥ Act 4 | 139

Concluding Postscript: Reading Biblical Literature | 145

Appendix: Ruth in the Jewish and Christian Bibles | 147
    Ruth in the Jewish Bible | 147
    Ruth in Christian Bibles | 149

Bibliography | 153
Author Index | 161
Ancient Document Index | 165

Acknowledgements

I have been teaching the Book of Ruth to my Hebrew students for over a decade now. It's the first biblical book that they read from front to back. Many of the observations in this little book were first suggested by them or only became clear to me because of their questions. They are too numerous to name, but they each have my gratitude. Several students (past and present) and my nephew read chapters along the way. Sam, Sheree, Jonny, Cameron, Tobias, Andy, and Katie you have my thanks. Your questions and suggestions for clarification have made this book much better than it would have been otherwise. Thanks are also due to Robin Parry. This book came about due to a chance conversation with Robin at some conference or other. Thank you, Robin. This was probably the most fun I have had writing a book, so you can be assured that my thanks are not just obligatory. The greatest thanks are due to Marian Kelsey who has been my principal conversation partner. Her keen eye for faulty arguments, underappreciated facts, and biblical witticisms has made this a much better book.

—WT

My first in-depth encounter with the Book of Ruth was in Bill's seminar, where we read through the Hebrew and together explored the numerous inner-biblical connections in the text. It turned out to be a much darker, and more absorbing, tale than the pastoral idyll I had previously

Acknowledgements

assumed it to be. As with the Book of Jonah, I credit (or blame?) Bill for an interest that has since swallowed up many a delightful hour of mine. My thanks also go to Karo, without whom the last few years of research would not have been possible.

—MK

Abbreviations and Symbols

‖	"parallel"; indicates that two biblical texts or specific elements from two texts are presented as alike in some way (e.g., 1 Sam 1:18 ‖ Ruth 2:13; Ruth ‖ Hannah; water jar ‖ well)
AB	Anchor Bible
ABRL	Anchor Bible Reference Library
AJSN	*Association for Jewish Studies Newsletter*
AT	*Acta Theologica*
BI	*Biblical Interpretation*
BKAT	Biblischer Kommentar zum Alten Testament
BT	*The Bible Translator*
BZ	*Biblische Zeitschrift*
BZAW	Beihefte zur Zeitschrift für die alttestamentliche Wissenschaft
CBQ	*Catholic Biblical Quarterly*
CC	Continental Commentary
CI	*Critical Inquiry*
EKK	Evangelisch-katholischer Kommentar zum Neuen Testament
EstBib	*Estudios bíblicos*
FAT	Forschungen zum Alten Testament

Abbreviations and Symbols

FBBS	Facet Books Biblical Series
GCAJS	Gratz College Annual of Jewish Studies
GKC	Wilhelm Gesenius, *Hebrew Grammar*, edited and enlarged by E. Kautzsch, 2nd English ed., revised by A. E. Cowley. Oxford: Clarendon, 1910.
HAR	Harvard Annual Review
HS	Hebrew Studies
HTKAT	Herders Theologischer Kommentar zum Alten Testament
HUCA	Hebrew Union College Annual
Ibn Ezra	Abraham ben Meir ibn Ezra was a twelfth-century Jew from Spain (Al-Andalus) who wrote commentaries on much of the Hebrew Bible (born c. 1090; died c. 1165).
ILR	Israel Law Review
JAJ	Journal of Ancient Judaism
JBL	Journal of Biblical Literature
JBQ	Jewish Bible Quarterly
JLA	The Jewish Law Annual
JM	Paul Joüon and Tamitsu Muraoka, *A Grammar of Biblical Hebrew*, 2nd ed. Subsidia biblica 27. Rome: Pontifical Biblical Institute Press, 2006.
JNSL	Journal of Northwest Semitic Languages
JQR	Jewish Quarterly Review
JR	Juridical Review
JSem	Journal for Semitics
JSOT	Journal for the Study of the Old Testament
JSOTSup	Journal for the Study of the Old Testament Supplement Series
JTT	Journal of Translation and Textlinguistics
LHBOTS	Library of Hebrew Bible/Old Testament Studies
LXX	The label given to pre-Christian Jewish translations of the Hebrew Bible into Greek

Abbreviations and Symbols

ML	Mikra Leyisraèl: A Bible Commentary for Israel
Naḥmanides	Rabbi Moses ben Nahman (also called by the acronym "Ramban") was a thirteenth-century Jew from Spain who wrote commentaries on the Torah (born 1194, died 1270).
NICOT	New International Commentary on the Old Testament
NJPS	New Jewish Publication Society Tanak Translation
NRSV	New Revised Standard Version
NSKAT	Neuer Stuttgarter Kommentar/Altes Testament
OBT	Overtures to Biblical Theology
OTE	*Old Testament Essays*
OTL	Old Testament Library
PMLA	*Publications of the Modern Language Association of America*
Rashi	Rabbi Shlomo ben Yitzhaq (the name "Rashi" is an acronym), a eleventh-century Jew from France who wrote commentaries on the whole Hebrew Bible (born 1040, died 1105).
RB	*Revue biblique*
SB	Subsidia biblica
SBET	*The Scottish Bulletin of Evangelical Theology*
SJOT	*Scandinavian Journal of the Old Testament*
ST	*Studia Theologica*
SWR	Studies in Women and Religion
TB	*Tyndale Bulletin*
TDOT	*Theological Dictionary of the Old Testament*. 14 vols. Edited by G. Johannes Botterweck and Helmer Ringgren. Translated by Geoffrey W. Bromiley et al. Grand Rapids: Eerdmans, 1974–2004.
Tradition	*Tradition: A Journal of Orthodox Jewish Thought*
USQR	*Union Seminary Quarterly Review*
VT	*Vetus Testamentum*
VTSup	Vetus Testamentum Supplement Series

Abbreviations and Symbols

WBC	Word Biblical Commentary
WTJ	*Westminster Theological Journal*
ZABR	*Zeitschrift für altorientalische und biblische Rechtsgeschichte*
ZAW	*Zeitschrift für die alttestamentliche Wissenschaft*
ZBK	Züricher Bibelkommentare

Translations of biblical texts are my own unless indicated otherwise.

Introduction

THIS IS BOOK ABOUT a book. More accurately, it is a book about how to read a book, the ancient Hebrew book of Ruth. People have been writing commentaries and guides to biblical books since at least the turn of the first millennium, so this little book is part of a very long tradition.[1] In fact, anyone reading this paragraph has probably already found half a dozen similar works on Ruth currently on the market. So, why read this one?

What This Book Does and How It Does It

This book is not like others. Like most books of this kind, this one will work through the chapters of Ruth one by one, explaining its parts and building up the meaning. I will also spend some time thinking about the ideas presented in Ruth, its themes and topics. Two things make it different though. A part of my goal is to help readers better understand ancient Hebrew literature on its own terms. I will argue that ancient Hebrew narratives do not work like modern narratives, and particularly not like novels. They operate by a unique set of rules, which require a different set of reading skills, skills that must be learned. One aim of this book is to help readers see those differences more clearly, so that they can begin to read differently. This points to the second way that this book is unique. Ruth engages, even dialogues, with many other biblical books, books like Deuteronomy,

---

1. Among the oldest are the *pesharim*, ancient biblical commentaries found among the Dead Sea Scrolls.

Introduction

Judges, Samuel, Job, Proverbs, and (especially) Genesis. Some books outside of the Jewish scriptures engage with Ruth too, books like Tobit and the Gospels. Every introduction to Ruth discusses some of these relationships. In this one, though, Ruth's literary connections are a central focus. How Ruth engages with other scriptural books and how they engage with Ruth will be explored in detail. I do this, not because it is fun (and it is fun), but because I am persuaded that this is essential to understanding Ruth as a work of literary art, and that is what Ruth is: a work of art.[2]

In the first chapter, I describe some of the distinctive features of biblical narratives in general and Ruth in particular. This chapter is important orientation to Ruth as whole—its design, literary features, and how its parts relate to one another. In the following chapters, I will work though Ruth from front to back, paragraph by paragraph and chapter by chapter. Each chapter of Ruth presents its own mini-plot, subordinate to the main plot. This part of the book is about *discovery*. In it, I try to replicate the reading experience. I will do my best to let the story unfold in the order and time that its writers chose. As much as possible, I will avoid revealing the outcome of a sub-plot or a theme before it reaches its natural crescendo. Nor will I divulge how characters or themes change. Instead, I will let them develop according to their natural courses.

There are many topics and issues to be discussed, though, that cannot be constrained by the storyline. These require a wide-angle lens, a perspective on the book of Ruth as a whole. Some of these are topical like "the significance of names" or "the meaning of *ḥesed*" ("loving kindness" or "steadfast love" in many translations). Others are inter-textual. Ruth, as I will explain in chapter 1, is filled with analogies: analogies between its characters and other biblical characters; analogies between its events and other biblical events. These can only be discussed by comparing a fully developed character or story to another character or story. So, explaining these analogies often requires a wider lens too. All these wide-angle discussions will appear as little self-contained essays called *excurses*. The *excurses* will interrupt the *discovery* reading, but to avoid disrupting it excessively, I have placed them between paragraphs or scenes in the storyline. Nonetheless, the excurses assume that the reader is familiar with the whole story, so it is important to have read Ruth before *(Re)reading Ruth*. If you have not read

---

2. Scholars are sharply divided on the question of the Bible's literary credentials. For a little window onto this controversy, see the dispute between Kugel, "Bible and Literary Criticism," 217–36 and Berlin, "Bible as Literature," 323–37.

Introduction

the book of Ruth before, or not for a while, I would encourage you to read it through at least once or twice before continuing to chapter 1 of this book.

What This Book Does Not Do and Why

This book does not concern itself with questions of history and historical background. I will not take a position on the book's date, nor will I discuss the historicity of its events, characters, or cultural conventions. There are several reasons for this choice.[3] As Frederic Bush rightly observes, the identity of the book's writers is shrouded in mystery.

> Any attempt to discuss in any concrete manner the authorship of the book of Ruth is an exercise in futility for the simple fact that, like the rest of biblical narrative (except perhaps for the post-exilic "memoirs" of Ezra and Nehemiah), not only is the book anonymous, but it gives not the slightest hint, directly or indirectly, of the identity of the writer as a historical person.[4]

Scholars, then, must deduce the book's date from other evidence. But scholars do not agree on the value of the evidence that is available, which results in polarized positions. One view promotes the belief that the book is a product of Iron Age Israel from between c. 950 BCE and 700 BCE, during the time of the monarchy. The other sees the book as a product of the Persian period. Most who hold the latter view place it in the time of the

---

3. Despite this choice, I would not want anyone to think that I do not consider dating to be important, providing that it can be done accurately. The ways that dating can affect one's reading of the book are not trivial. When bringing historical information to bear on a book—cognate literature from surrounding cultures, ancient legal practices, ancient Near Eastern religious practices and traditions, and so forth—one must know which times and cultures this information could reasonably be drawn from. Which texts, institution, laws, practices, or beliefs did not exist yet when Ruth was written? Which are too far removed in time or location for us to expect that the writers of Ruth to be familiar with them? The cultures with which ancient Israel had significant interaction changed through the centuries, dramatically so between the tenth and fifth centuries BCE. To which of those cultures should we be looking?

4. *Ruth, Esther*, 17. In an intriguing thought-experiment, S. D. Goitein compared biblical literature to the types of songs and poetry produced by Yemenite Jewish women. Though kept in social positions of low power, Yemenite women produced an immense volume of songs, prayers, poems, and laments, and within that musical-literary context they were permitted to be critical of men in power. Goitein found many salient parallels between the types and content of material produced by Yemenite women and select parts of the Bible, but none for prose narratives like Ruth or Esther ("Women as Creators," 1–33).

Introduction

post-exilic restoration when questions of inter-marriage were central to community identity (c. 525–400 BCE), as one can observe in the books of Ezra and Nehemiah. The two positions are divided over two issues: the accuracy of linguistic dating (a tool used to date the Hebrew of a biblical text), and the evidence suggested by the book's contents.[5]

Advocates of linguistic dating believe that biblical books and parts of books can be dated precisely based on features of their language: word-choice, word-usage, syntax, distribution of verbal forms, and so forth. Its detractors reject the scientific credentials of linguistic dating. Illustrating this latter point and despite its claims of objectivity and precision, scholars who date the book of Ruth based on linguistic features are divided about the results. Some claim that the book's language is what is called "Classical Hebrew," so they date it to the time of the monarchy. Others claim that the book's language includes later elements, so they date it to the Persian period.[6] Contradictions like this (which are not uncommon in this sub-discipline) have led me to conclude that linguistic dating is not yet a sufficiently sophisticated or accurate tool for dating biblical texts.

If Ruth cannot be dated based on its language, does it provide clues to its date from its content? Many scholars point to the importance of David, notably in 4:16–22, to suggest a date from the time of the monarchy. Some of these scholars have suggested that Ruth was included to defend David's Moabite roots. Others argue that it is an oblique defence of his right to the throne, or, more specifically, the right of the Davidic monarchs to rule all twelve tribes.[7] The difficulty with this approach is that the topic of the rights and responsibilities of the Davidic monarchy is a perpetual feature of biblical literature. Even texts from the Neo-Babylonian and Persian periods—after the kingdom of Judah came to an end and the heirs of David's throne were taken into exile—continue to discuss David and the future of his line (for example, Jer 33:14–26; Ezek 34:23–31; Zech 12:7–14). Looking past David, other features of the book could be taken to refer to the Israelite experience after the exile. Intermarriage is the most obvious of these features, but it is not the only one. Christian Frevel, for example, has argued that the

---

5. Incidentally, there is no camp that dates the book to the period in which Ruth is set, the days of the Judges before the monarchy.

6. For different positions on the linguistic dating of Ruth see, for example, Campbell, *Ruth*, 26–28 (monarchy); Hubbard, *Ruth*, 23 (monarchy); Zevit, "Dating Ruth," 574–600 (Persian); Rofé, *Introduction*, 100–109 (Persian); Sasson, *Ruth*, 240–52 (unknowable); Holmstedt, *Ruth*, 17–39 (possibly early Persian, but ultimately unknowable).

7. Gow, *Book of Ruth*, 183–210, especially 204–5; Sasson, *Ruth*, 250–52.

Introduction

tale of a homeward journey and rebuilding a family's hopes and fortunes is well suited to the Persian period, when the Babylonian exile ended.[8] But the story of the Hebrew people frequently addresses questions of intermarriage (Gen 24, 26–28, 34; Exod 34; Num 12; Deut 7; Josh 23; Judg 2; 2 Sam 11–12; 1 Kgs 11; Jer 29; Mal 2; etc.), and the return from exile did not happen all at once, in one historical moment, as it were. It spanned centuries. In fact, the hope for return remains a part of the Jewish experience and has been at least from the days of the Neo-Babylonians until today. The contents of the book, then, do not clarify the book's date either. So, it remains unknown, and there is no definitive evidence (yet) that can clarify the issue.

There is a second reason that I will not attempt to relate the book to the time of the monarchy or the Persian period. This has to do with my understanding of the composition history of the Hebrew Bible generally and Ruth in particular. No one disputes that the books of the Hebrew Bible evolved over time. The only dispute is how extensive this evolution might have been. Did the scribes who passed the book down through the years, copying and recopying, limit themselves to updating archaic terms, correcting grammatical errors, and adding the occasional marginal notation? Or was their work more extensive, reworking the story, much as one might rewrite an essay several times before submitting it for a grade? As we can see from existing manuscripts and translations of Ruth from antiquity, both impulses were at work. Some scribes expanded and adapted the book quite freely.[9] Other scribes limited their activity to adding the occasional word, correcting grammatical infelicities or misspellings, and other small adjustments. In truth, more is unknown about Ruth's literary history than is known. The oldest manuscripts of the book are from the first century BCE, but those manuscripts are fragmentary.[10] The oldest *complete* copy of the book that we possess is from the fourth century CE.[11] In other words, even by the most conservative estimate (based on a Persian period date for the book) Ruth was copied and updated for at least seven centuries before the oldest complete copy that we possess was penned. If all the scribes who

---

8. Frevel, *Das Buch Rut*, 34. Dommershausen points out the dense repetition of the word "return," *šwb*, at the beginning of the story (1:6, 7, 8, 10, 11, 12, 15 [2x], 16, 21, 22 [2x]); "Leitwortstil," 394–407.

9. As we see in the Aramaic translations of Ruth, for example.

10. The oldest existing manuscripts are 2QRuth^a, and 4QRuth^a from the Dead Sea Scrolls. 2QRuth^a only includes parts of 2:13—3:8 and 4:3–4 and 4QRuth^a parts of 1:1–12.

11. The Greek translation of the Ruth from *Codex Vaticanus* (LXX^B) is the oldest complete copy of the book.

Introduction

touched the book in those centuries only made small adjustments, they would still accumulate. Any existing manuscript must contain many dozens of differences from the earliest drafts of the book. If the adjustments were more substantial, the differences would be too. In short, many people from many times had a hand in creating the book of Ruth. I cannot see how the book of Ruth has a singular date at all. We can date specific manuscripts of Ruth, to be sure, but the object that we think of "the book" is, in fact, a constantly changing entity that does not belong to a single time or place.

What this little book, *(Re)reading Ruth*, analyses and describes is one of the oldest Hebrew manuscripts of Ruth, a manuscript that goes by the name *Codex Leningradensis* or by the badge B19a. *Codex Leningradensis* was penned by medieval Jewish scribes called the masoretes in 1008 CE. This manuscript is the basis of virtually all English translations of the Hebrew Bible that have been produced since the middle of the twentieth century, so readers can be assured that I am describing the same book of Ruth that they are reading in English. One of the main advantages of focusing on *Codex Leningradensis* is that the Codex is a collection. It includes the whole Hebrew Bible, and the Book of Ruth has been integrated with this larger collection. Considered this way, Ruth is not an independent short story, untethered from the rest of the Hebrew Bible. It is part of a larger work—the Hebrew Bible—and it engages with that larger work. This, then, is the context in which we will read Ruth. Our focus is not the story of Ruth as it circulated in the context of an ancient culture; our focus is the Book of Ruth as it is set in the context of the Hebrew Bible.

There is one final reason why traditional historical questions will not be considered here. Most books on Ruth work through a common set of topics: date, authorship, language, canonicity, genre, historical context, and theology.[12] Most of these are historical topics, and most of them have little to do with the practical work of reading and understanding the story. In fact, historical questions and historical methodologies dominate in biblical studies today. In many other fields, literary studies sit alongside historical studies, the two approaches contesting and correcting one another. There is a large and ever-growing body of historical research on the works of Shakespeare, Dante, and the Homeric epics, for example. This scholarship

---

12. "Historical context" includes a set of common topics, too, like ancient Israelite family and kinship structures, widowhood, legal practices (especially, intermarriage, *levirate* marriage, and inheritance), Israelite-Moabite interactions, and the book's literary precursors in the ancient Near East. Excellent summaries of most of these topics (and more) can be found in Eskenazi and Frymer-Kensky, *Ruth*, xv–lv.

Introduction

is balanced by an equally large body of scholarship concentrated on the literary and artistic qualities of those works. This happy condition is less of a reality in biblical studies. In biblical studies, literary reading—reading books as completed works, bracketing questions of origin and evolution to focus on artistic features—is sometimes acknowledged as a necessary first step in the process of analysis, but the proper work of scholarship is historical and begins where literary reading ends.[13] In my view, this attitude has the effect of impoverishing both approaches. The reasoning and conclusions of historical scholarship should be corrected or nuanced by considering the results of literary research and vice versa. We will see a good example of the mutually correcting quality of the two approaches in Ruth 4 when I discuss its relationship to *levirate* law. Scholars working from a historical point of view disagree sharply about whether Boaz and his rival redeemer are adhering to some form of Iron Age law or custom. I will argue that they are not, but the evidence for that judgement will be based on literary observations. In this case, a literary argument supports one historical judgement against another, evidence that historically oriented scholars should be able to weigh up when making their own decisions. Viewed this way, *(Re)reading Ruth* is something of a corrective. It focuses somewhat narrow-mindedly on the literary qualities of Ruth, on Ruth as a work of art.[14] It can (and should) be set alongside more historically focused introductions. The two—being in creative tension—can correct and nuance one another's conclusions. From this point of view, if I were to flatter myself, I might call this a work of protest literature. In truth, it is a modest attempt to add a bit more width to the literature on Ruth.

God, Scripture, and Hebrew

Some of the language used in this book may be unfamiliar. To avoid any misunderstanding, it is important to explain the titles that I will use for God, for the Jewish and Christian scriptures, and explain a little bit about how I will refer to Hebrew words and phrases.

---

13. In my own experience, this point of view is most evident at research universities, as opposed to liberal arts colleges or religious institutions in higher education.

14. The two commentaries that pursue Ruth's literary qualities most rigorously (and not at the expense of historical research) are those of Fischer, *Rut*, and Zakovitch, *Ruth* (Hebrew).

Introduction

God. In most English Bibles, God's personal name is rendered as Lord (all capital letters). English "Lord" (lower case) represents the Hebrew title *ʾădōnāy*, which means "lord" or "master." English "God" represents Hebrew *ʾĕlōhîm*, which can mean either "God" or "gods." (The context determines which is correct.) A less common title for God, *Šadday*, appears in Ruth 1:20–21, which traditionally has been translated as "Almighty." I will follow the practice of translating *ʾădōnāy* as "lord" and *ʾĕlōhîm* as "God." The proper translation of *Šadday* is disputed, and I will render it as *Shadday* (pronounced shah-die).[15] For the divine name, called the tetragrammaton, I will use *Yhwh*, which is an English equivalent of the four Hebrew letters of God's name.

Scripture. With respect to the Jewish and Christian scriptures, I will not use the phrase *Old Testament*, which is a Christian label. In Judaism, these books are just *Bible*, but I will not use that term either. Instead, I will refer to the scriptures shared by Judaism and Christianity as the *Hebrew Bible*, a neutral title in common use among scholars. I will refer to the various Christian canons as *Christian Bible*.

Hebrew. Most of this book's readers will be reading Ruth in English. There are many occasions, though, when a bit of Hebrew understanding is needed. For example, English has a huge vocabulary, one of the largest among spoken languages today. The Oxford English Dictionary has over 250,000 headwords alone.[16] The Hebrew Bible, though, has a vocabulary of less than 7,000 words. (The exact number depends on how one counts them.) This means that for each Hebrew word there are usually several English words that could be a suitable equivalent.[17] In fact, biblical scholars spill quite a lot of ink arguing over the most suitable English translations for Hebrew words employed in specific contexts. So, if an important Hebrew word appears multiple times in Ruth, and if it is not translated with the

---

15. For discussion of *Shadday* and its possible meanings, see Niehr and Steins, "שׁדי," *TDOT* 14: 418–46.

16. A headword is a word that one looks up in the dictionary, like "hedgehog." Derivatives, like the plural "hedgehogs," appear under the headword.

17. We will see an example in *Excursus 2*, where one English version of the Bible translates a particular Hebrew word in twenty-one different ways. The opposite is rarely true. It is rare that Hebrew has multiple words for which English has a single equivalent. One of these exceptions is "lion." In English (excluding its Latin zoological classification) there is only one word for referring to a lion, namely "lion." In biblical Hebrew, though, there are seven words for "lion" (*ʾărî*, *ʾaryēh*, *lĕbî*, *kĕpîr*, *gûr*, *layiš*, *šaḥal*). It is not clear which of these are synonyms and which refer to different kinds of lion, distinguished by age, maybe, or by appearance.

Introduction

same English word in each case, we cannot spot the repetition in English. In a case like this, the translation has obscured something that might well be worth observing. For reasons like this, I will frequently provide an English *transliteration* of a Hebrew word or phrase. A transliteration is just a phonetic representation of the Hebrew word. For example, when discussing the word חֶסֶד, I will sometimes represent it, not with an English *translation*, but with its *transliteration*: ḥesed. (The opening letter ḥ is a guttural-*h*, pronounced similarly to the -*ch* on the Scots word lo*ch*, and the accent is on the first letter of the word.)

In addition, most Hebrew words are based on a root word made up of three-consonant. Specific words are created from root words by adding vowels, prefixes, and suffixes.[18] Prefixes and suffixes we have in English too, but the idea that vowels are not a part of the root is quite different from English. When Hebrew writers choose to repeat a word for literary effect, that word may not be identical in each case. The specific grammatical role it plays will require that it has certain vowels, prefixes, or suffixes. The reason that I am mentioning this fact is that sometimes I will present Hebrew words in full transliteration, as they sound in Hebrew, like: *hašōpṭîm*, "the judges." On other occasions, to make things easier for the reader, I will present just the root word, without the vowels, prefixes, or suffixes, like *špṭ*, the root that "judges" is formed from.

---

18. These adaptations signal things like person (1st person, 2nd person, or 3rd person), number (singular or plural), gender (masculine, feminine, or common), and other features that go by titles like "transitivity," "fientivity," "causativity," and so on. It is not important to unpack these categories. It is enough to know that the root *dbr*, for example, can be adapted to form the noun *dābār* ('word" or "thing"), or the verb *dābartî* ("I spoke"), or a host of other possibilities.

CHAPTER 1

Reading Ruth

WHY WOULD ANYONE NEED help reading Ruth? Compared with long, intricate narratives like *Paradise Lost*, *War and Peace*, or *Ulysses*, Ruth is very short and very easy to read. In fact, Ruth is sometimes characterized as the simplest of biblical stories. Armstrong Black thought it "unadorned and homely."[1] Ronald Hals found it difficult to praise Ruth's "simple style" and settled on indistinct adjectives like "warm" and "straightforward."[2] Thomas Paine believed it to be so artless as to be stupid. Ruth is "an idle, bungling story, foolishly told, nobody knows by whom, about a strolling country-girl, creeping slyly to bed with her cousin Boaz."[3] But, is Paine's caricature accurate? Is Black's or Hals'?

What I will attempt to show in this chapter is that Ruth is quite simple in some ways and highly complex in others. It is simple enough that any reader can understand the basic contours of the story: the characters' personalities, the problems they must overcome, and many of the twists and turns along the road from crisis to resolution. But this, I will argue, is a flat representation of the story, a mere sketch, reflecting only a rudimentary understanding of the story's intricacies. Ruth, like all biblical narratives, operates by a different set of conventions ("rules" if you like) from modern narratives. If we want to arrive at a better understanding of its ideas and

---

1. Black, *Ruth*, 7.
2. Hals, *Theology*, xi and 1.
3. Paine goes on to declare it one of the "best books in the Bible" because "it is free from murder and rapine." *The Age of Reason*, quoted by Sasson, *Ruth*, 196.

artistry, we will need to learn to appreciate these rules. Our first step, then, is to recognize how biblical storytelling differs from modern storytelling and to become aware of the ways that those conventions can extend and develop our comprehension and our pleasure.

Three Distinctives of Biblical Hebrew Narrative

Terseness & Density

One of the most obvious features of biblical narrative, when compared with modern literature, is its terseness. All the little details that give authenticity to a novel—descriptions of settings, weather, clothing, colors, meals, facial expressions—are rarely mentioned in the Bible. At best, we might be told that an encounter happed on a street or in the country, or we might be given a character's name. Physical features of characters are almost never described. Whether indoors or outdoors, settings are seldom described. Bare events and one-to-one dialogue are the stuff of biblical storytelling. The biblical writers do not attempt to make their stories seem more realistic by filling them up with detail.[4] There are small exceptions to this rule, to be sure. We know that Ehud was left-handed, that Abraham fed roast goat to three angels, and that Joseph was a beautiful man. In all these cases, though, no further details are offered that would add realism and authenticity to the story world. Even these sparse details are only provided because they introduce or reveal something essential about the characters and events in the story. This, in a nutshell, is what accounts for biblical terseness. *Biblical writers only provide readers with essentials.*[5]

This is also what makes biblical literature difficult to read and assimilate. It is *dense*. Events occur quickly, one after another in staccato. Dialogue is bereft of all the conversational cul-de-sacs and start-and-stop elements that we experience every day in nearly every conversation. In the Bible, almost every sentence is a topic-sentence. But biblical stories are not just dense in their contents and quick in their pacing. Poetic elements also

---

4. In a famous essay by Eric Auerbach, in which he compares the terseness of biblical storytelling with Homer's verboseness, he says this about the binding-of-Isaac story in Genesis 22: "In this atmosphere it is unthinkable that an implement, a landscape through which the travellers passed, the serving men, or the ass, should be described, . . . they do not even admit an adjective: they are serving men, ass, wood, and knife, nothing else." *Mimesis*, 9.

5. Fishbane, *Text and Texture*, xii–xiv; Auerbach, *Mimesis*, 11.

occur more densely in biblical literature than in modern prose. "Poetics" is the literary term for the forms, conventions, and aesthetics of literature. It refers to features like cadence, figures of speech, imagery, characterization, repetition, plot structure, and wordplay. In short, it refers to all the things that make literature artistic, everything additional to the meaning of the words. As an example, observe this (seemingly) unadorned scene between Ruth and Boaz in 3:14–15:

> **14** So she lay down at his feet until dawn. She got up and, before one person could recognize another, he thought, "Let it not be known that the woman came to the threshing floor." **15** And he said, "Take the cloak on you, and hold it firmly." So, she held it, while he measured out six barley. And he put it on her, and he came to the town.

Consider, first, the order of its contents. When we arrange the first clauses of verse 14 in the following way, we see more easily that the contents are patterned:

> And she lay down at his feet until morning,
> and she arose before one person could recognize another.

"Lay down" and "arose" are opposites. "Until . . ." and "before . . ." are both expressions of time. "Morning" and "before one person could recognize another" are partial synonyms, the second specifying the time of morning. The two clauses have similar content, expressed in a similar order, which gives the verse symmetry.

Verses 14b–15 are dense with repetition:

> he thought, "Let it not be known that the woman *came* to the threshing floor." And he said, "Take the cloak *on you*, and *hold it* firmly." So, she *held it*, while he measured out six barley. And he put it *on her*, and he *came* to the town.

In Hebrew, these clauses roll off the tongue in a way that they do not in English translation. Repetition of words and sounds in Hebrew creates rhythm. The two opening sentences have a similar syntactic structure: "and he said . . . that . . ." The verbs "hold it" and "held it" give cohesion to juxtaposed clauses. "On you" (*ʿālayēk*) and "on her" (*ʿāleyhā*) are alliterative. The opening and closing sentences deploy variations of the word "came" (*bwʾ*). Finally, notice the order of the repeated words, which create a mirror pattern *came–on you–hold it . . . held it–on her–came*.

(Re)reading Ruth

The rhythms and patterns created by repeated sounds and words are not the only poetic devices at work in this little paragraph. It is also replete with wordplay that exploits the reader's curiosity about what happened at the threshing floor during the night. Did Ruth come for sex? Did Ruth and Boaz have sex? What do "uncover the feet" and "spread your cloak over your servant" mean anyway? We will deal with those questions when we reach Ruth 3. What I want to observe here is that the writers seem to be aware that the previous night's events have presented something of a puzzle to the reader, and they cannot resist the opportunity to have some fun with that uncertainty. Three times in these two verses the writers employ words that are used in other contexts for sex—"lay down," "come to," and "know"[6]—to say nothing of "foot," which is a common enough euphemism in the Hebrew Bible.[7] And yet, these acts of wordplay do not help to answer our questions. That is not their purpose. They don't tell us what happened. They gesture at the questions we are asking, amplify our curiosity, and impel us to seek answers.

There are many additional poetic elements of these verses, their allusions and metaphors, point of view, and foreshadowing, for example. But the purpose of this little book is not to analyze each verse in that kind of fine-grained manner. Rather, I have offered these observations about Ruth 3:14–15 to illustrate an essential point about Biblical Hebrew narrative. *It is not like modern prose fiction.* Even a short and simple book like Ruth is dense with poetic elements that permeate the fabric of the story from front to back, more so than most English prose literature. No part of the Hebrew Bible, not even Ruth, can be appreciated by casual reading.

Repetition

Considering the terseness of biblical prose, it is ironic that it is also quite repetitive. Everything from individual sounds and words to whole stories, poems, oracles, and books are repeated in the Hebrew Bible. English prose literature has a strong disinclination for repetition, which is labelled

---

6. "Lay down," *šākab*: Gen 19:33, 35; 30:15, 16; Exod 22:15; Lev 15:33; Deut 22:22; 1 Sam 2:22; 2 Sam 13:14, etc. "Come into," *bô'* : Gen 6:4; 16:2; 30:3; 38:8, 9; Deut 22:13; Josh 15:18; Judg 1:14; 15:1; 16:1; 2 Sam 12:24; 16:21; 20:3; etc. "Know," *yâda'* : Gen 4:1, 17, 25; 24:16; 38:26; Num 31:17, 18, 35; Judg 11:39; 21:11; 1 Sam 1:19; Judg 19:22, 25; 1 Kgs 1:4; etc.

7. For example, Deut 28:57; Judg 3:24; 1 Sam 24:4; 2 Kgs 18:27; Isa 7:20; 36:12; Ezek 16:25.

Reading Ruth

"redundancy" and dismissed. In the Hebrew Bible though, no literary device does more work to shape the literature.

As we have already seen in 3:14–15, repetition is used to divide texts into their constituent parts (lines, paragraphs, stories, etc.), to connect the discrete segments, to thematize, to allude, and to accentuate. Those two verses are filled with repeated sounds and words that give structure and tempo to the language. Repetition operates in similar ways and in more complex ways when applied to a larger canvas. Take, for example, Ruth 1:6–22, which is the first Act in the story.[8] (Ruth 1:1–5 is a prologue, setting the scene and introducing the problem that must be resolved.) It opens with the line: "She arose, she and her daughters-in-law, and she returned from the country of Moab" (1:6a). It closes with: "Thus Naomi returned from the country of Moab; she returned with her daughter-in-law Ruth the Moabite" (1:22a). The repetition of "return," "country of Moab," and "daughter(s)-in-law" indicate that the Act has reached its resolution. They bring Naomi's initial action (departure) to a conclusion (arrival).[9] Within the Act, repetition also gives structure to the women's dialogue. For instance, the term "turn/return" (from the root *šûb*) occurs no less than twelve times in these seventeen verses (1:6, 7, 8, 10, 11, 12, 15 twice, 16, 21, and 22 twice) and each occurrence is necessary. Four occurrences, two at the opening and two at the closing, are used to help establish the parameters of the Act.[10] During their conversation, Naomi repeatedly tells her daughters-in-law to turn back, "each of you to her mother's house" (verse 8). She commands them to return home (1:8, 11, 12), but the two women refuse, repeating the word *return* in their rebuttal (1:10). After Orpah does depart, Naomi once again repeatedly commands Ruth to turn back (1:15), and Ruth refuses again, repeating the word *return* again (1:16). So, the term *return* is employed to give structure to all of 1:6–22, inscribing its boundaries and patterning the dialogue. But it does more than that. *Return* is one of the book's themes. This idea, the notion of *returning*, will be developed later in *Excursus 14*.

---

8. As a convenience, I use the term Act to describe the major parts of the book (capitalized for clarity). My use of this term does not suggest that Ruth was performed like a stage-play in antiquity. There is no historical evidence to suggest that it was.

9. The literary term for opening and closing a text or text-segment in a similar way is "ring composition," on which see Douglas, *Thinking in Circles*.

10. "She started out with her daughters-in-law to *return* ... they took the road to *return* to the land of Judah" (1:6–7). "Thus, Naomi *returned* from the country of Moab; she *returned* with her daughter-in-law Ruth the Moabite" (1:22).

(Re)reading Ruth

For the moment, I want to note that the (almost absurd) repetition of the word suggests that it is important.

In the Hebrew Bible, repetition is neither incidental nor accidental. It is not redundancy. It is a tool that the biblical writers employ continuously to craft their books into works of literature. Our modern reading habits do not serve us well in this respect. If we are to understand biblical literature according to its own conventions, we will have to acquire new habits of reading. We need to restrain our impulse to skip over repetition or dismiss it as superfluous. We need to be attentive to Ruth's many repetitions and be prepared to ask again and again what the function and significance of a repetition might be.[11]

Allusion & Analogy

There is a third way in which biblical narratives are fundamentally different from modern prose stories. Phrases, clauses, characters, events, conversations, and even complex plotlines can be crafted to resemble phrases, clauses, characters, events, conversations, and plotlines found elsewhere in the Hebrew Bible. When these resemblances are noticeable, when we are expected to recognize the other text or texts that use the same words or patterns, we label it "allusion." E. E. Kellett has a very simple and very helpful description of allusion. Describing a writer who crafts an allusion, he says:

> Here is a man who steals and boasts of his thefts: he covers his walls with paintings, and openly proclaims they are taken from a National Gallery. He is not like the Spartan boy who stole and gained glory if undetected: he desires to be detected, and deliberately leaves clues to guide his pursuers to their prey.[12]

Kellett's point is that we are supposed to observe allusions. We are supposed to pick up on the clues left by the writer that can lead us to the source text. We are supposed to do this because allusions *add* to the story. What is added might just be a bit of color, but it might be the significance of an action. It might even make a paragraph or storyline clear that is otherwise incomprehensible.

Allusions work by creating *analogies*. By reminding us of characters or objects or events in other stories or books they invite us to compare and

---

11. Sternberg, *Poetics*, 365–440.
12. Kellett, *Quotation and Allusion*, 3 (emphasis original).

contrast them. They force us to consider adjusting our understanding of the story we are reading.[13] Allusions are common enough in modern novels that we are all familiar with them. What makes biblical allusions unique is their omnipresence. Biblical writers allude all the time. They allude relentlessly. The reason for the robust use of allusion and analogy in biblical stories arises from something we have already discussed: terseness. Creating analogies is one of the principal ways that biblical writers add depth and dimension to their pithy stories, because analogies have the power to profoundly complicate the significance or the meaning or the power of any element in a story.

Now, many of the Hebrew Bible's allusions have small effects. They merely add detail or depth to something in the immediate context. For example, when Ruth makes her vow to Naomi in 1:16–18, her words echo Laban's speech to Jacob in Gen 31:43–50 (most notably in verses 43–44). We will talk about this allusion in the next chapter. My point here is that this allusion sets up a contrast between Ruth and Naomi, on the one hand, and Jacob and Laban, on the other. This contrast adds depth to our appreciation of the characters, but if overlooked we would not have missed out on something essential to the story. Allusions like this enrich the book and reward the knowledgeable and attentive reader. They might have a profound effect on our *appreciation* of the book, but their effect on our *understanding* is small.

Other allusions have more profound effects. They might alter our understanding of a whole chapter or even a whole book. They might permanently change our view of a series of events or a character. For example, when Boaz first speaks to Ruth, he tells her what he has heard about her and pronounces a blessing upon her (Ruth 2:11–12). As part of his blessing, he says "how you left your father and your mother and the land of your kindred and went to a people whom you did not know before." In doing so, he echoes words spoken by God to Abraham in Gen 12:1: "*Go* from *the land of your kindred* and from the house of *your father* to a land which I will show you." This, of course, raises important questions about Ruth's identity. By using words shared by God's blessing on Abraham in his blessing of Ruth, Boaz signals that she is like Abraham. In what way is this true? What is the

---

13. One phrase used to describe this phenomenon is *narrative analogy*. The following is a small sampling of the secondary literature on analogical allusions (alphabetically): Berman, *Narrative Analogy*; Beyer, *Hoffnung in Bethlehem*, 203–6; Garsiel, *First Book of Samuel*; Gordon, "David's Rise," 37–64; Grossman, "Dynamic Analogies," 394–414; Malamat, "The Danite Migration," 1–16; Michael, "The Achan/Achor Traditions," 730–60; Zakovitch, *"You Shall Tell Your Son."*

significance of relating Ruth, a gentile immigrant, to Abraham, the first Hebrew? Does the blessing depend upon the analogy in some way? Through the simple act of placing words from the past into Boaz's mouth the writers open new plotlines for development and pose questions that require resolution. They are developed and resolved by following the thread of the analogy as it evolves through the book and by coordinating this thread with observations drawn from the book's other analogies.

In biblical storytelling, allusions are like themes in that they are only rarely announced. More often than not, they must be puzzled out by careful reading. Though veiled, they are an organic part of a book's design and key to understanding its purposes. This does not mean that readers must somehow intuit them or are granted permission to posit whatever analogies they can imagine. Allusions, as we will see, are signaled in three major ways: (1) when the raw materials of the story—the names, places, objects, relationships, and events—correspond between two or more stories, (2) when distinctive words, phrases, and clauses are repeated from other stories, and (3) when texts share an identical plot-sequence.[14]

Reading for a story's analogies occurs in three steps. In the first step, the reader must be attentive to any elements of the story that (arguably anyway) serve to coordinate the story with another. In many cases, there will be a clear link like this between two stories, a link like a repeated name, an identical outcome, an evocative or scandalous moment, or a distinctive phrase that recalls another text. For example, in Ruth 4:11–12 the people at the city gate bless Ruth and Boaz's imminent union by comparing Ruth to Rachel and Leah, and Ruth and Boaz's new family to the household of Perez, child of Judah and Tamar. This is as explicit as allusion can be. Having made the initial link between elements (characters, in the case of Ruth 4:11–12), the reader must then discover how broad the analogy might be by searching the surrounding paragraphs, possibly the whole book, for additional links to the same context. These links may be more subtle, observable *only* after having made the initial connection.[15] In this way we learn whether

---

14. I should qualify here that stories can be inverted too; that is another species of analogy. Inversions, or mirror stories, reverse elements from two analogous stories. More precisely, a character and his or her actions are rendered as the *antithesis* of those in another story. Yair Zakovitch explores several examples of biblical mirror stories in: "Through the Looking Glass," 139–52.

15. The more obvious link is sometime called the "trigger" or "marker" and the more subtle connections called "confirming allusions." Compare Ben-Porat, "Literary Allusion," 105–28.

the analogy is limited to the initially identified items (like Ruth, Leah, and Rachel) or if it involves a larger constellation of related items, additional people and events from Ruth and the Jacob-story in our example. The third step is more difficult. It involves comparing and contrasting the analogous items. It explores what emerges from the analogy, what making the analogy adds to or changes in our understanding. How do we perceive Ruth differently once we discover she is analogous to Tamar? Does it reveal or resolve something about the book's themes or arguments? Does it tie Ruth into some larger complex of stories, continuing their narrative pathways?

Analogies are commonplace in both Jewish and Christian scriptures. Some are well-recognized, like the analogies constructed between the lives of Elijah and Moses, Saul and Gideon, John the Baptist and Elijah, and Jesus and Moses. Others are not commonly appreciated, like the analogy between the stories of Achan and Jonathan (Josh 7; 1 Sam 14), the analogy between David and Uriah (2 Sam 11–12), or the analogy between Rahab (Josh 2; 6) and David (1 Sam 19:11–18). One of the principal goals of this little book is to reveal the many under-appreciated analogies in Ruth and to explore how they contribute to Ruth's message.

Structure

What Is Structure?

"Structure" refers to nothing more than the organization of information in a literary work. All stories have a structure of one sort or another. To be accurate, *all texts have several structures*. The plot has a structure: a movement from problem to resolution, arrived at as the characters pass through various settings and times and events. The development of some characters is similar, an evolution from some simpler condition to one that is more complex, or problematic, or sublime. Poems (even free-verse poems) have an aural structure: a cadence or rhythm created by repeated sounds, or repeated stresses, or by the imposition of a meter. In the Hebrew Bible, dialogue often has an aural structure too, which is sometimes more and sometimes less prominent. Almost all biblical books switch between genres, at least from time to time, and these shifts may occur in patterned ways. Arguments have structure, as anyone who has written an argumentative essay at school will know. The structure of a poem's argument, for example, will not necessarily correspond to its poetic structure. In fact,

(Re)reading Ruth

the whole story-world of the Bible has a careful configuration. Ruth, for example, mentions Israel and Moab, but the horizon of the story is limited to Bethlehem and its environs, or, more specifically, to one road, one field, one house, one threshing floor, and one gateway. For some books, the spare setting is situated within a multi-layered world, a tiered world like a layer cake with celestial realms above, the human world in the center, and a world below, belonging to the dead (as the world is depicted in Ezekiel, for example). In short, biblical narratives abound with structures.

When biblical scholars discuss literary structure, they usually have a particular type of structure in mind: how the story is *divided into segments*. Biblical books *are* carefully divided into parts. They are like pearls on a string. The pearls are the individual scenes, or poems, or paragraphs. The string is the work as a whole. The segmentation into parts (pearls) can be signalled by a number of features like: repeated words and phrases; changes in setting, or time, or actors; changes in theme or argument; changes in genre; changes in rhythm, and so on. The problem in biblical studies is that the evidence scholars cite to validate a proposed structure often comes from different strata of the work. A suggested structure might be based on bits and pieces of many structural strata: the repetition of words, phrase, and clauses (graphic/visual stratum), patterns of sound (aural stratum), changes to variables in the story-world like time and place and actors (stratum of the story-world), and shifts in ideas and themes (stratum of ideation). In other words, biblical scholars tend to mix and match evidence from different strata of the literary work, without considering whether they work together in harmony or whether they represent different structures, laid one upon the other.[16] I do believe that the emphasis on text-segmentation in biblical scholarship is right and good. The tendency to grab whatever bit of evidence can be used to validate a *singular* structure is less good, unless it can be shown that all the different structural strata work in harmony with one another.[17]

---

16. In the case of Ruth, one notable exception is Adele Berlin. Her discussion of the book's structure is restricted to a single stratum, to plot-structure. *Poetics and Interpretation*, 101–10.

17. Many biblical scholars are suspicious of proposals regarding structure in narrative texts. The most common reason offered is that structure is "subjective." As R. P Gordon puts it, "Unfortunately in most such exercises there is a high degree of subjectivity involved and the discovery of patterns in the text can depend in substantial measure on the discoverer's decisions as to what is, and what is not, significant" ("Simplicity of the Highest Cunning," 69–80, quote at 74). Gordon's charge is surely correct. To be precise, when readers fail to distinguish between types or layers of literary structure (aural,

Ruth has precisely this sort of structure. Changes in the plot, changes in genre, changes in theme, and changes to time, place, and characters all seem to occur in harmony with each other and with the natural breaks between Acts. In the following pages, I describe Ruth's structure (as I understand it), and I describe why it is essential for readers to see and grasp the structure, how *it profoundly complicates a singular linear reading,* and creates a framework for comparing and contrasting characters and events *within* the Book of Ruth.

The Structure of the Book of Ruth

We begin with the opening and closing verses of the book, which I refer to as the Prologue (1:1–5) and Epilogue (4:18–22). The Prologue introduces the main character (Naomi), the protagonist (Ruth), and the chief problem that the book must resolve, a lack of both sons and the partners needed to produce them. The Epilogue reveals the book's ultimate results and points forward to the main character of the Book of Samuel, King David:

> 1 And it came about, in the days of the judging of the judges, that there was a famine in the land. And a man from Bethlehem of Judah went to reside as an alien in the fields of Moab, he and his wife and two of his sons. 2 And the name of the man was Elimelek, and the name of his wife was Naomi, and the name of his two sons were Maḥlon and Kilyon, Ephrathites from Bethlehem of Judah. And they entered the fields of Moab, and they stayed there. 3 And Elimelek, Naomi's man, died, but she survived him, she and her two sons. 4 And they took wives for themselves, Moabites. The name of the one was Orpah, and the name of the second was Ruth, and they dwelt there about ten years. 5 And the two of them also died, Maḥlon and Kilyon, and the woman was left behind by her two children and her husband. (Ruth 1:1–5)

> 18 These are the descendants of Perez: Perez fathered Hezron, 19 Hezron fathered Ram, Ram fathered Amminadab, 20 Amminadab fathered Nahshon, Nahshon fathered Salmon, 21 Salmon fathered Boaz, Boaz fathered Obed, 22 Obed fathered Jesse, and Jesse fathered David. (Ruth 4:18–22)

---

graphic, generic, argumentative, world-structure, etc.) and deploy evidence from more than one stratum to construct a single structure for a book, the results certainly appear to be a convenient hodge-podge of evidence.

(Re)reading Ruth

In addition to the simple fact that 1:1–5 opens the book and 4:18–22 concludes it, two other features link these paragraphs: their antithetical themes and matched triads. The Prologue is about death, the death of three men—Elimelek, Maḥlon, and Kilyon—which, as we come to discover, entailed the death of Elimelek's line. In contrast, the Epilogue is about life. Ruth, grafted into a new family tree, becomes part of a new line stretching from Perez to David. After Ruth joins the family, three generations are enumerated, culminating in the birth of David (Obed → Jesse → David). In this way, the Epilogue sets three generations of Ruth's posterity against the three dead men and the death of Elimelek's line in the Prologue.[18]

The body of the book (1:6—4:17) occurs in four Acts, which (unusually and helpfully) correspond with the chapter divisions in our Hebrew and English Bibles: 1:6–22; 2:1–23; 3:1–18; 4:1–17. The beginning and end of each Act signals clearly that it is a beginning or ending of a part of the story. Some sub-plot is revealed at the beginning of each Act that reaches resolution in the ending. In effect, these four Acts are the four pearls, and the Book of Ruth is the string.

We have already observed how 1:6 and 1:22 form a frame around Act 1. Act 2 (2:1–23) begins and ends in this way:

beginning
> ¹ And Naomi had a kinsman of her husband, a mighty man of strength from the clan of Elimelek, and his name was Boaz. ² And Ruth the Moabite said to Naomi, "Let me *go into* the fields, and let me glean the heads of grain after the one *in whose eyes I find favor.*" And she said to her, "*Go*, my daughter."

ending
> ²² Naomi said to Ruth, her daughter-in-law, "It is better, my daughter, that you *go out* with his young women, so *others will not molest you* in another field." ²³ So she *clung to* the young women of Boaz, gleaning until the barley and the wheat harvests were finished. And she lived with her mother-in-law.

At the beginning of Act 2, Ruth asks permission to *go out*, to provide for Naomi and herself by gleaning, though there is some risk in doing so. At the end, she is encouraged to *stay* with Boaz's female harvest workers, who are shielded from molestation. The need expressed by Ruth in 2:11–12 has been safely met by 2:22–23. Signalling this completion, the Act is framed

---

18. It is also worth noting that several of the names in the Prologue and Epilogue rhyme. Maḥlon and Kilyon rhyme with Hezron, Nahshon and Salmon.

both by the repetition of *go out* and by the deployment of two pairs of antonyms: *go* versus *cling*, *molested* versus *find favor*.

In Act 3 (3:1–18), the plot reaches its apogee with the drama at the threshing floor.

beginning	1 Naomi, her mother-in-law, said to her, "My daughter, should I not seek a resting-place for you, where things *will be better for you*. 2 Now, is *Boaz not our kinsman, whose young women you were with?*"
ending	16 And she came to her mother-in-law, and she said, "Who are you, my daughter?" She reported to her everything the man had done for her. 17 And she said, "These are six barley he gave to me, because he said to me, 'You should not come to your mother-in-law empty handed.'" 18 And she [Naomi] said, "Sit, my daughter, until you learn how the matter turns out. For the man will not rest, but he will finish the matter today."

The Act opens with Naomi's offer to "seek some security" for Ruth and concludes with Ruth's report to Naomi about the success of the scheme. The beginning and ending of this Act have some clear affinities with the beginning and ending of Act 2. The first verse repeats a clause, slightly reworded, from the close of Act 2. *She stayed close to the young women of Boaz, gleaning* (2:23) is reworded as *with whose young women you have been working* (3:2).[19] It also echoes the beginning of Act 2, repeating *kinsman*, *Boaz*, and a common sentiment in the lines *I may find favor* (2:2) and *it may be well with you* (3:1).[20] If we widen our perspective slightly, we will also notice that the action in Acts 2 and 3 culminate in the same way too: Ruth returns to Naomi with a report and a generous gift of grain from Boaz.

Act 4 is the denouement (4:1–17) and transitions smoothly into the Epilogue. Its beginning and ending differ from those in the preceding Acts. These are crafted to be antithetical to Act 1. The two beginnings read:

---

19. Note the correspondences, which occur in the same order:
"She stayed *close* to the *young women* of Boaz, *gleaning*..." (2:23)
"... *with* whose *young women* you have been *working*" (3:2)

20. We could also add that the terms "security" (*mānôaḥ*, 3:1), and "rest" (*yišqōṭ*, 3:18), are synonyms in Hebrew (cf. Isa 14:7).

(Re)reading Ruth

beginning of Act 1	**6** And she arose, she and her daughters-in-law, and she *returned from the fields of Moab*, because she had heard (while in the fields of Moab) that Yhwh had visited his people to give them bread. **7** So she *departed* from the place where she was, and her two daughters-in-law with her. And they set out on the road to return to the land of Judah.
beginning of Act 4	**1** And Boaz went up to the gate, and he sat down there. And behold the redeemer was passing by (the one Boaz had spoken about). And he said, "Turn aside, sit down here Nobody." So he turned and he sat. **2** Then he took ten men from the elders of the town, and said, "Sit here." So, they sat. **3** He then said to the redeemer, "Naomi—the one *returned from the fields of Moab*, is selling the allotment of farm-field that belonged to our brother Elimelek."

Naomi, in crisis, sets out for the town of Bethlehem with her daughters-in-law. Boaz sets out for Bethlehem's gate to find his next-of-kin and resolve Naomi's crisis. If this seems a rather impressionistic connection, that is because it is. The correspondence between the two Acts is more evident from Boaz's words in 4:3, which echo 1:6, but it is not unmistakable until we reach the conclusion of Act 4 (4:14–15) and recall the end of Act 1 (1:20–21):

ending of Act 1	**20** "Call me Mara, for Shaddai has dealt very bitterly with me. **21** I went out full, and Yhwh has returned me empty. Why do you call me Naomi, since Yhwh has testified against me, and Shaddai has afflicted me?"
ending of Act 4	**14** Then the women said to Naomi, "Blessed be Yhwh, who has not withheld a redeemer from you today. May his name be spoken in Israel. **15** He will restore your life and sustain your old age. Because your daughter-in-law who loves you bore him. She is better to you than seven sons."

Act 1 culminates in Naomi's arrival in Bethlehem and her accusation of God. Though she survived the deaths of her man and her sons, she returned with no redeemer and no one to support her in old age. Adopting the language of a legal complaint, she accused God of testifying against her and dealing out affliction. Act 4 culminates with the arrival of a child and "the women" blessing God. Naomi's life was renewed. Quite by surprise, she was granted a redeemer and offspring to sustain her in old age. So, the woman of Bethlehem call blessings on God for these gifts, all of which are the fruit of Ruth's love. Indeed, Ruth's love has dissolved Naomi's bitterness.

The way that the women's blessing counters Naomi's accusation suggests another piece of evidence that corroborates the four-Act structure. Each Act includes a liturgical moment. Act 1 concludes with Naomi's accusation, Act 4 with the women's blessing. Acts 2 and 3 also crescendo in blessings:

Act 2	19b "May the one who noticed you be blessed" So she told her mother-in-law with whom she had worked, and said, "The name of the man with whom I worked today was Boaz."
Act 3	10 "Blessed are you to Yhwh, my daughter! Your latest kindness is greater than the first, in that you did not go after younger men, whether poor or rich."

These speeches stand out because of the shift in register. Register is the linguistic term for the ways that speakers use language differently depending on circumstances.[21] Naomi's speech shifts into a legal register, as she testifies against God. The other three shift into a liturgical register. Their importance for the structure of the book is clear when we realize that each of these utterances is also a tolerable summary of the central event in their Act: Naomi's loss (accusation); Boaz's regard for Ruth (blessing 1); Ruth's choice of Boaz (blessing 2); and God's generosity, assuring that Boaz could act as redeemer (blessing 3).[22]

Combining our observations to this point, we arrive at the following basic structure:

---

21. One does not speak in a law court, for example, in the same way that one speaks with a neighbor on the street. "Registers are usually characterized solely by vocabulary differences; either by the use of particular words, or by the use of words in a particular sense." Trudgill, *On Dialect*, 101.

22. Novick, "Liturgy and the First Person," 279–83. As an accusation, Naomi's speech is different from the three blessings, but it is less different than it appears. We will see in the next chapter that her accusation is modelled on a blessing uttered by another biblical character.

(Re)reading Ruth

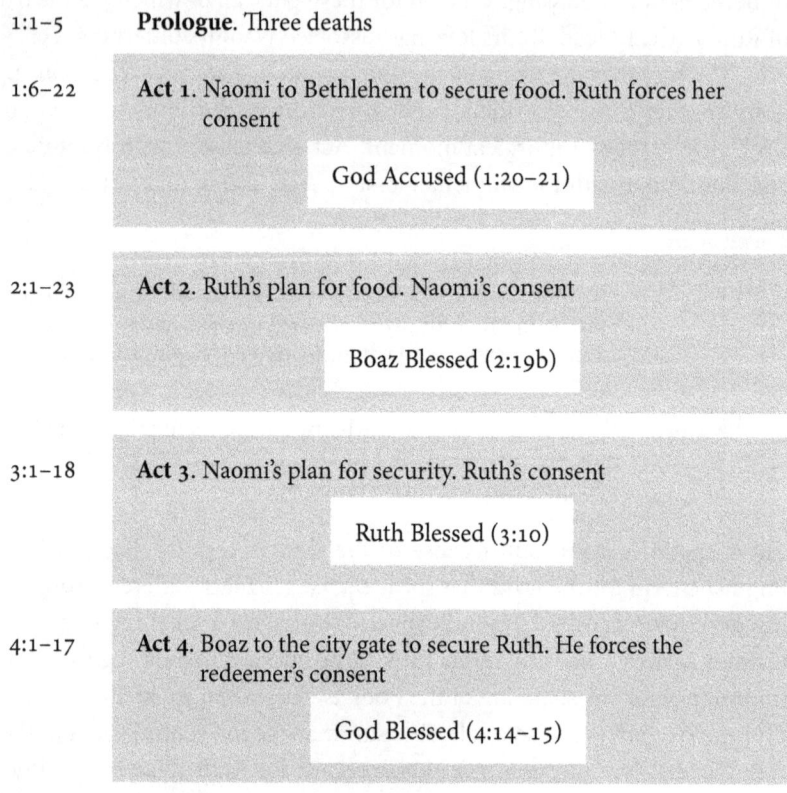

1:1–5	**Prologue.** Three deaths
1:6–22	**Act 1.** Naomi to Bethlehem to secure food. Ruth forces her consent
	God Accused (1:20–21)
2:1–23	**Act 2.** Ruth's plan for food. Naomi's consent
	Boaz Blessed (2:19b)
3:1–18	**Act 3.** Naomi's plan for security. Ruth's consent
	Ruth Blessed (3:10)
4:1–17	**Act 4.** Boaz to the city gate to secure Ruth. He forces the redeemer's consent
	God Blessed (4:14–15)
4.18–22	**Epilogue.** Three new generations

This basic structure is almost satisfactory. If we add the following observations (based on a consideration of each stratum of the story) to those that we have made so far, we will notice that they also uphold a four-Act structure.

- Regarding the genre of the Acts, the body of each is dominated by dialogue. In fact, it would not be incorrect to think of the Book of Ruth as little more than a sequence of conversations. To be precise, fifty-five of Ruth's eighty-five verses are dialogue.
- The central dialogue in each Act is framed by transitional paragraphs narrated in the third person, introducing the Act or summing up the Act.
- A group of women of unknown identity and size appear at the conclusion of Acts 1 and 4 and speak to Naomi (1:19; 4:13–17). When they first appear, their words inspire Naomi's accusation of God. When

they reappear in Act 4, they bless God and declare her accusation void. I will call them the "chorus," since they perform a similar function to the chorus in a Greek play.

- Considering characters, locations, and times we will notice three other features that align with what we have observed to this point. (1) The main actors in Act 1 are all women; in Act 4 they are all men. In Acts 2 and 3 the actors are Ruth and Boaz. (2) The primary location changes between Acts too: on the road to Bethlehem, in Boaz's field, at Boaz's threshing floor, and at the city gate of Bethlehem. (3) Of the two scenes on Boaz's property, the first occurs in the daytime (Act 2) and the second in the nighttime (Act 3).
- In Act 2 Boaz gifts Ruth with extra barley (2:16). In Act 3, he again gifts her with barley (3:15). Both Acts end with Ruth returning to Naomi with the gift and discussing the day's (or night's) events.

Combining all these observations results in the following structure:

(Re)reading Ruth

	Principle Events & Genre	Act	*Themes, Actants, Times, Places*
1:1–5	**Prologue**. Three deaths		death
1:6–7	Introduction: Naomi sets out for Bethlehem	1	Naomi's ill fortune,
1:8–19a	**Dialogue**: Who will go with Naomi? Consent forced		God accused, women + chorus
1:19b–22	Conclusion: "is this Naomi?"		Divine gift (grain)
2:1–3	Introduction: Ruth's plan. Naomi's consent		Boaz's field,
2:4–17	**Dialogue**: Boaz shows favor to Ruth + barley gift	2	Boaz blessed, daytime
2:18–23	Conclusion: Naomi and Ruth discuss the day		gift of grain
3:1–6	Introduction: Naomi's plan. Ruth's consent		Boaz's threshing floor,
3:7–15	**Dialogue**: Boaz shows favor to Ruth + barley gift	3	Ruth blessed, nighttime
3:16–18	Conclusion: Naomi and Ruth discuss the night		gift of grain
4:1–2	Introduction: Boaz goes to the city gate		Naomi's good fortune,
4:3–12	**Dialogue**: Who will redeem Ruth? Consent given	4	God blessed, men + chorus
4:13–17	Conclusion: "a son is born to Naomi"		Divine gift (child)
4:18–22	**Epilogue**. Three new generations		birth

Some readers will have observed immediately that Acts 1 and 4 and Acts 2 and 3 possess some remarkable correspondences. Some of these are identical and some antithetical. The chorus only appears in Acts 1 and 4. Act 1 stresses Naomi's ill fortune, and Act 4 declares her renewed fortune. God is cursed in Act 1 and blessed in Act 4, and the moment of consent in Acts 1 and 4 happens at the end of each Act's dialogue. Considering Acts

2 and 3, both occur on Boaz's land, and both feature Ruth and Boaz as the main characters. Consequently, in Act 2 it is Boaz who is blessed, and in Act 3 it is Ruth. The two central Acts revolve around the execution of a plan, one of Ruth's devising (Act 2) and one of Naomi's (Act 3). The moment of consent in Acts 2 and 3 happens at the beginning of each Act. As we work our way through Ruth in the subsequent chapters, we will observe many other correspondences between these paired Acts.[23]

This brings us to the central point of our discussion on structure. *Certain Acts within our story are designed to be compared and contrasted.* They are analogous and encourage comparison and contrast just as allusions do with stories from other biblical books.[24] This is what I meant when I said that structure has the power to profoundly complicate a single linear reading. When we read Act 3, for example, we are encouraged by its similarities to Act 2, to compare and contrast elements in these two Acts. The same is true of Acts 1 and 4. This indicates that the book's composers expected readers to operate on two axes at once. Obviously, everyone will continue to read in a linear fashion, following the development of plot, characters, themes, and so forth from the beginning of the book to its end. Once a reader arrives at Act 3, though, she must also reach back in her memory to ask which elements of Acts 2 correspond to which elements of Acts 3 and how those correspondences affect her understanding of Act 3. With my students, I sometimes refer to this comparative, non-sequential way of reading as *vertical reading* (as opposed to linear reading).[25] Due to these factors, beginning in Act 3 the process of describing the contours of the

---

23. Similarly, Porten, "Scroll of Ruth," 23.

24. Bertman is one of the few to argue this point. Unfortunately, after showing that the first two Acts in Ruth are analogous to the second two, he stops. He does not explore what effects this has on a reader's understanding of the book's storyline, characters, and themes. "Symmetrical Design," 165–68. (So too, in part, Fischer, *Rut*, 26–28, 47–48.)

25. It is commonplace for scholars to assert that structure reveals those segments that are emphasized or central. Jerome Walsh, for example, contends that "in a symmetrical structure, certain positions (ends, centers) are often points of greater emphasis" (*Style & Structure*, 11). However, if my earlier assertion is correct that biblical narratives only provide essential information, no part is less important than another. To my mind, recognition of a text's structures enhances reading in two major ways: (1) it signals which segments of the story, which are not adjacent to one another, should be compared and contrasted, and (2) it serves memory, making the parts of a story, the order of those parts, and the variations in those parts easier to recall.

(Re)reading Ruth

story will become more far more complex as we undertake linear and vertical reading simultaneously.[26]

Reading the Book of Ruth is a complex process. It is unlike any literature in the modern world with which I am familiar. Because of this, it requires a different kind of reading than comes naturally. We must cultivate new habits and develop new skills to read it well. As it happens, these habits and skills will not be orphaned when we are finished with Ruth. They are the reading competencies required by all biblical literature.

---

26. A nearly identical phenomenon, which also anticipates "vertical reading," can be observed in Dante's *Divine Comedy*, whereby corresponding cantos in *Inferno*, *Purgatorio*, and *Paradiso* have been systematically coordinated by means of complex constellations of allusions. See Corbett and Webb, "Introduction," 1–11.

CHAPTER 2

Act 1 ~ Ruth 1:1–22

RUTH 1 DOES ALL the things that a good beginning should. It introduces the main characters. It introduces the problems those characters must face, setting the plot in motion. It introduces the dynamic between the main characters, establishing how they will relate to one another along the way. It sets up one of the book's major plot-twists.

Ruth 1 consists of two major parts, and it has two principal characters. Its two parts are the *Prologue* to the whole book (1:1–5) and the *first Act* in the story (1:6–22). The first Act has an unadorned structure. A short introduction (1:6–7) and a short conclusion (1:22) frame a lengthy dialogue between Naomi and her daughters-in-law (1:8–19a). So, it would not be inaccurate to think of Ruth 1 as containing a *prologue* followed by a *dialogue*. The only additional element to appear in chapter 1 comes at the end, in verses 19b–21. The chorus, who are identified only as "the women of Bethlehem," briefly address Naomi, and she responds by making an accusation against God. The chorus will not appear again until the final scene (4:14–17) just before the book's *Epilogue*.

The two principal characters in Act 1 are Naomi and Ruth. Though she does very little after chapter 1, Naomi is the book's main character. All the other characters are described in relationship to her. For example, Ruth and Orpah are almost always referred to as Naomi's daughters-in-law rather than Maḥlon and Kilyon's wives. Boaz is identified as Naomi's near-kinsman not Elimelek's (2:1). When Elimelek and his sons die, the narrator, ignoring Orpah and Ruth, says that Naomi was left behind (1:5). Likewise, the plot

(Re)reading Ruth

is focused on Naomi, on overcoming her personal dilemmas. At the close of the story, when all the crises confronting Naomi and Ruth are resolved, it is Naomi who is declared the recipient of God's kindness (4:14–17). Ruth is mentioned not as a recipient of God's care but as one of God's blessings on Naomi (4:15). So, the book is centered on Naomi. True as this is, it is Ruth who is the protagonist.[1] She is the character that the camera-eye will follow most of the time. It is her plans and her actions that will determine how the plot plays out, not Naomi's. Because of her extraordinary loyalty to Naomi and the risks that she takes to solve Naomi's problems, she is the character for whom we most wish good things.[2] It seems only right, then, that the book takes its name from her.[3]

Prologue (1:1–5): From Israel to Moab; from Life to Death

> [1] *And it came about, in the days of the judging of the judges, that there was a famine in the land. And a man from Bethlehem of Judah went to reside as an alien in the fields of Moab, he and his wife and two of his sons.* [2] *And the name of the man was Elimelek, and the name of his wife was Naomi, and the names of his two sons were Maḥlon and Kilyon, Ephrathites from Bethlehem of Judah. And they entered the fields of Moab, and they stayed there.* [3] *And Elimelek, Naomi's man, died, but she survived him, she and her two sons.* [4] *And they took wives for themselves, Moabites. The name of the one was Orpah, and the name of the second was Ruth, and they dwelt there about ten years.* [5] *And the two of them also died, Maḥlon and Kilyon, and the woman was left behind by her two children and her husband.*

---

1. The protagonist is usually the main character of a story, but not always. The protagonist is the character who drives the story forward.

2. Useful character sketches of Naomi and Ruth can be found in Berlin, *Poetics*, 83–91; Ostriker, "Love of the Land," 347–50; Ziegler, *Ruth*, 123–35, 153–66 (focused on Act 1).

3. As we progress, I will argue that both Naomi and Boaz are depicted in relationship to Ruth, Naomi as her opposite and Boaz as her equal.

Act 1 ~ Ruth 1:1–22

The story is set after the conquest of Canaan and before the rise of the monarchy. Elimelek and his family, who were from the tribe of Judah, lived in Bethlehem. Although Bethlehem means "house of bread," there was no bread to be found due to the onset of a famine. In the hope that the deprivation had not reached Moab, Elimelek moved his family east to that neighboring country. When Elimelek died, his widow Naomi and his two sons chose to remain in Moab. The sons married Moabite woman and settled down for ten years. But the two sons also died, without having fathered any children. The three women—Naomi, Orpah, and Ruth—were left with no means of support. With these bare facts, the Prologue has established all the information necessary for the story to unfold.[4] We now know the time, the setting, the characters, and the obstacles that the key characters need to overcome. It also injects suspense into the story: suspense about the fate of the surviving characters, how they will meet the hurdles that stand between them and security.

The original problem that motivated Elimelek to emigrate to Moab was a famine in Israel. The famine must have been severe, for, as we will learn, Elimelek gave up his ancestral lands when he emigrated. Though Naomi learns in the very first verse of the next paragraph that "Yhwh had visited his people to give them bread" (1:6), problems surrounding food and land will persist throughout the story, because Naomi has no obvious way to secure food even though it is now available. The Moabites, of course, are cousins of the Israelites, descended from Abraham's nephew Lot. But the relationship between Israel and Moab in the time of the judges was one of conflict, not harmony (for example, Judg 3 and 11). This introduces a second problem that the book will confront directly: the challenges of living as a foreigner. Unexpectedly, it will not be Naomi who will have to learn to live and thrive in a foreign country, but Ruth, Naomi's Moabite daughter-in-law.[5] The third

---

4. There are many gaps in 1:1–5. Why did the family stay in Moab after Elimelek's death? Why did Maḥlon and Kilyon not father any children? What happened that caused the three men to die but left the three women alive? The writers will not explain any of these gaps. They have established enough information for the story to proceed, and they expect us to tolerate the unanswered questions.

In fact, all texts have gaps. Any scene, or character, or idea could be described endlessly without ever achieving perfect completion. It is difficult to determine when writers expect their readers to fill gaps based on their own knowledge or deductions they draw from the work, and when they expect readers to simply tolerate those gaps. The only way to decide is to wait and see if the writers provide clues that suggest missing information should be supplied. In the case of Ruth 1:1–5, there is no information in the book of Ruth that would allow one to fill the gaps that I have identified here.

5. Siquans, "Foreignness and Poverty," 443–52.

problem, the one that seems most insurmountable, is the long-term security of the women. In ancient Israel, property was typically handed down from father to son. Daughters could inherit property, but only on the condition that they marry within the extended family. This way the land did not pass out of the family (Num 27:5–11; 36:5–9). There is no evidence that widows like Naomi could inherit their husband's property.[6] Instead, widows relied on male relatives to support them. But Naomi's sons died too, and no close relative steps forward in the story to volunteer aid. As a result, when she returns to Israel, Naomi has no land and no home of her own.[7] Naomi and Ruth are in desperate need of security, the kind of security that male relatives were expected to provide.[8] Three basic human needs, then, establish the trajectory of the story: the need for food, the need to navigate the dangers of living as an alien, and the need for men to provide security.[9] Two of these needs belong to both women. One is Ruth's alone.

The writers of the Prologue emphasize the problems confronting the widows through wordplay. In the Hebrew Bible, the word *bayit*, "house" can refer to a dwelling, but more often it designates a "household" or "family."[10] Moshe Garsiel has described the ironic use of the name Bethlehem in the Prologue, which is based, in part, on the meaning of *bayit*.

> The departure of Elimelek's family from Bethlehem ["house of bread"] . . . to the "field of" Moab is more than an ordinary movement from one place to another, for it means the abandonment of the *byt*, the "house," and even the loss of *lḥm*—of bread; and indeed the "house" in the sense of "family" falls apart and is destroyed when Elimelek and his two sons die.[11]

In addition, the writers tell us that Elimelek's family were "Ephrathites." Ephrathite is a family name, sometimes called a "clan name." Elimelek is from the tribe of Judah and the family of Ephraim (not to be confused with

---

6. Westbrook, *Property and Family*, 65, 83. See also Num 27:8–11, where property could pass to a daughter but not a wife.

7. What has happened to Elimelek's land will be discussed in Act 4 and *Excursus 13*.

8. Westbrook raises the possibility that there was an obligation on the near kinsman (who appears in 4:1) to care for Naomi and Ruth as members of his wider family (*Property*, 67). The near kinsman does not do so in Ruth. See also Greengus, *Laws*, 11, 73–76.

9. Barbra Green unifies the women's needs under the theme of "seed" (not including the dangers of life as an alien). "Plot," 55–68; similarly, Sutskover, "Land and Fertility," 283–94.

10. Chapman, *House of the Mother*, 1–32.

11. Garsiel, *Biblical Names*, 250.

the tribe Ephraim). It is unusual for the biblical writers to offer a character's family name. They do so here because "Ephrathite" is derived from the Hebrew word *prh*, "fruitful," which creates another pun on the tragedies this family experienced. Not only did Naomi's husband die, eliminating any chance she might have had to bear more children, but her two sons died childless, eliminating any chance of grandchildren.[12]

Before leaving the Prologue, it is important to note that it has carefully directed our attention to other parts of the Hebrew Bible. Verse 1 points overtly to the Book of Judges. Locating the story in "the days of the judging of the judges" encourages readers to wonder where and how Ruth fits among the stories of the judges. It must be acknowledged, though, that Ruth does not give us sufficient information to locate it *within* the Book of Judges.[13] What it does do is orient itself *between* the Books of Judges and Samuel. We will see as we progress that the Book of Ruth interacts with some of the last stories in Judges (see *Excursus 7*), and several of the stories in Samuel, including its opening chapters (see *Excursus 5*).[14] The story of Ruth appears to have been carefully crafted to fit between Judges and Samuel.[15] That such an explicit invitation to consider Ruth's relationship with another biblical book occurs in the first sentence should lead us one to wonder if inter-textual

---

12. Many interpreters speculate that Elimelek or his family must have committed some sin. The sin is usually identified as national infidelity (leaving his people and land for another), lack of trust in God to provide, or intermarriage with Moabites. This interpretive impulse reflects a typical human reaction to misfortune, namely the need to identify a cause for it. It is an impulse that biblical wisdom literature works hard to overcome. Sin does not need to occur for tragedy to occur, and humans are not always permitted to know why tragedy befalls them (Job, for example). The narrator does not suggest or even hint that either Elimelek or his family have sinned. The only action in 1:1–5 that might be identified as a sin is the intermarriage of Maḥlon and Kilyon with Moabites. As we will see in *Excursus 8*, that judgment is based on a particular interpretation of Deut 23:4–9, an interpretation that the writers of Ruth do not sympathise with.

13. This has not always stopped interpreters from trying to fit Ruth into the Book of Judges. The ancient Aramaic translation of Ruth, called the Targum, claims (at Ruth 1:3) that Orpah and Ruth are the daughters of King Eglon of Moab, who was killed by Ehud, in Judg 3:12–30. Though this is pure speculation, it does underline the peril to Ruth when she relocates to Israel.

14. Samuel is a single book in the Hebrew Bible. It is not divided into two books, as it is in Christian Bibles.

15. Note also, the family name "Ephrathite" only appears in one other text, 1 Sam 17:12. "David was the son of an Ephrathite of Bethlehem in Judah, named Jesse." The name "Ephrathite," then, is one of many connections between the Book of Ruth and the Book of Samuel.

connections like this will be important to the story.¹⁶ Indeed, there are other potential allusions in the Prologue. Some are implied by the character's names (notably Elimelek; see *Excursus 1*), but another is suggested by the miniature plotline of the Prologue. The Hebrew Bible contains other stories about a severe famine prompting a family to move to a foreign land and live as aliens there, stories recorded in Genesis 12, 26, and 41–46. As we read on, we should be wondering if the book will develop narrative analogies with any of these stories or with any of their characters.¹⁷

Excursus 1. The Significance of Names

In Hebrew, as in most languages, names have meanings. English names have meanings too, but many people do not know the meanings of their names (including myself). Fewer still choose their children's names based on the meaning. In Hebrew Bible, though, the meanings of names are important. More often than not, a character's name is relevant to the themes or events of the stories in which they appear. Sometimes the connection between a name and a story is obvious. Adam's name is derived from the word *soil* (*'ădāmāh*), because he was formed from the ground. Nabal's name means "fool," and as his wife Abigail says "as his name is, so is he" (1 Sam 25:25). Saul's name means "asked" because the people asked (*ša'ûl*) for a king (1 Sam 8:4–5). In other cases, the connection between a name and a story is less obvious. The name Abel is derived from the word "vapor" or "unsubstantial" (*hevel*) and sure enough, like a vapor, his presence in his own story is momentary (Gen 4:1–16).

To complicate matters slightly, the meaning of a Hebrew name is not always based on the same word as the name itself. For example, the meanings of many biblical names are based on puns. In Gen 5:28–29 Lamech names his son Noah, a name based on the word *nûaḥ*, "rest." But, he explains Noah's name by saying "this one shall bring us relief (*nḥm*) from our work and from the toil of our hands." "Relief" (*nḥm*) is an entirely different root-word than "rest" (*nwḥ*), but that does not matter in

---

16. The phrase "in the days of the judging of the judges" is obviously a *textual* reference not a historical one.

17. We will not be able to explore every allusion in Act 1, including some that begin in this Act but extend beyond it (like Gen 12:10–20 and 20:1–18) and several closely related texts (like Gen 16, 21, and 34).

biblical storytelling. What matters is that they *sound alike*. Complicating things still further, biblical storytellers will sometimes derive the meaning of a name from one word, but then make a pun (or some other wordplay) based on another word. Moses' name, famously, is derived from his having been "drawn out" (*mšh*) of the water (Exod 2:10). But because Moses' name sounds like "save" (*yš*ʿ) the writers of the Exodus story cannot refrain from making that pun (Exod 2:17). Jacob was named because he came out of the womb clutching his brother's "heel" (ʿ*āqēb*; Gen 25:26), but after losing his blessing to Jacob's deception, Esau proposed a more appropriate meaning for his name: "that is why his name is called *Jacob* (*yaʿăqōb*), for he *deceived me* (*yaʿqĕbēnî*) these two times" (Gen 27:36; also, Hos 12:4). Sometimes, the reasons given for a name are not connected to the name itself, but to people or places later associated with it. When Esau was born, he was "red, like a hairy mantle all over, so they named him Esau" (Gen 25:25). None of the words in the explanation are connected to the name "Esau" in any obvious way. Nonetheless, Esau is the father of the Edomites whose traditional homeland was Seir (Gen 36:8). "Red" (ʾ*admoni*) is a pun on "Edom," and "hairy" (*sēʿār*) alludes to "Seir."

In light of this, it is not surprising that the names of the characters in Ruth are significant.[18] In the Prologue alone, six names appear: Elimelek, Naomi, Maḥlon, Kilyon, Orpah, and Ruth. All the names in Ruth are connected to the storyline, though it must be admitted that the meaning of Orpah and Ruth are opaque (perhaps deliberately so).[19]

- *Elimelek* means "my God is king." It was chosen, I suspect, to underline the Book of Ruth's relationship to the books of Judges and Samuel. At the end of Judges, the narrator twice says, "there was no king Israel" (Judge 19:1; 21:25). The second occurrence adds "everyone did what was right in their own eyes, because there was no king Israel." This expression betrays the writers' hope in the monarchy, a hope that when the king comes, he will be able to rectify the social ills associated with the days of the judges. The Book of Ruth ends happily, and David's name arises twice in that ending (4:17, 22). Perhaps the writers of Ruth share the same hope? Conversely, the Book of Samuel views the people's request for the king as a foolish risk. Samuel warns the

---

18. Fischer, *Rut*, 33–36. Lest one doubt the importance of names in Ruth, the writer repeats the word "name" (*šēm*) five times in the Prologue alone, and its sound-alike word "there" (*šām*) twice. Porten, "Scroll of Ruth," 24–25; Ziegler, *Ruth*, 109.

19. For more detail, see Demsky, "Names and No-Names," 27–37.

(Re)reading Ruth

people at some length of its dangers, but they are unmoved (1 Sam 8:11–18). God interprets the people's request as a rejection of his kingship: "they have rejected *me* from being king over them" (1 Sam 8:7). Even though it appears in a book that looks forward to the coming of David, Elimelek's name seems to reflect the sentiment held by the writers of 1 Samuel 8. His name reminds readers that risks accompany the monarchy. It adds a note of caution to a story that otherwise has a hopeful view of the coming of David.

- *Naomi.* The name Naomi means "pleasantness, kindness" (from the word *nōʿam*).[20] When a biblical Hebrew name ends in /i/ it is sometimes an abbreviated form, with God's name (the "theophoric element") missing from the end. In other words, it is possible that Naomi's name is an abbreviated form of *Noʿŏmîyāh*, "kindness of Yhwh" or "kind (woman) of Yhwh."[21] The meaning of her name is closely related to the plotline and the characterization of Naomi, as we will begin to see in this chapter when we reach 1:20.

- *Maḥlon* and *Kilyon.* Elimelek's and Naomi's sons, Maḥlon and Kilyon, have been give appropriate but unfortunate names. Maḥlon is based on the word *ḥŏlî* and means "sickly."[22] (The /ma/ on the front of his name is a prefix.) Kilyon is based on *kālāh* and means "dying" or "ending." Indeed, neither one of them survives beyond the Prologue.

- *Orpah*'s and *Ruth*'s names are something of a puzzle. Scholars have arrived at several possible meanings for them, but none are certain. In Hebrew, *ʿorep* is the back of one's neck, so some ancient Jewish interpreters connected Orpah's name to her decision to turn back, that is, to show the back of her neck to Naomi (1:10–14). Other suggestions have included "cloud," "dew," and "mane," but all of those are based on words in other Semitic languages, not Hebrew.

  Ruth's name is not based on a recognizable Hebrew word at all. Those who treat it as Hebrew usually point to the root *rwh* (or *rwy*) "to saturate" or "to drench," which has no obvious connection to the

---

20. Though traditionally Naomi's name is pronounced with an /a/ as the first vowel, in Hebrew her name is *Noʿ omî*, with two long /o/ sounds, one after the other (phonetically: *Nō-ō-mee*).

21. Jeneane Fowler, *Theophoric Personal Names*, 149–69; Holmstedt, *Ruth*, 59.

22. In 4:10 Boaz will make a different pun on Maḥlon's name (see discussion of 4:7–10).

Act 1 ~ Ruth 1:1-22

story.²³ Some ancient translations—expecting Ruth's name to be significant—make puns of their own. For example, the Syriac translation (called the Peshiṭta) consistently renders Ruth as "friend" (see Gen 38:12; 1 Sam 30:26), and indeed, Ruth (*rût*) and "friend" (*rĕ'ût*) sound alike. Others think that the meaning of her name eludes us because it is Moabite and not Hebrew.²⁴ I suspect that the writers avoided assigning a meaning to Ruth's name because they wanted her actions to define her. As Kristin Saxegaard put it, "She is simultaneously a foreign Moabite and a faithful daughter-in-law, a seductive handmaid, and a worthy woman. Thus, the narrative gives an ambiguous picture of Ruth's character, which coheres well with her unidentifiable name."²⁵ In fact, Ruth is called by titles like "daughter-in-law," "daughter," and "Moabite" more than three times as often as she is called by her name.²⁶

- *Moab/Moabite*. Moab is the son of Abraham's nephew Lot, by his oldest daughter (Gen 19:30-38). After tricking her father to impregnate her, Lot's oldest daughter "bore a son and named him Moab" (verse 37), which sounds like "from father" (*mĕ'ab*). Moab became father of the Moabite people. Despite Ruth's vow to Naomi that "your people are my people" (1:16), the narrator continues to call her a Moabite (see note 70). The name is important because the writers of Ruth will develop an extensive allusion to Gen 19:30-38, that culminates in chapter 3.

- *Boaz*. The meaning of Boaz's name is key to the plot in Acts 2 and 3 and helps define his relationship to Ruth. There is no Hebrew word based on the letters *b'z*, so it appears to be a compound. The *Midrash Ruth Rabba*, a Palestinian Jewish commentary from Late Antiquity or the early Middle Ages, suggests that *bō'az* is a pun on *bĕ'ōz*, "in strength" (*b-* "in" + *'ōz* "strength"; cf. Prov 31:17). The Septuagint, the pre-Christian Jewish translation of the Hebrew Bible into Greek, gives his name as Boos, which appears to read the Hebrew as "in him is

---

23. Campbell, *Ruth*, 56; Rendsburg, "Philological Notes (2)," 27-32.
24. Gerleman, *Rut*, 14-15.
25. Saxegaard, *Character Complexity*, 128.
26. Ruth's name appears eleven times (1:4, 14, 16, 22; 2:2, 8, 21, 22; 3:9, 4:5, 10). Other titles are used for her on thirty-five occasions: *daughter-in-law* seven times (1:6, 7, 8, 22; 2:20, 22; 4:15), *daughter* eleven times (1:11, 12, 13; 2:2, 8, 22; 3:1, 10, 11, 16, 18), *Moabite* six times (1:22; 2:2, 6, 21; 4:5, 10), *girl* twice (2:5; 4:12), *foreigner* once (2:10), *slave* once (2:13), *servant* once (3:9), *wife of Maḥlon* once (4:10), *wife of the deceased* once (4:5), and *woman/wife* four times (3:11; 4:10, 11, 13).

strength" (*b-* "in" + *ō* "him" + *'ōz* "strength"). These similar interpretations have in their favor the fact that they correspond to the description of Boaz as a "mighty man" in Ruth 2:1.²⁷ We will return to the issue of Boaz's name at 3:10–11 and in *Excursus 11*.²⁸

- *Pĕlōnî 'almōnî*. The last character to be introduced is a man lacking a name (4:1). Several characters in Ruth lack names, like Boaz's harvest-manager, the group of women who appear in chapters 1 and 4, and the group of elders in chapter 4. This man, though, is directly addressed by Boaz and called *pĕlōnî 'almōnî*, which means "so-and-so" or "nobody." (Some English Bibles translate "friend," which is misleading.) In other words, just when his name *should* be introduced, the writers withhold it. Why this character is so openly and awkwardly nameless will be discussed when he appears in 4:1. I will call him Nobody.

Act 1. Naomi's Ill-Fortune (1:6–22)

> ⁶ *And she arose, she and her daughters-in-law, and she returned from the fields of Moab, because she had heard (while in the fields of Moab) that Yhwh had visited his people to give them bread.* ⁷ *So, she departed from the place where she was, and her two daughters-in-law were with her. And they set out on the road to return to the land of Judah.*

While still in Moab with her daughters-in-law, Naomi receives news that the famine has ended in Israel, and she decides it is time to return home. Naomi and Elimelek left Bethlehem for Moab to find food. More than a decade later, now a widow, she retraces her steps for the same reason. The

---

27. Garsiel, *Names*, 251; Bal, *Lethal Love*, 71–75. Note also, in front of Solomon's Temple were two columns called Yachin and Boaz. The Septuagint translated the second one, *bō' az*, not as name but as a title, "strength" (2 Chr 3:17), indicating that it understood the title of the pillar in a similar way to the name Boaz.

28. A long list of alternative explanations of Boaz's name can be found in Sasson, *Ruth*, 40–42. They are all based on a modern understanding of Semitic etymology and comparative philology. As was described in *Excursus 1*, a biblical name will often take on a meaning that does not correspond to the name's root-word.

human reality is that most people in ancient Israel were subsistence farmers. They lived from season to season and harvest to harvest, their health and welfare pinned to the success of the annual yield. In this light, it is hardly surprising that Naomi would find herself having to pursue her food. Many people would have found themselves in the same circumstances at one point or another.[29]

The unexpected thing in this paragraph is not that Naomi leaves Moab but that Orpah and Ruth set out with her. We do not know about Moabite customs, but in ancient Israel a woman who separated from her partner would typically return to her father's house (Judg 19:1–2). A widow could do the same, if she was without support from a male relative of her husband's family (Gen 38:11; Lev 22:13).[30] Not only could a widow return to her father's house, in most cases she needed to do so. Widows who were not part of a man's household were vulnerable and could discover themselves lacking in physical safety, legal protection, and material care (1 Kgs 17:10–16; Job 24:21). Widows were so vulnerable in the ancient world that the Hebrew Bible goes to some length to warn against taking advantage of them. Exploiting a widow is depicted as a particularly heinous crime (Exod 22:21; Deut 10:18; Isa 10:2; Jer 7:6; Ps 94:6), and God directs ferocious anger against those who misuse widows in any way (Deut 10:18; Isa 1:12–17). That Orpah and Ruth chose to accompany Naomi—three widows alone on the road—is not just unexpected, it is alarming. While it must be admitted that the story's plot requires the three women to set out together, it also underlines the precariousness of the women's situation.

> 8 *And Naomi said to her two daughters-in-law, "Go, return, each to her mother's house. May Yhwh deal faithfully with you, just as you have dealt with the dead and with me.* 9 *May Yhwh grant that you find a resting-place, each in the house of a husband." And she kissed them, and they lifted up their voice, and they wept.*

For reasons that are never explained, Naomi is determined to break from her daughters-in-law. Abruptly and with no discussion she commands them to return to Moab. Her exhortation to them is part of another elaborate

---

29. Meyers, "In the Household," 21–22.
30. Meyers, "In the Household," 23.

(Re)reading Ruth

witticism on the name of her hometown, continuing the play-on-words that began in the opening paragraphs. Naomi heard that God had "visited his people to give them *bread* (*leḥem*)," so she set off for *Bethlehem* (*bêt-leḥem*). Rather than encouraging her daughters-in-law to do exactly what she did years earlier and emigrate, she exhorts them to turn back, "each to her mother's *house*" (*bêt*).[31] This double pun combined with Naomi's blessing on the younger women reiterates two of the major problems faced by the women: lack of bread and lack of security. In her blessing, Naomi says "May Yhwh deal faithfully with you" (see *Excursus 2*) and then specifies what she would like God to do for them: "May Yhwh grant that you find a resting-place, each in the house (*bêt*) of a husband."[32] In Naomi's mind, "rest" for her daughters-in-law is synonymous with remarriage. She believes that, without husbands, they are unlikely to find any peace in life.[33] They should be pursuing a permanent place in a man's household, not pursuing an old woman to a foreign country. In fact, if the women press ahead, there is no guarantee that a "house" (*bayit*) awaits them in Bethlehem, not in either sense of the word: a dwelling or a family.

---

31. The expression "mother's house" is unusual. The typical expression being "father's house." "Mother's house" is chosen here for two reasons. The first is contrast. Naomi is emphasizing that a widow should return to her *mother* and not remain with her *mother-in-law*, as Porten has observed ("Scroll of Ruth," 26). The second reason is allusion. Apart from this verse, the phrase "mother's house" only occurs in Gen 24:28 and Cant 3:4; 8:2. The Book of Ruth, as will be described in *Excursus 8*, develops a complex allusion to several betrothal scenes, including Genesis 24. Part of the phrase is also one element of an allusion to Gen 2:24, which will be described in the closing pages of this chapter.

Carol Meyers makes the observations that every story to use the expression "mother's house" involves a female perspective, which I take to mean a female character's perspective, not a female writer's perspective (which is highly unlikely, historically speaking). "Her Mother's House," 39–51, 304–7.

32. Garsiel, *Biblical Names*, 251.

33. "Resting place," *mānôaḥ*, is a charged word in the Hebrew Bible. The noun, and its related verb *nwḥ*, can be used to refer to a range of ideas, literal and metaphorical. God "rested" his newly made human in the garden in Eden (Gen 2:15). Noah (whose name is based on this word) sends out a dove that can find no "resting place" because the earth is still covered in water (Gen 8:9). The mourner of Lamentations says his people have no proper "resting place" in exile (Lam 1:3). Often, though, the writers of the Hebrew Bible use the word (both the noun and verb) to refer to the "rest" Israel will experience if she obeys the Torah and will lack if she does not (see, for example, Deut 28:65). Naomi does not use it in this theologically charged way. "Rest," for Naomi, is the security a woman has when she belongs to the household of a man ("a resting-place, each in the house of a husband"). Her wish in 1:9 is a subtle reminder of the instability of the women's position in the world now that they are all unattached widows.

Act 1 ~ Ruth 1:1-22

Excursus 2. Ḥesed

There is an enduring interpretive tradition in Judaism that the purpose of the Book of Ruth is to teach *ḥesed* by exemplifying it. This is famously expressed by *Midrash Ruth Rabba*:[34]

> Rav Z'eira said: This book contains neither [laws of] impurity or purity, nor [laws of] prohibition or permission. Why then was it written? To teach how good is the reward of those who bestow *ḥesed* on others.[35]

But what does *ḥesed* mean? In Ruth 1:8, Naomi says to her daughters-in-law "may Yhwh deal faithfully with you." The word that I have translated as "faithfully" is *ḥesed*. *Ḥesed* is an important word in the book and one that is often misunderstood. It occurs three times in Ruth. The first is in Naomi's wish for Orpah and Ruth (1:8). The second is part of a blessing on Boaz: "May Yhwh bless him, who has not forsaken his *ḥesed* to the living or the dead" (2:20). Finally, it occurs at the book's climax when Boaz agrees to marry Ruth: "May Yhwh bless you, my daughter. This last instance of your *ḥesed* is better than the first" (3:10). English Bibles vary their translations of *ḥesed* quite a lot. If we consider the whole Hebrew Bible, the NRSV translates *ḥesed* in a bewildering number of ways: steadfast love, kindness, kindly, loyal, loyalty, loyally, unswerving, constancy, mercy, merciful, love, faithful love, faithfulness, faithful deeds, devout, devotion, gracious deed, favor, righteousness, and good deed. The NRSV uses "steadfast love," most often, but variations on "kind" and "loyal" are common too.[36]

---

34. *Midrash* (plural *midrashim*) is the name for a whole genre of ancient and medieval Jewish biblical commentaries.

35. *Midrash Ruth Rabba* 2 §14. See discussion in Prager, "Megillat Ruth," 15–22.

36. A few examples: steadfast love (Gen 24:14, 27; 39:21; Exod 20:6; 34:6-7; 2 Sam 7:15; 1 Kgs 3:6; Isa 54:10; Hos 2:21; Ps 5:8 [7]; 13:5 [6]; 31:7 [8]); kindness (Gen 19:19; 1 Sam 15:6; 2 Sam 9:7; Mic 6:8); kindly (Josh 2:12; Judg 1:24; 1 Sam 20:8); loyalty (Deut 7:9, 12; 2 Sam 2:5; Hos 4:1); loyal (Prov 20:6); loyally (Gen 24:12); unswerving loyalty (Mic 7:20); constancy (Isa 40:6); mercy (Ps 23:6); merciful (1 Kgs 20:31); love (Isa 54:8; 55:3; Hos 12:6; Ps 52:8 [10]); faithful love (1 Sam 20:14); faithfulness (Jer 31:3); faithful deeds (2 Chr 35:26); devout (Isa 57:1); devotion (Jer 2:2; Esth 2:17); gracious deed (Isa 63:7); favor (Esther 2:9; Dan 1:9); righteousness (Prov 20:28); good deed (Neh 13:14; 2 Chr 32:32). Though I interact with the NRSV in this excursus, I am not trying to single it out for criticism. It is one of the two translations that I use most often (along with the NJPS). I chose it simply because it was handy.

(Re)reading Ruth

Not all the NRSV's translations are synonyms, which indicates that *ḥesed* may have more than one meaning. It is common enough for words to have more than one meaning, to be "polysemous" as semanticists say.[37] The English word "bar," for example, can refer to a length of metal, a place where alcoholic drinks are bought and consumed, a lawyer's qualification, or a segment of a musical composition with a fixed number of beats. It can also be a verb meaning "to prevent," or it can be an archaic preposition, as in "she's the best musician, bar none." No occurrence of "bar" means all these things at once. Ordinarily, it can only support one of these meanings in any instance. In the sentence "she passed the bar on her first attempt," more than one meaning is possible, but only one is likely. *Ḥesed* is like "bar." It has more than one meaning, but only one is active in most cases. It is our task as readers to determine which definition best suits the word when we encounter it, to decide on the most appropriate meaning based on the context. In fine literature, of course, a writer can create a play-on-words that activates more than one meaning at once, but this exceeds normal practice in which a particular occurrence of a word has a particular meaning.[38]

So, what can *ḥesed* mean, and are all the translations of *ḥesed* in the NRSV possible?[39] In fact, *ḥesed* has two meanings:

- *Fidelity* or *loyalty*, referring to actions born out of some obligation or commitment to another person. Loyalty does not require love or even fondness. Though used between wives and husbands (Gen 20:13) and friends (1 Sam 20:8), it is also used between hosts and guests (Gen 19:19), allies (1 Kings 20:31), kings and people (2 Sam 3:8), and servants and masters (Deut 33:8).

- *Kindness* or *goodness*, referring to actions rather than courtesy or politeness. In many cases, this meaning also springs from some sense

---

37. Semanticists and lexicographers label words that have multiple meanings *polysemic*, from Greek *poly*, "many," and *sema*, "sign."

38. Kukharenko, "Properties of the Text," 240–41. A few translations of *ḥesed* in the NRSV combine two definitions into one, creating compound translations like *faithful love* or *steadfast love*. There are two problems with these cases. First, there is usually no reason to think that the writer is deliberately employing a double-meaning, and second, "love" is not a demonstrable meaning of *ḥesed*.

39. In fact, there are two different words in Hebrew that have the root *ḥsd*. One means "be suspicious" or "be ashamed." The other is the word we are discussing.

of connection or obligation (Exod 20:6; 34:7; Deut 7:9; Mic 7:18; Ps 136:1–26; Dan 9:4; for example).[40]

Some of the definitions for *ḥesed* in the NRSV, definitions like "love," "mercy," and "devout" confuse the meaning of the word with ways that God or people can show loyalty or kindness. Consider Psalm 136, for example, which describes God's *ḥesed* in detail. The psalmist names God's killing of the Egyptian firstborn (136:10), Egyptian army (136:15), and various foreign kings (136:17–20) as evidence of his *ḥesed* toward Israel. *Ḥesed* does not *mean* "killing" or "death" any more than it means "love" or "mercy." God's killing of Pharaoh's army and showing mercy to Israel are both actions he has taken that demonstrate his *ḥesed*, they are not *ḥesed* itself. Equally, though many of the characters in the Bible who share *ḥesed* have affection for one another, that is not a necessary element of it. People who do not entirely trust one another can still be loyal to each other (Gen 24.22–24), and *ḥesed*, like a skill, can be taught and learned (Prov 31:26). Other translations of *ḥesed* in the NRSV are synonyms for "loyalty" or "kindness" and are perfectly acceptable: kindness, loyal, loyalty, constancy, faithfulness, devotion, and (if we stretch a bit) good deed.

Ḥesed, then, means "loyalty" or "kindness." When Naomi invites her daughters-in-law to return to their mother's houses, she wishes them well. Her expression of this wish is a rather precise one: "may Yhwh deal faithfully with you" (1:8). It is Naomi's wish that God does not neglect Orpah and Ruth, even though they are no longer married to Israelites. Though he is under no such obligation, she hopes that God will continue to be committed to them. When Naomi declares her blessing in 2:20, the meaning of *ḥesed* is not immediately obvious. She says, "May he be blessed by Yhwh, who has not forsaken his *ḥesed* to the living or the dead" (2:20). At first glance, Naomi appears to be praising Boaz's filial piety, his loyalty to his relatives, both living (herself) and dead (Elimelek and his sons). If so, "kindness" does not fit this example well. Naomi is referring to Boaz's very first generous act toward Ruth and herself, so the expression "has not *forsaken* kindness" does not make sense. However, there is a second way to read the blessing. The subject of the relative clause "who has not forsaken his *ḥesed* to the living or the dead" could equally be Yhwh. In fact, this is the more likely option.[41] Read this way, Naomi perceives a fulfilment of the

---

40. Sakenfeld, *Faithfulness*, 2–5.

41. The head of a relative clause is usually the nearest possible antecedent, which in this case is Yhwh. See discussion in Holmstedt, *Ruth*, 141–42. Alternatively, Mordechai

wish that she declared in 1:8. God *is* maintaining loyalty to Ruth, not by placing her in the house of new husband but by means of Boaz's generosity. This, of course, foreshadows the plot's eventual outcome. Boaz's interest in Ruth will blossom until she does enter his household as his wife. Thus, Naomi's original wish, in 1:8, will eventually come true for Ruth because of Yhwh's loyalty to her. Finally, in Ruth 3:10, neither "loyalty" nor "kindness" is a perfect fit. In this case, Boaz seems to be deliberately exploiting the polysemy of *ḥesed*. He says, "your latest *ḥesed* is better than the first." Boaz is referring, of course, to Ruth's loyalty to Naomi (her first *ḥesed*), and he compares it with her treatment of him, which he also names *ḥesed*. Ruth's *ḥesed* toward Boaz cannot mean "loyalty" because she has no fixed relationship with him. She is not under any familial obligation to him, and the two have not exchanged promises of any kind. With respect to him, it must mean "kindness." Boaz's clever line, then, deploys both meanings at once: Ruth's kindness to him is even better than her loyalty to Naomi.

The word *ḥesed* serves to underscore one of the book's governing themes: *choice* or, to be more precise, *choosing to be responsible for another*. Both Ruth and Boaz choose to care for and be faithful to persons whom they are under no legal or familial obligation to support. Their motives are complex, to be sure, but the fact remains that they do it.[42] Naomi makes clear that Orpah and Ruth are absolved of any responsibility to their mother-in-law (1:8–9), and that she no longer considers herself to be under any family-obligation to her daughters-in-law (1:11–13). Despite this, Ruth chooses to be loyal to her and enacts that loyalty in extraordinary ways. Boaz, as we will see, is under no legal obligation to take responsibility for Naomi or Ruth. And yet, he not only chooses to take on that responsibility; he does so gladly. It is this broader theme—the choice to be loyal—that the word *ḥesed* highlights, and it is one of Ruth's and Boaz's shared virtues.[43]

Cohen has argued that the syntax is deliberately ambiguous, retaining both reading possibilities: "*Ḥesed*: Divine or Human?" 11–38.

42. As Eskenazi sums up, "*Ḥesed* in Ruth is not so much a case of good people doing good things, but rather an example of how ordinary people with mixed motives become extraordinary through the cultivation of *ḥesed*" (Eskenazi and Frymer-Kensky, *Ruth*, l). See further, Bohlen, "Die Rutrolle," 1–19.

43. Schept, "*Ḥesed*: Feminist Ethics," 27–28. Some readers will be wondering why I did not mention Naomi as a person who shows *ḥesed*, as most interpreters do. Naomi has been cast as a negative character and Ruth's opposite. My reasons for reading her this way will become apparent in time.

> ¹⁰ *And they said to her, "We will return with you to your people." ¹¹ And Naomi said "Return my daughters. Why would you go with me? Do I still have sons in my belly who could be husbands for you? ¹² Return my daughters. Go. For I am too old to get a husband. Even if I thought there was hope for me—even if I had a man tonight, and even if I bore sons—¹³ would you really wait until they grew up? Would you really withhold yourselves, and not take a husband? No, my daughters. Truly, it is more bitter for me than for you. For the hand of Yhwh has struck out against me." ¹⁴ And they lifted their voice, and they wept again, and Orpah kissed her mother-in-law, but Ruth clung to her.*

Naomi's instruction and good wishes do not move Orpah and Ruth (1:8–9), so she becomes more insistent. Assuming that the younger women are only accompanying her to profit from her in some way ("Why would you go with me? Do I still have . . . ?"), Naomi tries to shift them with a double-argument. The first part cuts straight to what it is that she assumes they want. She announces that she has no more sons to give to her daughters-in-law. Naomi's argument about hypothetical sons may seem baffling, but it makes good sense within her cultural context and in the context of a story about marriage. Naomi is referring to the practice of *levirate*.⁴⁴ *Levirate* is described in Deut 25:5–6:

> ⁵ When brothers reside together, and one of them dies and has no son, the wife of the dead brother will not be married outside [the family] to a stranger. Her brother-in-law will go to her and take her to himself as a wife and perform the duty of a brother-in-law to her. ⁶ Then the first son whom she bears will be established in the name of his brother, the deceased one, so that his name is not blotted out of Israel.

According to this law, if a man died without having produced a male heir, his widow should not be married outside the family. Instead, the deceased man's brother was expected to "take her to himself as a wife" and "do his

---

44. *Levir* is a Latin word meaning "brother-in-law." *Levirate* means, literally, "being a brother-in-law," but it refers to the specific legal practice described in Deut 25:5–6.

duty as a brother" by giving her children. The oldest son born to parents in a *levirate* marriage was given the name of the dead spouse and added to the family tree in the dead man's place. So, *de facto*, the child was the son of the brother-in-law, but *de jure*, he was a brother of his genetic father. The effect of all this was that the widow's new son could inherited property alongside his uncles as if he was their brother. In this way, no shoot from the family tree was pruned, and the widow was provided with someone to shelter and care for her.[45] Understanding this as the background of Naomi's comments, she is announcing that she cannot provide either daughter-in-law with a *levir*. Her first argument, then, can be unfolded as three assertions: "I have no sons"; "I will have no more sons"; "even if I did have sons immediately, you would never wait for them to be old enough to perform the duty of a brother-in-law."[46]

The second part of Naomi's argument is an implicit one. She claims that God has been harsh with her. As she says, he has "struck out against me." The implication of this complaint is that the younger women should not put themselves in the way of God's disfavor too. Rather than gaining something by accompanying Naomi, Ruth and Orpah are risking more woe. Naomi hopes that this double argument will scupper whatever reasons her daughters-in-law might have for following her.[47] She is half right. Orpah appears to accept Naomi's reasoning and departs. Ruth did not.[48]

---

45. See Weisberg, *Levirate Marriage*, 1–22. Ordinarily, someone who slept with a brother-in-law or sister-in-law was guilty of incest, but *levirate* was a legal exception (Lev 18:6–18; 20:10–21, esp. verse 21).

46. There may be a pun in verse 13 that supports Naomi's argument. The word "wait" (*śbr*) sounds similar to "bereaved" (*š' r*; 1:3, 5). If the young women did wait, they would be bereaved indeed, because there are no sons left in Naomi's womb.

47. It is worth noting that Naomi does not say "if Elimelek had a brother, and if I had him tonight" (verse 12). She refers, instead, to "a man." Her argument, then, may be a reference to an unknown marriage practice like *levirate* but not identical to it, or she may simply be drawing on *levirate* practice for persuasive effect. (We will see a similar lack of correspondence to *levirate* law in Act 4, discussed in *Excursus 13*.)

48. Naomi's speech is anaphoric. That is, each part is introduced by a nearly identical line. The first argument is in two parts, both of which are introduced by the command "return my daughters" (verses 11–12). Her second argument is introduced by the line "no, my daughters." This technique underlines her authority as their mother-in-law and senior. Ruth defies her authority in, perhaps, the only way that she could without impropriety.

> 15 *And she said, "Behold, your sister-in-law has returned to her people and to her gods. Return after your sister-in-law.* 16 *And Ruth said, "Do not urge me to forsake you, to return from following you. For where you go, I will go. And wherever you lodge, I will lodge. Your people will be my people. And your God will be my God.* 17 *Wherever you die, I will die; and there I will be buried. Thus-and-more may Yhwh do to me. . . . Only death will part me and you!"* 18 *And she saw that she was determined to go with her, so she stopped arguing with her.* 19 *And the two of them went until they came to Bethlehem.*

Naomi tries again. She orders Ruth to follow Orpah back to Moab, back to "her people and her gods." Before she can say any more, Ruth interrupts, and what she says has become one of the most famous speeches in the Hebrew Bible. To add force to her declaration, Ruth speaks in verse.[49]

> *Do not urge me to forsake you,*
>   *to return from following you.*
> *For where you go, I will go.*
>   *And wherever you lodge, I will lodge.*
> *Your people will be my people.*
>   *And your God will be my God.*
> *Wherever you die, I will die;*
>   *and there I will be buried.*
> *Thus and more may Yhwh do to me. . . .*
>   *Only death will part me and you!"*

Even in English translation her speech has a cadence and rhythm that gives additional weight to her words. Each pair of lines is topically and syntactically parallel, fixing them in our memories, and the staccato lines land powerfully: I go where you go; I stay were you stay; your people are my people; your God is my God. But as memorable and as clear as Ruth's vow seems to be, it is hard to avoid the sense that we, as modern people, are missing something, something implicit, something obvious perhaps to ancient Israelites

---

49. "Verse" and "poetry" are not exact synonyms. All poetry is verse, but not all verse is poetry. Verse is characterized by recurrence, whether alliteration, rhyme, meter, accent, parallelism, or whatever. Nursery rhymes are a classic example of verse. What elevates some verse to the level of poetry differs from culture to culture. See Jakobson, "Closing Statements," 350–77.

but not to us, something that makes these words more than a declaration of personal loyalty offered in a moment of heightened emotion.

And we would be right. Every facet of Ruth's vow is carefully chosen: the vow to stay with Naomi, the vow to join her people, the vow to adopt her God, even the invitation to be cursed if she fails at any part of the vow. Ruth's vow is a *covenant*. Her words are much more than a heartfelt intention. She has pronounced a unilateral, verbal contract between herself and Naomi.[50] Lacking witnesses, she calls on God himself to seal and enforce it. Any enforcement will fall on her alone, because all the obligations are hers. Ruth does not ask Naomi to make any commitments to her, and Naomi does not offer any.[51]

So, what marks this as a legal commitment, as a personal covenant?[52] There are four stories in the Hebrew Bible in which one character forges a covenant with another, stories that sound remarkably like Ruth's vow. In the first examples, the kings of Israel and Judah ally together against a common enemy (similar language to Ruth 1 in italics):

> And he [Ahab] said to Jehoshaphat, "*Will you go with me* to battle at Ramoth-gilead?" Jehoshaphat answered the king of Israel, "*I will do what you do;*
> *My troops will be your troops.*
> *My horses will be your horses.*" (1 Kgs 22:4)

> As he went, he [king Jehoram] sent word to King Jehoshaphat of Judah: "The king of Moab has rebelled against me; *will you go with me to Moab* to war?" He replied, "*I will go up.*
> *I will do what you do.*
> *My troops will be your troops.*
> *My horses will be your horses.*" (2 Kgs 3:7)

A verbal pledge between kings is binding, and in both these stories the king who made the vow honored it. But the covenant is a legal mechanism that is used not just between kings and nations. It is also used in family life to extend one's bonds beyond the immediate clan or to clarify individuals' rights and responsibilities in family life. It also can be used in personal

---

50. Some Christian theologians make a distinction between a covenant and a contract. I do not fully understand what motivates this distinction, but it is not a relevant distinction in the Hebrew Bible.

51. Ziegler, "So Shall God Do . . ." 59–81, esp. 64–65.

52. For more on Ruth's vow as a covenant, including parallels in ancient Near Eastern literature, see Mark Smith, "Family and Covenant," 242–58.

relationships too, either to bind friendship (as in 1 Sam 20:42) or to express loyalty between people of different rank or class. Ruth's vow is more like one of these private covenants. It shares many parallels with the covenant between Laban and Jacob (Gen 31) and the vow made by Ittai to David (2 Sam 15).

In Genesis 31, Jacob decides to return from Haran to Canaan. Back in Canaan, he had fallen out with his brother Esau when he stole Esau's birthright and blessing. Esau vowed to kill Jacob, so the journey is a risk. Jacob is driven to take this risk because he has also fallen out with his brothers-in-law. He married his uncle Laban's daughters and then stole most of Laban's wealth in sheep and goats (30:25–43). God tells Jacob to depart before the situation can boil over (31:1–3). Jacob decides to flee secretly. Unknown to Jacob, Rachel (acting just like him) steals her father's household gods and takes them along too. When Laban learns of all this, he pursues Jacob in anger. Jacob, always the lucky man, is protected by God who warns Laban to do nothing "either good or bad" to Jacob (31:22–30). Their confrontation ends in a covenant. There is no love lost between Laban and Jacob, but because they are kin, they choose to divide the world between them, Jacob will stay to the West of Gilead, and Laban will stay East. The story of their family-covenant has many parallels not just to Ruth's vow, but to the whole of Ruth 1 (similar language in italics):

> **43** Then Laban replied and said to Jacob,
> "*The daughters are my daughters,
> the children are my children,
> the flocks are my flocks,*
> and all that you see is mine.
>
> Yet what can I do today about my daughters, or about their children whom they have borne? **44** Come now, let us make a covenant, you and I; and *let it be a witness between you and me*." **45** So Jacob took a stone, and set it up as a pillar. **46** And Jacob said to his kinsfolk, "Gather stones," and they took stones, and made a heap; and they ate there by the heap. **47** Laban called it Yegar-sahadutha: but Jacob called it Gal-ēd.[53] **48** Laban said, "This heap is a witness between you and me today." Therefore, he called it Gal-ēd, **49** and the pillar Mizpah, for he said, "May Yhwh watch between you and me, when we are away from one another.[54] **50** If you treat my daughters badly,

---

53. The name that Laban suggests is Aramaic for "mound (or stone-heap) of witness." Jacob's is Hebrew and means the same thing, but it is also a pun on *Gilead* from verse 23.

54. The name "Mizpah" entails a sound-play on *yiṣep*, "watch."

(Re)reading Ruth

or if you take wives in addition to my daughters, though no one else is around, remember that *God is witness between you and me.*" **51** Then Laban said to Jacob, "See this heap and see the pillar, which I have set between you and me. **52** This heap is a witness, and the pillar is a witness, that I will not pass beyond this heap toward you, and you will not pass beyond this heap and this pillar toward me, for harm. **53** *May the God of Abraham and the God of Nahor" (the God of their fathers) "judge between us."* So, Jacob swore by the Fear of his father Isaac. **54** And Jacob offered a sacrifice on the hill and called his kinsfolk to eat bread, and they ate bread and tarried all night in the hill country. **32:1** Early in the morning Laban *rose* and *kissed* his grandchildren and his daughters and *blessed* them; then he *went* and *returned home.*[55] (Gen 31:43—32:1)

Laban uses the same formulaic language as Ahab, Jehoram, and Ruth, namely "my/your X is your/my X" (Gen 31:43 ‖ Ruth 1:16). Also, like Ruth, Laban summons God to witness the covenant. In Ruth's vow, the punishment for breaching the covenant is never expressed (Ruth 1:17), and it is not expressed in Laban's either (Gen 31:53). And as in Ruth, Laban *rises* (‖ Ruth 1:6), *kisses* his kin (*nšq* ‖ Ruth 1:9), *blesses* his kin (*brk* ‖ Ruth 2:4, 19, 20; 3:10), and *returned* (‖ Ruth 1:6, 7, 8, 10, 11, 12, 15 twice, 16, 21, 22 twice) *to his place* (*māqôm* ‖ Ruth 1:7). The point of the allusion to Gen 31 is not to forge a direct analogy between Ruth and Naomi, on the one hand, and Laban and Jacob, on the other. It is an antithesis. Jacob's and Laban's story is the story of the deterioration of a family. Jacob, as he has done before (Gen 25:27—34; 27:1—28:5), has fractured his family and burned his bridges. In Ruth, the opposite is true. She is not exploiting Naomi. She is not continuing the devolution of Naomi's family. She is tying her fate and fortune to Naomi's with bonds of loyalty. She is reconstituting Naomi's crumbing family. Ruth is an anti-Jacob. While he deceives, she is sincere. While he shatters family ties, Ruth forges them. While Jacob fails at his family obligations, Ruth adopts them and shoulders them. The Hebrew patriarch lacks family virtue. The foreign widow has a surplus.[56]

---

55. In Christian Bibles, Gen 32:1 is the last verse of the previous chapter; it is 31:55.

56. Ruth is an anti-Jacob in this analogy, but there are also ways that Naomi is coordinated with Jacob. She is similar in some ways and antithetical in others. Naomi leaves Moab with two daughters-in-law, and Jacob leaves Haran with two wives. Naomi is poor, and Jacob is wealthy. Naomi's daughter-in-law Ruth renounces her people's gods, and Jacob's wife Rebecca steals her father's gods. Naomi tries to persuade her daughters-in-law to turn back from following her, and Jacob (with some divine help) persuades Laban to abandon following him. The equation between Naomi and Jacob is not straightforward.

Act 1 ~ Ruth 1:1-22

What distinguishes Ruth's story from 1 Kings 22, 2 Kings 3, and Genesis 31 is that all three of those stories are about covenants between Hebrew people or blood-relatives, whereas Ruth is a gentile who pledges herself to an Israelite. There is still one more story, though, that echoes Ruth's words, a story about a private covenant between an Israelite and a gentile. When David flees Jerusalem to escape Absalom's rebellion, he is in a state of shock and grief. He has already lost his son Amnon, killed by Absalom (2 Sam 13:23-33). Now Absalom has turned his knives on David. On the first day of the rebellion, David chooses to flee Jerusalem rather than becoming trapped there (2 Sam 15:13-16). As David is departing, with his Canaanite bodyguard, he has a curious exchange with one Ittai the Gittite. Ittai, it seems, is from Gath, the Philistine city where David stayed when hiding from Saul (1 Sam 27:3). It hardly needs mentioning that Philistines are paramount among Israel's enemies in the Book of Samuel. In a scene that is reminiscent of the Philistine rejection of David in 1 Samuel 29, David tries to deter Ittai and his men from joining his army because he is a "foreigner" (*nōkrî*). The similarities between David's words and Naomi's are impossible to miss:

"Why will you also *go with us*?[57] *Return*, and dwell with the king [Absalom]; for you are a *foreigner*, and an exile from your *place*.[58] You came only yesterday, and today should I make you wander, *going with us*? I am *going* wherever I can *go*. *Return*, and make your kinsfolk *return with you*. And *may loyalty* and faithfulness *be with you*."[59] (2 Sam 15:19-20)	And Naomi said to her two daughters-in-law, "*Go, return*, each to her mother's house. *May Yhwh deal faithfully with you*, just as you have dealt with the dead and *with me*. (Ruth 1:8)

Ittai, the foreigner, responds to David, the Judahite from Bethlehem, in much the same way that Ruth, the foreigner, responds to Naomi, the Judahite from Bethlehem. He refuses. Instead, he vows his loyalty to David, loyalty unto death: "As the Lord lives and as my lord the king lives, wherever my lord the king may be, whether for death or for life, there your servant will be!" (15:21). I hardly need to spell out the similarities to Ruth's vow in Ittai's words. In this analogy, the characters involved are not antithetical;

---

57. Ittai's name (*'ittay*) means "with me." Note the repeated puns on his name in these two verses.

58. Foreigner (*nōkrî*), and place (*māqôm*) appear in Ruth 2:10 and 1:7.

59. The translators of the Septuagint (the pre-Christian Jewish translations of the Hebrew Bible into Greek) recognized the similarity to Naomi's words and made it more obvious by adding: "*the Lord will deal* with you [in] mercy and truth." ("Mercy" is how the translators understood *ḥesed*.)

they are alike. David, the man who has received so much benefit and protection from foreigners, behaves like Naomi, rejecting Ittai's assistance and loyalty. Ittai behaves like Ruth. He swears his loyalty at any cost. In both cases, the foreigner has been absolved of any duty by the Israelite. In both cases, the foreigner will not be refused. It may be unwanted, but Naomi and David receive the loyalty of Ruth and Ittai anyway.

These four texts (1 Kgs 22; 2 Kgs 3; Gen 31; 2 Sam 15) reveal Ruth's words as a personal covenant between herself and Naomi. But there is still one element of Ruth's vow that has no parallel in any of these four stories. Ruth also vows to adopt Naomi's God. There is a good reason why this part of the vow does not appear in any tale of a covenant between kings, relations, or retainers. It is because it is derived from the covenant between God and Israel. It appears for the first time in Exod 6:7, "I will take you as my people, and I will be your God" (cf. Deut 4:20), though its classical expression is "you will be my people, and I will be your God" (Jer 30:22; 31:33; Ezek 14:11; 36:28; Zech 8:8; cf. Gen 17:7). Scholars refer to this divine pledge as the covenant-formula. It is a pithy summation of the commitment of God to Israel and Israel to God, and it occurs all over the Hebrew Bible.[60] When Ruth echoes these words, she is invoking the covenant between God and Israel and placing herself squarely inside that relationship. Why she thinks she is permitted to do this is not indicated. Is it a wish? Is it an invocation? Whatever her expectations, Ruth's motives are clear: she will be loyal to Naomi, whatever that entails, and that (she believes) entails becoming an Israelite, nationally and religiously.[61]

So, how does Naomi respond to all this? "And she saw that she was determined to go with her, so she stopped arguing with her" (1:18). Based on her silence in response to Ruth's vow, Phyllis Trible describes Naomi as "withdrawing" from Ruth. Though I will characterize it differently, Trible's observation is apt.[62] Naomi does not acknowledge Ruth's vow, let alone re-

60. The even more pithy "I am Yhwh your/their God" (Exod 20:2; 29:46; Lev 11:44; 18:2, 4; 26:1) and "I am Yhwh" (Lev 18:21; 19:12; 21:12; Num 3:13, 41) usually function as reminders that the covenant between Israel and God is operative, and its obligations cannot be ignored.

61. Zechariah 8 describes the restoration of Jerusalem in the future, sometime after the Persian period. Verse 23 reads, "Thus says Yhwh of hosts, 'In those days, ten men from nations of every language will seize every Jew by the hem of the garment and say, "Take us with you, for we have heard that God is with you." Act 1 of Ruth is a vivid illustration of the same act: a gentile clings to Jew in the hope of being adopting by the God of Israel.

62. Trible, *Sexuality*, 172–73.

ciprocate it, which is certainly a curious blank in the story. Admittedly, this is only our first glimpse of Naomi's true nature. We will have to see how her character develops. We will not need to wait long, though. We will be granted a second look in the very next paragraph.

Excursus 3. Did Ruth Convert?

Conversion is a complex and varied thing. For many Christians, conversion is identified with a singular internal act: belief. For Jews, though, the ways that a gentile might approach or cross the boundary into Judaism are diverse. In his seminal book *The Beginnings of Jewishness*, Shaye Cohen argued that it was only in the second century BCE that Judaism opened its boundaries and allowed gentiles to enter the Jewish community.[63] From that time on, there were a variety of ways that ancient persons might identify with Judaism: (1) admiring some aspect of Judaism, (2) acknowledging the power of the God of the Jews or incorporating him into one's pantheon, (3) benefitting Jews or being openly friendly with Jews, (4) practicing some of the rituals of Judaism, (5) venerating the Jewish God and denying or ignoring all others, (6) joining the Jewish state or community, and (7) converting to Judaism and "becoming a Jew."[64] The final category, "converting," was more than just a matter of belief. Cohen limits the term "conversion" to those who practiced Jewish laws, were exclusively devoted to the God of Israel, and integrated with the Jewish community.[65] All three are required. Cohen sees "harbingers" of this openness already in the Persian period

---

63. Cohen, *Beginnings of Jewishness*, 109–39.

64. Cohen, *Beginnings of Jewishness*, 141. Shifting perspective from the convert to conversion, Martin Goodman has provided a four-fold classification of the varieties of "mission" undertaken by Jews between, roughly, 300 BCE and 300 CE. Goodman's four types are: informative missions, educational missions, apologetic missions, and proselytizing missions. Only proselytizing missions had the principal goal of persuading people to become Jews. *Mission and Conversion*, 1–19, esp. 1–5.

65. Cohen, *Beginnings of Jewishness*, 156–57. Cohen identifies this three-fold expectation in several ancient sources. To cite just one example, in the Book of Judith when Achior the Ammonite "saw all that the God of Israel had done, he believed firmly in God, and he was circumcised, and he joined the house of Israel, remaining so to this day" (14:10).

(Re)reading Ruth

(sixth to fourth centuries BCE), but, for him, the fact remains that in the Hebrew Bible "the idea [of conversion] itself is not yet in evidence."[66]

Now, it is important to recognize that Cohen's list of ways that a gentile might identify with Judaism are shaped by and suited to the evidence from Late Antiquity.[67] The Hebrew Bible is not his focus, and there is no *prima facie* reason to think that the two did or should match. Still, it must be admitted that several the possibilities that Cohen itemizes are already evident in the Hebrew Bible. Gentile sailors acknowledge the power of Jonah's God and pray to him (Jonah 1:14–16; Cohen's #2). The Torah permits gentiles to practice part of the Passover rite (Exod 12:19, 43–45) and to make certain sacrifices to the God of Israel (Lev 17:8; 22:18; Cohen's #4). Esther 8:17 mentions a group of gentiles, the *mityahădim*, who "professed to be Jews" (Cohen's #6).[68] There are many similar examples. So, was Ruth's vow to Naomi an act of conversion or not? Is she the exception to the rule, a gentile who converted to Israelite religion before conversion was typically accepted or practiced?

Christian and Jewish interpreters have different ways of answering this question. This is largely because they have different understandings of what conversion entails. Many Christian interpreters through the ages have seen Ruth as a prefiguring the church, which was "called by God from the Gentiles."[69] In this roundabout way, "she" does convert, albeit to Christianity and not to ancient Israelite religion. Other Christian interpreters—those who read Ruth as a human drama and not an allegory or type—still tend to interpret Ruth 1:16–17 as a genuine conversion. Nicholas of Lyra (1472) interpreted Ruth's vow in this way, and more than five-hundred years later Robert Hubbard (1988) did the same.[70] For these Christian interpreters,

---

66. Cohen, *Beginnings of Jewishness*, 122. In "Conversion to Judaism," Louis Feldmann describes a profound rise in the Jewish population of Palestine between 586 BCE and the first century CE that he believes can most readily be attributed to conversion (pages 115–56).

67. Late Antiquity is a title that originated in the study of European history and refers to the period from the third to the eighth centuries CE, or from about 230 CE to the early Islamic conquests in 622–750 CE. In the study of Judaism, the beginning of Late Antiquity is reckoned from either the First Jewish-Roman War in 66–70 CE, or the Second Jewish-Roman War and the deportation of Jews from Jerusalem in 132–35 CE.

68. There is a question, with this last example, as to whether those who "professed to be Jews" were genuine or not. See Berlin, *Esther*, 80–81.

69. Isidore of Seville, *On Ruth*, quoted from Smith, *Medieval Exegesis*, 7.

70. Hubbard *Ruth*, 117–21, esp. 120. Hugh of St. Chair, in his *Postills on Ruth* (Paris, 1533), accuses Naomi of sinning because she encouraged Orpah and Ruth return home and (by implication) to remain in idolatry.

conversion is a matter of belief in and commitment to the God of Israel. It is a matter of faith and will.

Jewish opinion is more divided, in part because conversion is a less fixed notion. For some interpreters, Ruth's actions do not rise to the level of "conversion." For others they do. Ancient interpreters tend to argue that Ruth was a convert. In *Midrash Ruth Rabba* (2 §22), Ruth is quoted as saying to Naomi: "For in any event, my intention is to convert, but it is better through you [with your help] and not through another" (on Ruth 1:17). Others thought she already had already converted when she married Maḥlon:

> R. Pedas asked the son of R. Yosi, man of Soko: Since Ruth converted [when she first married], why did they not give her a new [Jewish] name? He said to him: I received a tradition that she had another name. When she married Maḥlon... they called her Ruth, for she converted when she married Maḥlon and not afterwards.[71]

For modern Jewish scholars like Cohen, the matter is not so simple. Yael Ziegler, for example, does not identify Ruth's vow with conversion. For her, Ruth's actions represent loyalty and devotion, love even, but not conversion. The telling issue, for Ziegler, is Ruth's motive. For Ziegler, "Ruth's choice to remain with Naomi is a courageous and compassionate display of human love and devotion. Even if Ruth's motivation is exclusively in the realm of her interpersonal relations, her behaviour can illustrate the proper way to serve God."[72] Tamara Eskenazi sees it in still another way. For her, the vow is just a first step. There is an evolution in Ruth from Moabite widow to Israelite wife.

> She begins as a Moabite and remains so for most of the book. . . . But despite retaining her Moabite marker, the book also charts her journey through specific stages whereby her initial pledge is gradually affirmed by others—by, Boaz, by the people of Bethlehem, and finally by God. . . . Most significantly, the very last time that she is named, in Ruth 4:13, Ruth is no longer labelled as a Moabite.[73]

---

71. *Zohar*, Ruth §79a; cited by Jackson, "Ruth's Conversion," 53–54. Similarly, Japhet, discussing the issue of foreign wives in Ezra-Nehemiah, says, "the very marriage [of foreign women] to Israelite men entailed in fact their conversion." If this is so, it rather undercuts Ruth's vow, making it superfluous and irrelevant. "Expulsion of the Foreign Women," 141–61, quote at 154.

72. Ziegler, *Ruth*, 161.

73. Eskenazi and Frymer-Kensky, *Ruth*, xliv–xlv. Wünch holds a similar view. He sees Ruth as moving from Moabite to "a full member of the house of Israel" ("Ruth, a

(Re)reading Ruth

For Eskenazi, conversion is not only a matter of religious affiliation, not in the ancient world. In deep antiquity, it entailed membership in a community, not just religious practice. In the ancient Near East, gods were affiliated with communities and places, not just with beliefs and practices. For Eskenazi, conversion in the sense of "conversion to a new religion or god" is too narrow an idea to account for what we witness in Ruth. The Book of Ruth is fundamentally about Ruth's assimilation into a community.[74] So, in this small sample of Jewish interpretations, we have three different opinions, based on three different standards for what constitutes "conversion."[75]

Whether or not Ruth's vow is considered a conversion, or even a first step on a road to conversion, depends on what is required to call something "conversion." For the Christian interpreters named above, Ruth's vow expresses belief and dedication. Conversion requires nothing else. For Cohen, conversion requires adoption of Jewish law, exclusive devotion to the God of Israel, and integration with the Jewish community, and Ruth says nothing explicit about the first of these. As a result, for him, Ruth's attempt to become Israelite cannot be called "conversion." For the writers of *Ruth Rabba*, it can. For Ziegler, it is not conversion, because she was motivated by her love for and dedication to Naomi, not to God alone. For Eskenazi Ruth does, eventually, integrate herself into the Judean community, successfully adopting a new identity for herself. So, it seems that there is no straightforward answer to our original question. The answer depends on one's definition of "conversion." It is hardly surprising, then, that different interpreters answer the question differently.

> [19b] *And it came about, when they entered Bethlehem that all the town was in a stir because of them, and they said, "Is this Naomi?"* [20] *And she said to them, "Do not call me Naomi. Call me Mara, for Shaddai has dealt very bitterly with me.* [21] *I went out full, and Yhwh has returned me*

Proselyte," 36–64, quote at 51). For an exploration of Ruth's metamorphosis from one identity to another see Hyman, "Changing Identity," 189–201.

74. Eskenazi is building on the work of Neil Glover regarding ethnicity and post-exilic identity. "Your People, My People," 293–313.

75. For an analysis of religious identify in Ruth that brings all the book's relevant themes into the frame, see Wetter, *"On Her Account,"* 42–60.

Act 1 ~ Ruth 1:1–22

empty. Why do you call me Naomi, since Yhwh has testified against/afflicted me, and Shaddai has injured me?

As Naomi and Ruth enter Bethlehem the village people are in an uproar (*hûm*, "noisy" or "confused"). We are not told precisely why they respond to the arrival of the two widows in this way, though commentators almost never avoid speculating. The hubbub creates a situation where Naomi can address the whole town, and she does so with venom. Naomi is angry. In her anger, Naomi is eloquent, and she has four accusations: God has dealt bitterly with her; he has emptied her; he has afflicted her (or possibly "testified against her"); and he has injured her.

Call me Mara

1. *for Shaddai has dealt very bitterly with me.*
2. *I went out full and Yhwh has returned me empty.*

Why do you call me Naomi?

3. *since Yhwh has testified against/afflicted me,*
4. *and Shaddai has injured me*

Except the imperative "call me Mara" and the parallel question "Why do you call me Naomi?", each line is an accusation. Naomi renames herself Mara: "Do not call me Naomi (pleasantness). Call me Mara (bitterness), for Shaddai has dealt very bitterly with me." Surely readers are meant to wonder if Naomi's fate will match her name, as her sons' fates did. If so, which name will it match: her given name or her new self-given name? Naomi's new name, Mara, is also a pun on "bad/injured" in the fourth accusation. Notice the sequence of sounds: *mārāʾ* (Mara/bitterness), *hēmar* (dealt bitterly), *hēraʿ* (injured/done bad). These two accusations, the first and last, sum up Naomi's feelings and her claim. The two central accusations offer Naomi's specific charges against God.

In Naomi's second accusation—*I went out full, and Yhwh has returned me empty*—she gives voice to one of the book's main themes. When discussing the Prologue, we identified Naomi's two major needs. She needs food and she needs security. In this single line, Naomi's sums up her losses and her needs in a single word: *empty*. This is the main theme of the chapter and, indeed, is half of the larger theme *emptiness and fullness*.[76] The book opened with the declaration that the land, even Bethlehem ("house of

---

76. Rauber, "Literary Values," 27–37, esp. 29–30.

bread"), was empty of food (1:1). In the following verses, Naomi's household emptied of men, as first her husband and then her sons died (1:3, 5), until only Naomi was left (1:5). Naomi then gave the emptiness theme a literal twist during her dispute with her daughters-in-law who wanted to follow her to Israel. As she argued, "Do I still have sons in my womb who could be husbands for you?" Her body, Naomi claimed, is empty of children. What's more, her heart is empty of hope. She does not believe that she could succeed at the task of establishing a new household in Israel, because "I am too old to get a husband" (1:11). Here in 1:20–21, at the close of Act 1, Naomi expresses all these losses as an emptiness. "*I went out full, and Yhwh has returned me empty.*" As the book progresses, the two women's needs and Ruth's efforts to meet them will often be viewed through the lens of emptiness and fullness. As we are about to see, the point of Act 1 is to direct our attention to the single solution to all Naomi's problems, to her emptiness, a solution that Naomi will fail to appreciate.

In the third accusation, Naomi uses another polysemic word, ʿnh. The word ʿānāh means "*testified* against me." In this case, her words are a legal charge with juridical force. Naomi is accusing God of treating her unfairly in his role as divine judge, of corrupting justice. But the same word spelled slightly differently, as ʿinnāh, means "to humiliate" or "be harsh." This is not a mild word. It is one of the words used to describe the brutal conditions the Israelites endured while slaves in Egypt (Exod 3:7, 17; 4:31; 10:3; etc.). If this reading is correct, Naomi is accusing God of treating her in a way that makes him angry when others do the same. She is accusing him of hypocrisy. Until late antiquity, Biblical Hebrew was written without any vowels. That means that some readers would have assumed that the vowelless word ʿnh was ʿānāh and others that it was ʿinnāh. English Bibles are divided over the proper way to read the word. Some translate "testified against me" and others "dealt harshly with me." Jack Sasson rightly observes that both readings make good sense here, and the writers of Ruth may have chosen ʿnh to exploit this dual possibility.[77] If he is correct, neither translation is right, and neither is wrong.

---

77. Sasson, *Ruth*, 35–36

Act 1 ~ Ruth 1:1-22

Excursus 4. Naomi and Job

The stories of Naomi and Job are tales of disaster and loss. At the beginning of Ruth, Naomi owns property and has a family, like Job did. She loses both, like Job did:

> 13 One day, as his sons and daughters were eating and drinking wine in the house of their eldest brother, 14 a messenger came to Job and said, "The oxen were plowing and the she-asses were grazing alongside them 15 when Sabeans attacked them and carried them off, and put the boys to the sword; I alone have escaped to tell you." 16 This one was still speaking when another came and said, "God's fire fell from heaven, took hold of the sheep and the boys, and burned them up; I alone have escaped to tell you." 17 This one was still speaking when another came and said, "A Chaldean formation of three columns made a raid on the camels and carried them off and put the boys to the sword; I alone have escaped to tell you." 18 This one was still speaking when another came and said, "Your sons and daughters were eating and drinking wine in the house of their eldest brother 19 when suddenly a mighty wind came from the wilderness. It struck the four corners of the house so that it collapsed upon the young people, and they died; I alone have escaped to tell you." (Job 1:13-19, NJPS)

When Naomi eventually returned to Bethlehem, with just an impoverished Moabite daughter-in-law for support, the townsfolk were so startled that they had to ask, "is this [really] Naomi?" Job's friends responded in a similar way to his change of fortune:

> 12 When they saw him from a distance, they could not recognize him, and they broke into loud weeping; each one tore his robe and threw dust into the air onto his head. 13 They sat with him on the ground seven days and seven nights. None spoke a word to him for they saw how very great was his suffering. (Job 2:12-13, NJPS)

Neither character knows why they are suffering, but both assume God is to blame. (This assumption is true in Job's case, as the reader of Job is permitted to learn. Although Job is never allowed to learn this. No cause is ever suggested for the tragedies that Naomi endures.)[78] In the end, both characters are restored. In Ruth, Naomi's family-property is redeemed and a new generation springs from the marriage of Ruth and Boaz. In Job, his property is restored, and he fathers ten new children: "Thus Yhwh blessed

---

78. See chapter 2, note 12.

the latter years of Job's life more than the former. He had fourteen thousand sheep, six thousand camels, one thousand yoke of oxen, and one thousand she-asses. He also had seven sons and three daughters" (Job 42:12–13).[79] As Yair Zakovitch says, Naomi is a "female version of Job."[80]

These similarities are suggestive, to be sure, but they do not imply a literary relationship between the two books. They might be *similar* stories without being *related* stories. (Think of all the romantic comedies you have seen or detective novels you have read that follow a prescribed storyline. They may be alike, even strikingly so, without being purposefully related to one another.) There is, however, a strong clue in Ruth 1:20–21 that Job is more than just a fellow sufferer, that Naomi and Job are analogous characters.[81] Notice the remarkable similarities between Naomi's and Job's accusations against God, which make use of a common constellation of words and are delivered in a legal register:[82]

Naomi: 20 And she said to them, "Do not call me Naomi. Call me *Mara* (*mārāʾ*), for *Shaddai* (*šadday*) has *dealt* very *bitterly with me* (*hēmar . . . lî*). 21 I went out full, and Yhwh has returned me empty. Why do you call me Naomi, since Yhwh has afflicted/*testified against me* (*ʿānāh bî*), and *Shaddai* (*šadday*) has injured me?

Job 27:2 As God lives, who has taken away *my right* (*mišpāṭî*), and *Shadday* (*šadday*), who has *made my life bitter* (*hēmar napšî*).[83]

For all the similarities between the two accusations, there is an important difference between Job and Naomi. The difference is evident in their responses to a reversal of fortune. Naomi—assuming that God was responsible for her "emptiness" (*rēqām*)—renames herself Bitterness and accuses

---

79. The similarity may be incidental, but it is worth noting that Job has seven sons (42:13) and Ruth is "better than seven sons" (4:15).

80. Zakovitch, "Halakhic Creativity," 145–51.

81. Numerous modern scholars have noted the stylistic similarities between the framing narrative of Job (chapters 1–2, 42) and Ruth, which are usually attributed to an "old epic style" or some similar chimera. To my knowledge, the first modern commentator to recognize the allusion to Job found in Naomi's retort to the women of Bethlehem is Zakovitch, *Ruth*, 63–66 [Hebrew]; compare Fischer, *Rut*, 152–54.

82. Both use legal language in their accusations. Naomi charges God with "testifying against me" (*ʿānāh bî*), and Job cites him for withholding "my rights" or, perhaps, "my due justice" (*mišpāṭî*).

83. Similarly, Job 7:11; 10:1; 13:26.

God of injustice, of injuring her unfairly.[84] Job also believes that God has treated him unfairly, but he still responds with a blessing: "Naked (*ʿārûm*) I came from my mother's womb, and naked (*ʿārûm*) will I return there. Yhwh gave, and Yhwh has taken away. Blessed be the name of Yhwh" (1:21). In this one way, Naomi and Job are antithetical characters. One exemplifies a natural and all-too human response to misfortune: to blame God for unkindness, if not out-and-out cruelty. The other exemplifies an *un*natural and *un*likely response: to hold the same grievances against God but to acknowledge his right to "give and take" as he sees fit.

In the end, both characters thrive. It is not entirely clear why Job eventually prospers. It is connected to his intercession for his friends, but it clearly is not a reward for how he responded to his own suffering (Job 42:7–10). Perhaps the cosmic bet had simply run its course. Although the reasons for Job's eventual good fortune are obscure, Naomi's are crystal clear. Naomi will prosper because of the kindness and the loyalty of others (Ruth 4:14–15).

---

22 So, Naomi returned, and Ruth the Moabite her daughter-in-law with her, the one who returned from the fields of Moab.[85] They came to Bethlehem at the beginning of the barley harvest.

The Act concludes with a single transitional verse. The first half of verse 22 closes off Act 1 by summing up the main actions.[86] The second half serves as a transition to Act 2 by setting its scene. Act 2 will occur in Boaz's barley field, where Ruth will glean behind Boaz's harvest laborers.

Before turning to Act 2, it is essential that we observe one last allusion in Act 1. As we have already seen, narratives in the Hebrew Bible are dense with allusions. Allusions are used to craft terse stories like Ruth into complex, multifaceted dramas. We have discussed numerous allusions in Act 1, and each one informed a verse or two (as in 1:16–17 and 1:20–21).

---

84. Notice, in this regard, Naomi's pun on "bitter" in her complaint: God has made her life bitter (*hēmar . . . lî*), and he has "injured her" or "done wrong to her" (*hēraʿ lî*).

85. The second half of the verse, "the one who returned . . . ," refers to Ruth, who is the immediate antecedent of the verb. We will see why this is significant in *Excursus 14*.

86. It is also part of the ring-structure that surrounds 1:6–22, as described above on pages 12–13.

(Re)reading Ruth

This is how allusions often work. They are often quite limited in scope. Recognizing that Naomi's or Ruth's words echo another text, we readjust our understanding of the narrative moment, but they do not cause us to rethink the plot of the whole chapter or the whole book.

Sometimes though, an allusion has greater scope. Act 1 includes one such allusion that permeates and shapes the whole Act. Once recognized, it adjusts our understanding of the relationship between Naomi and Ruth quite profoundly. This allusion is to Gen 2:24.

> For this reason, a man forsakes his father and his mother and clings to his wife, and the two become one flesh.

Genesis 2:24 is the first description of marriage in the Hebrew Bible. It is also the closest thing in the Hebrew Bible to a definition of marriage. Act 1 evokes this verse again and again. It is not easy to see, but when we catalogue all the echoes of Gen 2:24 that are found in Ruth 1, they prove to be an impressive collection. The women's conversation revolves around the *subject* of marriage and the impossibility of Orpah and Ruth marrying again, if they stay with Naomi (especially verses 9 and 11–13). Naomi exhorts her daughters-in-law to return to the houses of their *mothers* (*'m*), dissolving the households they had established with Maḥlon and Kilyon by re-joining their families of origin (1:8). Ruth rebukes Naomi, "do not urge me to *forsake* (*'zb*) you" (1:15), and she *clings* (*dbq*) to her (1:14). Ruth vows "your people will be my people" (1:16), disavowing her ties of kinship to anyone in Moab. In the same way, marriage, according to Gen 2:24, entails the loosening of one set of kinship ties—with mother and father—to fashion a new family bond.[87]

It is in the light of this allusion that the weight of Ruth's vow becomes fully visible.[88] Although she has lost the family that she created though marriage, she voluntarily transfers her fidelity to Naomi. Ruth will live, die, and be buried with Naomi.[89] She vows loyalty to Naomi. She will not be

---

[87]. The Hebrew idioms "you are my bone" or "you are my flesh" (Gen 2:23) mean "you are kin." To "become one flesh" is to form a kinship bond. See, for example, Gen 29:14; 2 Sam 5:1.

[88]. On this allusion see esp. Fischer, *Rut*, 47–48, 142, 176–77; Beyer, *Hoffnung in Bethlehem*, 197–99.

[89]. In the ancient Near East, where one was buried had religious connotations. As Herbert Chanan Brichto puts it,

> Property too was essentially a religious concept, particularly real property. The family was attached to the soil as the notion of the burial place as the ancestral

separated from Naomi and she will not forsake her.[90] The story of Act 1 is the story of Ruth tying not just her fortunes but her person to Naomi with a vow that is as strong or stronger than the bond she shared with Maḥlon.

The tragedy unveiled at the close of Act 1 is not the one Naomi thinks it is. It is not Naomi's grief. It is not her loss of husband and sons (tragic as that is), and it is not God's behavior toward her. It is Naomi's self-centeredness. "I went out full, and Yhwh has returned me empty." Nothing could be further from the truth. Ruth has given everything that she owns to fill Naomi's emptiness; she has given herself. Not only is Naomi unaware of the powerful and poignant gift bestowed on her by Ruth; she is also unaware of Ruth. She neither acknowledges the gift nor reciprocates it. She is not empty; she is blind.[91]

---

    home was extended to the surrounding fields. Laws of primogeniture, succession and inheritance rights, indivisibility and inalienability of real estate, the sacrilegious nature of the crime of moving a landmark all derive from this concept of the family and its real holdings...."

For more on this idea see Brichto, "Kin, Cult, Land, and Afterlife," 9–24.

90. Ziegler observes (*Ruth*, 156–57) that Ruth's vow is not limited by Naomi's lifespan, because she vows to be buried alongside Naomi.

91. The allusion to Gen 2:24 will persist in Act 2, signalled most clearly by the repetition of *forsake* ('*āzab*) in 2:11, 16, 20 and *cling* (*dābaq*) in 2:8, 21, 23.

CHAPTER 3

Act 2 ~ Ruth 2:1–23

¹ And Naomi had a kinsman of her husband, a mighty man of strength from the clan of Elimelek, and his name was Boaz. ² And Ruth the Moabite said to Naomi, "Let me go into the fields, and let me glean the heads of grain after the one in whose eyes I find favor." And she said to her "Go, my daughter." ³ So she went. She entered and gleaned in a field behind the harvest workers. And by chance it was a portion of field belonging to Boaz, who was from the clan of Elimelek.

THE NARRATOR OPENS ACT 2 by presenting a new character, Boaz. His relationship to Naomi is mentioned twice, repeated at the beginning and end of the paragraph: "a kinsman of her husband . . . from the clan of Elimelek, and his name was Boaz" (2:1); "Boaz . . . from the clan of Elimelek" (2:3). Clearly, Boaz will be central to Act 2, and his kinship with Elimelek will define his role in the story. In verses 2–3, Ruth initiates a plan to solve one of the women's basic needs, the need for food. She gets permission from Naomi to take advantage of the timing of their arrival, "at the beginning of the barley harvest" (1:22) to glean in the fields for dropped grain. Ruth's plan will propel the plot of Act 2.[1]

---

1. We cannot explore every allusion from Act 2. The most notable omission is an allusion to the manna story in Exod 16.

Act 2 ~ Ruth 2:1-23

The new character is introduced by three important facts: he is a relative of Elimelek's; he is a "mighty man of strength"; and his name is Boaz. Israelites were distinguished by their family relationships, by tribe (*šebeṭ* or *maṭṭēh*), clan (*mišpāḥāh*), and extended household, often called the "house of the father" (*bêt ' ab*).[2] Boaz is from Elimelek's clan, the Ephrathites (1:3), a fact that will become increasingly important as the story progresses. He is not presented to readers as a blank canvas. He is characterized as an *' îš gibbôr ḥayil*, literally a "mighty man of *ḥayil*" or "a man, a mighty one of *ḥayil*." *Ḥayil* is yet another polysemic word. It can mean "strength," "power," "ability," or "wealth." The phrase "mighty man of *ḥayil*" is mostly used for warriors (Josh 1:14; Judg 6:12 [ironic]; 2 Kgs 24:14; 1 Chr 12:9) but, every once in a while, for the wealthy (2 Kgs 15:20) or for persons who are uniquely competent (1 Kgs 11:28).[3] At this point in the story, we obviously have no way of determining which of these is correct for Boaz. This will only become plain in the next Act.

Turning to the plan, Ruth suggests to Naomi that she begin to "glean," a practice governed by a set of laws from Deut 24:19-22.

> 19 When you reap the harvest in your field and overlook a sheaf in the field, do not return to retrieve it.
> It is for the foreigner, the orphan, and the widow, in order that Yhwh your God may bless you in all the work of your hands.
> 20 Once you beat your olive trees [to harvest the olives], do not go over them again.
> It is for the foreigner, the orphan, and the widow.
> 21 When you harvest your vineyard, do not pick it again.
> It is for the foreigner, the orphan, and the widow.
> 22 So remember that you were a slave in the land of Egypt.
> It is for this reason that I command you to do this.

The gleaning law is repeated and rephrased in Lev 19:9-10 (23:22).

> 9 When you reap the harvest of your land, you will not reap to the edges of your field nor gather what is dropped during your harvesting.
> 10 You will not pick your vineyard bare, nor gather your vineyard's fallen fruit. You will leave them for the poor and the foreigner.
> I, Yhwh, am your God.

---

2. This is just a sketch. Israelite family relationships can be described using other terms, as we saw in 1:8. See Blenkinsopp, "The Family," 48-103; Anderson, "Israelite Kinship Terminology," 29-39.

3. Bush, *Ruth, Esther*, 100-101; Kosmala, "גבר," *TDOT* 2:367-82, esp. 374.

(Re)reading Ruth

Deuteronomy 24 and Leviticus 19 specify that a part of every harvest must be left for the most disadvantaged: the poor, widows, orphans, and foreigners living in Israel. Naomi meets two of these criteria. Ruth meets three. Deuteronomy 24 encourages Israelites to follow this law in two ways. Verse 19 provides a negative motivation. The law implies that, should Israel not care for the humble and most desperate, God will not care for Israel. It summons Israel to imitate the providential care that God extends to Israel, in short, to be a blessing.[4] Verse 22 provides a positive motivation. It appeals to Israel's empathy. Israelites should not treat the disadvantaged in the way that the Egyptians treated Israel by oppressing them. Instead, they should follow the golden rule and treat foreigners in the way they would have wished to be treated. (Leviticus 19:10 offers a single motivation, "I, Yhwh, am your God," which is a common way that Leviticus reminds Israel of God's prerogatives over her.) What Ruth proposes to Naomi is that she follow behind the harvest workers who are tying up the cut grain into sheaves and collect whatever is dropped or overlooked. If the harvest laborers respect the harvest law (Deut 24:19–22 and Lev 19:9–10), they should recognize her right to do this. However, Ruth acknowledges that permission will require the favor of the foreman or owner (Ruth 2:2). She does not assume that her right to glean will be recognized. Indeed, as we will see, it is not just her rights that are at risk.[5]

Despite its risks, Naomi endorses Ruth's plan. The plan is essential to the story. It not only creates the appropriate conditions for Boaz to meet Ruth, it will provide him with the opportunity to meet one of the two women's needs.

> 4 *And behold, Boaz was coming from Bethlehem, and he said to the harvest workers, "Yhwh is with you!" And they said to him, "May Yhwh bless you."* 5 *And Boaz said to his young man, the one who was foreman over the harvest workers, "Whose is this young woman?"* 6 *And the young man, the one who was foreman over the harvest workers, answered, "A young woman, she is a Moabite, the one who returned with Naomi from the land of Moab,* 7 *and she said, 'Please let me glean and gather*

---

4. In keeping with Gen 12:3.
5. Compare Braulik, "Intra-Biblical Critique," 16–18.

Act 2 ~ Ruth 2:1-23

among the sheaves behind the harvest workers.' And she came, and she has been on her feet from morning until now. She has only sat in the house for a little while."[6]

Ruth does not need to do anything to attract Boaz's attention. When Boaz arrives from town, presumably to check on the progress of the harvest, he immediately notices Ruth.[7] The harvest, it seems, flies from his thoughts. He does not ask his foreman about the yield, or progress, or the harvest workers. The only thing that he asks is *"whose* is this young woman?" This particular question might seem an unexpected one. "*Who* is this young woman?" we would ask. But Boaz is not asking about her identity. The Hebrew Bible uses very simple language to describe when men and women become domestic partners, either by marriage, or concubinage, or any other domestic custom. The partners "take" (*lqḥ* or *nsʾ*) one another and each then "belongs to" (*lĕ-*) the other.[8] Likewise, the question "whose?" can be asked of a dependent, as in Gen 24:23, "whose daughter are you?" With this question, Boaz is inquiring *whose household* Ruth occupies. Is she single or married? Is she someone's daughter or ward?[9] The foreman explains that she is the woman everyone has heard about (1:19), the Moabite who returned with Naomi. She is a woman without a household. He goes on, though, to volunteer some additional information: "and she has been on her feet from morning until now." Ruth is a hard worker. The foreman does not know it, but he could not have said anything to enhance Boaz's attraction more. In this chapter and the next, Ruth's industriousness will be the centerpiece of Boaz's attraction to Ruth.

---

6. The last two clauses, which I have rendered idiomatically as "and she has been on her feet from morning until now. She has only sat in the house for a little while" are grammatically problematic. See discussion in Holmstedt, *Ruth*, 116–17.

7. The labourers' reply to Boaz is a line from the traditional priestly blessing (Num 6:24–26). It does not indicate that the labourers are pious God-fearers though. As Schipper and Bush observe, it is a formulaic greeting, that is similar to those found in ancient Hebrew letters and conventional Arabic salutations today (Schipper, *Ruth*, 118; Bush, *Ruth, Esther*, 112).

8. The language for permitting a marriage or other partnership is equally simple. One party, usually the father or a king, "gives" (*ntn*) his ward or subject to be a man's "woman" (*ʾišāh*). There are other ways to describe partnering in the Hebrew Bible, but these are among the most common.

9. Genesis 24:23 shows that the question "whose?" (*lĕmî*) can be asked without implying that the person is property as some modern interpreters assume.

(Re)reading Ruth

Once Boaz knows that Ruth is not attached to any man's household, he approaches her with a suggestion:

> ⁸ So Boaz said to Ruth, "Will you not listen, my daughter? Do not go out to glean in another field, and also do not go elsewhere, but cling to my young women. ⁹ Let your eyes be on the field which they harvest and follow them. Have I not ordered the young men not to touch you? And when you are thirsty, go to the jars and drink what the young men have drawn."

The conversation between Boaz and Ruth in verses 8–13 seems straightforward, but it is filled with allusions, puns, and figures of speech. Most are playful, broadening our appreciation of the characters' wit and foreshadowing events to come. Some, though, are profound, summoning memories of towering figures from Israel's past and setting this modest romance story against a backdrop of national drama.

With his first words (2:8–9) Boaz encourages Ruth to remain in his fields with his young women, and he offers her protection.[10] His question, "have I not commanded the young men not to touch you?" highlights the precariousness of Ruth's situation as a poor widow in a foreign country and the dangers Ruth must face just to find enough food to eat.[11] In the span of

---

10. The "young women" of Boaz are never explained. Based on the use of "young women" (*naʿărōt*) with a possessive pronoun ("*my* young women," "*her* young women," etc.), they are most likely servants (Gen 24:61; Exod 2:5; 1 Sam 25:42; Prov 31:15).

11. Koosed, *Gleaning Ruth*, x n. 19; Shepherd, "Women, Foreignness, and Violence," 528–43; Fewell and Gunn, *Compromising Redemption*, 42–44, 76–77, 84–85. Some commentators minimize the risk to Ruth, suggesting that the harvest workers might merely have prevented Ruth from working alongside Boaz's servant women or might have shooed her away from the water (Hubbard, *Ruth*, 158; Sasson, *Ruth*, 50). The most common meaning for the verb *ngʿ* is "to touch," resulting in the translation, "have I not ordered my young men not to touch you?" (2:9). When the verb is used of one person "touching" another, it typically indicates a violent (Gen 26:29; 32:25; Josh 9:19; 1 Sam 6:9; Isa 26:5) or sexual (Gen 20:6; 2 Sam 14:10; Prov 6:29) touch. Boaz repeats the command in verse 15, but uses the synonym *klm*. This term is used for humiliation (1 Sam 10:5; Jer 6:15), including physical humiliation (Judg 18:7; 2 Sam 25:7, 15). The fact that several verses later Boaz specifies that Ruth is not to be subjected to verbal abuse indicates that he is referring to physical abuse in 2:15. Finally, when Naomi repeats the same warning to Ruth in 2:23, she uses the synonym *pgʿ*, "touch, strike," which is also commonly employed to describe acts of violence (Exod 5:3; Judg 8:21; 15:12; 18:25; 1 Sam 22:17–18; 1 Kgs 2:25, 31–32; etc.).

two verses, Boaz has effectively spoken to all of Naomi's and Ruth's needs: the need for food, the need for security, and the need to navigate life as a powerless foreign woman. His offer, surely, is meant to draw Ruth closer to his household and to himself.[12] It is an obvious offer for an infatuated man to make. His language, though, hints at more than this. There is an allusion to Act 1 in Boaz's proposal. He urges Ruth to "cling" (*dbq*) to his young women, and he calls her "my daughter" (*bitti*). When Naomi commanded her "daughters" (1:11, 13) to return to Moab, Orpah obeyed, but Ruth refused and "clung" (*dbq*) to her (1:14). Boaz asks Ruth to glean only in his fields, to be loyal, so to speak, to his property, his servant girls, and himself. In the process, he unwittingly echoes the language used to describe Ruth's fidelity to Naomi in Act 1, language that itself echoes the Bible's first description of marriage.[13] He is, in effect, inviting more loyalty than he realizes. All this, of course, is for the benefit of the reader. As bystanders to the scene, we anticipate watching Boaz pursue his newfound romantic ambitions.

At first blush, the offer of water seems superfluous (1:9b). It does not speak to one of the major needs exhibited by the Prologue (1:1–5), and it is the most innocuous of Boaz's gifts, a small act of kindness that cost him nothing. So why is it mentioned? First of all, it is one of the triggers of an elaborate allusion that spans Ruth 2 and 3, and which will be described at the end of this chapter in *Excursus 8*. Second, it is an ironic echo of Deut 23:4. The law in Deut 23:3–8 (Hebrew 23:4–9) stands prominently in the background of the Ruth story. It will be alluded to on several occasions:

> **3** An Ammonite or Moabite will not enter into the assembly of Yhwh. Even the tenth generation will not ever enter to the assembly of Yhwh, **4** because they did not meet you with food or water on the way when you went out from Egypt, and because they hired against you Balaam son of Beor, from Petor of Aram-of-the-Rivers, in order to curse you. . . . **8** You will not promote their peace or their welfare for as long as you live.

The Book of Ruth faces questions about the marriage of Israelites and gentiles without flinching. Since many ancient interpreters understood the expression "enter the assembly of Yhwh" as a reference to marriage, Deut 23:3–8 is never far out of view. Ruth 2:9, though, is concerned with

---

12. Eskenazi and Frymer-Kensky even suggest that this might "reflect some formal reassignment of her status within the corporate household," but they admit that we cannot be certain (*Ruth*, 34).

13. See comments on 1:22. Compare Raskas, "Book of Ruth," 224.

a different dimension of this law. According to Deut 23, the reason for the lasting enmity between Israel and Moab is that the Moabites did not "meet you with food or water on the way when you went out from Egypt." Ruth 2:9 is a reversal of that historical memory. At their first meeting, Boaz the Israelite offers water to Ruth the Moabite, who has recently come out of Moab. He will offer her food too (2:14), actively pursuing her welfare. Whether this small irony merely signals that Boaz has resisted ethnic prejudice or whether it signals that the book will include a focused engagement with the law of Deut 23:4–7 remains to be seen.

Ruth's response to Boaz's protection and care is immediate and overwhelming:

> 10 *Then she fell upon her face, prostrating herself to the ground, and she said to him, "Why have I found favor in your eyes so as to recognize me when I am a foreigner?"*

Ruth's response might seem extravagant or overwrought, but in the Hebrew Bible it is appropriate. A person in a socially inferior position will act as Ruth did when asking for favor or expressing gratitude for kindness, particularly when the gratitude is directed toward a person in a socially superior position. When Abigail meets David for the first time (1 Sam 25:23) to plead for his mercy, she "hurried and dismounted from the donkey; she fell before David on her face, bowing to the ground." We can observe the same action again and again in the Bible (Gen 18:2–3; 33:3; Judg 1:14; 1 Sam 20:41; 2 Sam 14:21–22; 16:4).[14]

Ruth's words express more than simple gratitude, though. Her question "why have I found favor in your eyes?" is an echo of her own words to Naomi in 2:2. There she asked Naomi to allow her to glean "after the one in whose eyes I find favor." She does not know why Boaz has shown her favor, but she recognizes in this moment that she has attained her objective. At the same time, she is surprised that anyone would show kindness to her because "I am a foreigner." Despite hoping someone would be kind to her, Ruth clearly did not really believe that anyone would. She underlines her disbelief with a play on words: "Why have I found favor in your eyes so as *to recognize* (*nkr*) me when I am *a foreigner* (*nkr*)?" She wants Boaz to explain the reasons for his kindness. It is as if Ruth suspects it is too good to be mere kindness; it must come with strings attached.

---

14. Bridge, "Self-Abasement," 255–73.

Act 2 ~ Ruth 2:1-23

Excursus 5. Ruth and Hannah

The Book of Ruth is a bridge between Judges and Samuel. The Prologue announces that the story's events occurred during the days of the judges (1:1), and the book's Epilogue spells out Perez's linage, culminating with David (4:18–22).[15] But Ruth's writers did more than locate the story in the larger biblical storyline.[16] They also infused the story with connections to specific stories in Judges and Samuel, notably at the end of Judges and at the beginning of Samuel. Hannah's is the first story in the Book of Samuel, and its similarities to Ruth are startlingly apparent when one reads the two stories one after the other.

There are a few evocative phrases and clauses shared by Ruth and 1 Samuel 1–2 that first alert readers to the allusion. Three stand out. In 1 Samuel 1, Hannah despairs her inability to become pregnant. In a moment of obtuseness, her husband Elkanah asks her "am I not better to you than ten sons?" (1:8). Naomi too lamented her lack of sons (1:11–13), and at the end of her story the women of Bethlehem describe Ruth to Naomi as "better to you than seven sons" (4:15). Second, when Hannah goes to the tabernacle to beg God for a child, Eli believes her to be drunk and scolds her. When he realizes that she is pouring out her heart to God in grief and anxious hope, he extends a blessing to her: "may the God of Israel grant you what you have asked of him" (1:17). She observes, in gratitude, that "your maidservant has found favor in your eyes" (1 Sam 1:18), which is the very same line that Ruth says to Boaz in Ruth 2:13 (compare 2:10). Finally, when Hannah returns to the tabernacle year after year, her husband is blessed by Eli: "May Yhwh grant you seed by this woman" (1 Sam 2:19). Boaz is blessed in similar words by the people at the gate: "May Yhwh give you seed from this young woman" (Ruth 4:12). Both blessings come true.

---

15. As Jobling observes, "For this book [Ruth] achieves exactly the same journey that 1 Samuel does—from 'the days when the judges ruled' to 'David.'" "Ruth Finds a Home," 130.

16. As I describe in the Appendix, though the events in Ruth are *presented* as having occurred before Samuel in the biblical storyline, Ruth is often *physically located* in the HB immediately after Proverbs. The physical arrangement assists the reader in recognizing certain connections to Proverbs, just as the presentation assists one in seeing the connections to Hannah's story.

(Re)reading Ruth

Having noted these similar lines, readers may suspect a connection between Hannah's story and Ruth's. But is the connection compelling? There may not be many verbal parallels between the two stories, but there are many similarities between the stories' characters and plotlines.[17]

- Each story is about two wives: Orpah and Ruth ‖ Hannah and Peninnah (1 Sam 1:2 ‖ Ruth 1:4)
- The main character in each is childless (1 Sam 1:2 ‖ implied in Ruth 1; 4:13), and the plot of each is focused on the need to bear children.
- Each story features a meal in which a man gives a special portion to the woman (1 Sam 1:4–5 ‖ Ruth 2:14)
- In each story, a particular man can resolve the woman's need, and he is much older than her (1 Sam 1:12–18 ‖ Ruth 2:20; 3:10).
- Both Ruth and Hannah show special deference to the man who has the power to resolve their need (1 Sam 1:18 ‖ Ruth 2:13).
- Both men bless the woman (1 Sam 1:17 ‖ Ruth 3:10).
- Both women become pregnant by divine provision and have sons:

   > **13** So Boaz married Ruth; she became his wife, and he came into her and Yhwh gave her a pregnancy, and she bore a son.... **17** They called his name Obed. He was the father of Jesse, father of David. (Ruth 4:13, 17)

   > **19** Elkanah knew his wife Hannah and Yhwh remembered her. **20** Hannah conceived, and at the turn of the year she bore a son. She named him Samuel, meaning "I asked Yhwh for him." (1 Sam 1:19–20)

- The two sons have interrelated destinies. One is the progenitor of David. The other will establish David on the throne of Israel.

The similarities between Ruth's story and Hannah's certainly create cohesion between the Book of Ruth and the beginning of the Book of Samuel.

---

17. Fischer (*Rut*, 109–10), Jobling ("Home," 132–34), Raskas ("Book of Ruth," 223–32), Zakovitch (*Ruth* 14–15), and Ziegler (*Ruth*, 235–40) all discuss aspects of the analogy between Ruth's story and Hannah's. The notion that the two women's stories are connected is not just a modern proposal. *Pesiqta Rabbati*, a medieval midrash on select portions of the Torah and prophets (those read at festivals), also coordinates the lives of Ruth and Hannah (43 §179–82).

Act 2 ~ Ruth 2:1-23

But how does the analogy between Hannah and Ruth enhance either story? It is clear from Hannah's story, that God was caretaker of Samuel's birth and his destiny. From Ruth it is clear that God enabled her to conceive too (4:13), that David's destiny was also under God's providential direction. The lives of both men, who would change the course of Israel's history by establishing the Davidic monarchy, were divinely curated. The analogy between Ruth and Hannah does more than just present Samuel's and David's lives as divinely directed. It presents the lives of their mothers as the work of providence too. Before they were born, God orchestrated their mothers' lives, their births, and their vocations. As a way of prefiguring the intertwining of the two men's lives, the stories of their mothers are presented as reflections of one another too.[18]

Further, this analogy shows the God of Israel working through a gentile in precisely the same ways as he does with Israelites. Reminded of the fact, readers may recall that the lives of other gentiles are steered toward good or blessed by the God of Israel, like Pharaoh's midwives, Job, Obed-Edom, Cyrus, Ebed-Melech, and all gentiles in Isaiah 56–66. The analogy between Ruth and Hannah, indeed the whole Ruth story, is a vaccine

---

18. Psalm 89:19-21 (Hebrew 89:20-22) says that David's rise was foretold in a vision and that God was always with him:

> 19 Then you spoke to your faithful ones in a vision and said,
> "I have granted help to a warrior
> I have exalted the one chosen from the people
> 20 I have found David, my servant
> anointed him with my sacred oil
> 21 My hand will be with him constantly
> and my arm will strengthen him . . . ."

Verse 19 may well be speaking of Hannah. After being granted children through Eli's blessing, Hannah sings a song (1 Sam 2:1-10) that anticipates the coming monarchy. Note verse 10 in particular:

> Yhwh, his foes will be shattered
> He will thunder against them in the heavens.
> Yhwh will judge the ends of the earth.
> He will give power to his king,
> And triumph to his anointed one.

Because she predicted the coming of the monarchy, Hannah is remembered as a prophet in Jewish tradition. According to *Megillah* 14a, part of an ancient compendium of Jewish law called the Talmud (c. 500 CE), Hannah was one of only seven female prophets in ancient Israel's history. The others were Sarah, Miriam, Deborah, Abigail, Huldah, and Esther.

against jingoism and ethnocentrism, a more effective one, I imagine, than an essay or lecture could ever be.[19]

> 11 *And Boaz answered, and he said to her, "Everything that you did for your mother-in-law after the death of your husband has been reported to me: how you left your father and your mother and the land of your kindred and went to a people whom you did not know before.* 12 *May Yhwh reward your deed, and may your wage be complete from Yhwh, the God of Israel, whom you came to seek refuge beneath his wings."*

Boaz tells Ruth that he has no secret motive. His help is inspired by her virtue. Twice in the book, once in Act 2 and once in Act 3, Boaz will speak about Ruth's virtues. In each case, he will draw an analogy between Ruth and another character from the Bible. In this case, he alludes to the life of Abraham and equates Ruth with him. In verse 11, he alludes to Gen 12:1–3, and in verse 12, to Gen 15:1 (similarities of theme and language italicized):

11 "Everything that you did for your mother-in-law after the death of your husband has been reported to me: *how you left your father and your mother and the land of your kindred and went to a people whom you did not know before.*	12:1 Now Yhwh said to Abram, "*Go from your country and your kindred and your father's house to the land that I will show you . . .*"
12 *May Yhwh reward your deed, and may your wage be complete from Yahweh*, the God of Israel, whom *you came to seek refuge beneath his wings."*	15:1 After these things the word of Yhwh came to Abram in a vision, "Do not be afraid, Abram, *I am your shield; your reward will be very great."*

---

19. The prophet Amos is explicit about this. He contends that the God of Israel engages with all nations. Israel is not unique. "To me, O Israelites, you are just like the Ethiopians"—an utterance of Yhwh. "True, I brought Israel up from the land of Egypt, but also the Philistines from Caphtor and the Arameans from Kir." (Amos 9:7)

Boaz alludes to the first two promises made to Abraham.[20] In Boaz's eyes, by leaving her own people and land to travel to Bethlehem with Naomi Ruth has acted like Abraham who left Ur to travel to Canaan.[21] In a certain respect, Ruth's choice was the harder of the two. She did not have a divine promise to assure her of the wisdom of her choice. More than this, Boaz sees himself as participating in the divine promise. The promise to Abraham in Genesis 12, continues "I will make of you a great nation, and I will bless you, and make your name great, so that you will be a blessing. I will bless the ones who bless you, and the one who curses you I will curse. Indeed, in you *all the families of the earth will be blessed*" (12:2–3). Ruth certainly belongs to one of those "families of the earth." She has shown herself to be a blessing to at least one Israelite, Naomi. It is only appropriate, Boaz reasons, that an Israelite should reciprocate.[22] As Zvi Novick has observed, Boaz is offering Ruth hope, hope that God will reward Ruth for her past deeds toward Naomi.[23] I would go further. Boaz is prepared to pay Ruth's wage himself.

Ruth replies by repeating her question, but this time she makes it declarative:

> **13** *And she said, "I have found favor in your eyes, my lord, for you consoled me and indeed you spoke to your maidservant's heart, even though I am not one of your maidservants."*

This repetition highlights the importance of the "finding" theme. In Act 1, Naomi blessed her daughters-in law "May Yhwh grant that you *find* (*mṣ'*) security, each in the house of a husband" (1:9). In the introduction to Act 2, Ruth expressed hope that she could *find* (*mṣ'*) favor in the eyes of some landowner (2:2), and she questions Boaz when she does *find* (*mṣ'*) his favor (2:10). Here, she declares "I have *found* (*mṣ'*) favor in your eyes, my lord." Following the exchange between Boaz and Ruth, the question arises: will she indeed *find* security in the household of Boaz as Naomi hoped in 1:9?

---

20. See Smith, "Your People," 246; Beyer, *Hoffnung in Bethlehem*, 199–203.

21. As Robert Alter says at Ruth 2:11: "Ruth is conceived by the author as a kind of matriarch by adoption." *Biblical Narrative*, 59.

22. Porten sees an ironic play on Boaz's name at 2:11 and 20. The consonants of the verb "forsake," '*zb*, are an anagram for "Boaz," *b'z* ("Scroll of Ruth," 36; so too Garsiel, *Names*, 252).

23. "Wages from God," 708–22.

In verse 10, she asked Boaz why he was being kind to her. Now she describes the effect of his kindness: "you consoled me and indeed you spoke to your maidservant's heart." The verb "console" (*nḥm*) is used when one character reassures another, calming their fears (as in Gen 50:21), but it is also used for consoling the bereaved (as in Gen 37:35). Both possibilities suit Ruth's circumstances. The following line, "you spoke to your maidservant's heart," is more suggestive. In several passages, "speaking to the heart" describes a romantic exchange, amorous talk meant to win another's affection. In Genesis, for example, the young prince Shechem falls for the daughter of Jacob. As the narrator says, he "clung to Dinah; he loved the young woman, and *he spoke to the heart* of the young woman" (34:3). In Judges, an unnamed Levite has a lover's quarrel with his concubine. When she returns to her father's house, he follows and "*spoke to her heart*, to persuade her to return" (19:3). The phrase is not always used this way,[24] but considering the undertones of Ruth and Boaz's conversation so far, it is not farfetched to detect romantic hope in Boaz's phrasing. This inference is heightened when Ruth refers to herself as "*your* maidservant" while admitting "I am not one of your maidservants." She is clearly responding to Boaz's initial invitation to "cling to" his young woman and fields. He appealed to her loyal nature, and she responded.

> 14 *And Boaz said to her at mealtime, "Come here, and eat some bread, and dip your morsel in the vinegar." So she sat alongside the harvest workers, and he held out parched grain to her. Then she ate and was satisfied, so she had left over.*

Boaz continues to show Ruth attention and kindness, feeding her himself and making sure she is satisfied. It is the second time that Boaz has gone out of his way to meet one of Ruth's needs. Verse 14 continues the *emptiness-fullness* theme described at 1:22. Ruth, in this moment, is full. Her need for food has been met. In fact, she has an excess. This raises a few additional questions. Will her need for food continue to be met? Will her other emptinesses, and those of Naomi, be filled too?

---

24. For example: "Comfort, comfort my people, says your God. Speak to the heart of Jerusalem" (Isa 40:1–2).

Act 2 ~ Ruth 2:1-23

Excursus 6. Ruth and Judas

In the Gospels of Matthew and Mark, at the moment Jesus' betrayal is revealed, there is a strange interchange between Jesus and the disciples:

> 21 and while they were eating, he said, "Truly I tell you, one of you will betray me." 22 And they became greatly distressed and began to say to him one after another, "Surely not I, Lord?" 23 He answered, *"The one who has dipped his hand into the bowl with me will betray me."* (Matt 26:21-23 NRSV)

> 8 And when they had taken their places and were eating, Jesus said, "Truly I tell you, one of you will betray me, one who is eating with me." 19 They began to be distressed and to say to him one after another, "Surely, not I?" 20 He said to them, "It is one of the twelve, *one who is dipping bread into the bowl with me."* (Mark 14:18-20 NRSV)[25]

This is an obscure way to reveal that there is a traitor among the twelve. Why include the line about dipping in the bowl? Why not just say "one of you will betray me"? Commentators have tended to ignore this detail, offering no explanation or only a cursory explanation of it.[26] This instinct is understandable because it *is* superfluous to the scene. Whatever its function, it is not a plot-necessity. It was included because it is an allusion. In the Christian Bible, this rather specific action—dipping a grain product in a liquid at a shared meal—only occurs in Ruth and at the Last Supper.

In the Gospels, Judas is known principally as the disciple who betrayed Jesus. The Gospel writers remind their readers of this fact again and again (Matt 10:4; 26:14, 16, 25; 27:3; Mark 3:19; 14:10-11; Luke 6:16; 22:6, 48; John 6:71; 12:4; 13:2; 18:2, 5). Because of this, Matthew and Mark do not miss the opportunity to contrast him with the character in the Hebrew Bible who most exemplifies loyalty (*ḥesed*). Judas' actions at the Passover table mirror those of Ruth at the harvest meal. The allusion is transparently ironic. If Ruth most exemplifies loyalty, Judas most exemplifies disloyalty.[27]

---

25. Luke omits the dipping of bread. In Luke 22:21, Jesus merely says "the hand of the one who is betraying me is with me at/on the table," which illustrates that the act of dipping in a bowl is not a necessary detail.

26. There is a robust debate about whether dipping-into-the-bowl is a detail that was added to the text, since it is both unnecessary and awkward (especially in Mark). See summary comments in Markus, *Mark 8-16*, 950-51.

27. Some commentators see an allusion to Ps 40:10 in Matt 24:23 and/or Mark 14:20. Ps 10 reads (translated from the LXX), "Surely, the one at peace with me, in whom

(Re)reading Ruth

The Gospel of John makes the allusion to Ruth even more explicit:

> [21] After saying this Jesus was troubled in spirit, and declared, "Very truly, I tell you, one of you will betray me." [22] The disciples looked at one another, uncertain of whom he was speaking. [23] One of his disciples—the one whom Jesus loved—was reclining next to him; [24] Simon Peter therefore motioned to him to ask Jesus of whom he was speaking. [25] So while reclining next to Jesus, he asked him, "Lord, who is it?" [26] Jesus answered, "*It is the one to whom I give this piece of bread when I have dipped it in the dish.*" So when he had dipped the piece of bread, he gave it to Judas son of Simon Iscariot. [27] After he received the piece of bread, Satan entered into him. Jesus said to him, "Do quickly what you are going to do." [28] Now no one at the table knew why he said this to him. [29] Some thought that, because Judas had the common purse, Jesus was telling him, "Buy what we need for the festival"; or, that he should give something to the poor. [30] So, after receiving the piece of bread, he immediately went out. And it was night. (John 13:21–30 NRSV)[28]

John includes one additional detail not found in Matthew and Mark. Jesus dips the bread in the dish and hands it to Judas, just as Boaz handed the grain to Ruth after it was dipped in the sour wine (Ruth 2:14b). John also reminds readers that Judas kept the group's money purse. In John's Gospel, Judas steals from this purse, taking money meant for the poor (John 12:6; 13:29). That he is callous and has sticky fingers makes it unsurprising when he betrays Jesus for silver (John 13:2). It also reminds us (if we have noticed the allusion to Ruth) that Ruth was poor herself, and yet she never exploited those around her, which heightens the contrast.

Comparing Judas to Ruth has a heightening effect on the Gospel stories. It makes the betrayal more tragic, more heart-rending. Ruth, who owed nothing to Naomi, insisted on remaining loyal. Her loyalty was uninvited and unwavering. It was a loyalty that persisted beyond death (Ruth 1:16–17). Judas betrayed Jesus by his own volition. It was not an action taken under duress or need. He freely chose to be disloyal (Matt 26:14, 16; Mark 14:10), all the while knowing that his disloyalty would only lead to death. What he failed to recognize was that it would lead not to one death but to two.

I hoped / the one who eats my bread, has magnified his cunning against me." See, for example, Gnilka, *Evangelium nach Markus*, 236. I agree with the proposed allusion to Ps 40:10, but the expression was also included to allude to Ruth.

28. Gospel translations are light adaptations of the NRSV.

Act 2 ~ Ruth 2:1-23

> **15** *Then she rose to glean, and Boaz commanded his young men, "Let her glean even between the sheaves, and do not molest her,* **16** *and you will surely pull out some of the bundles of grain for her and leave[29] them for her to glean, and you will not scold her."* **17** *So she gleaned in the field until evening. Then she beat out what she had gleaned, and it was about an ephah of barley.*

Having fed Ruth once (verse 14), Boaz now makes sure that she and Naomi have food for the coming days.[30] This is already his third intervention on her behalf: he gave her permission to glean and extended protection to her (2:8-9); he fed her till she could not eat more (2:14); and now he makes certain that her work-day is successful beyond expectation (2:15-16). In addition, he emends two of his previous instructions to his harvest workers (2:9). Ruth is allowed to glean *among* the harvesters, not just where they already have passed (2:7), giving her first pickings ahead of the other gleaners. The harvest laborers are not just to avoid touching Ruth, they are to avoid speaking harshly with her as well (*g' r*, "rebuke, scold"). Clearly, the favorable impression Ruth made on Boaz has been enhanced though their interaction. His romantic pursuit appears to be well underway.

Excursus 7. Boaz and the Levite

In the same way that similarities between Hannah's story and Ruth's connect the Book of Samuel with the Book of Ruth (*Excursus* 5), similarities between the last story in Judges (chapters 19-21) and Ruth's story connect the books of Judges and Ruth. The last judge in the Book of Judges is Samson (chapters 13-16). No judge appears in the last five chapters of the book. Instead, it closes with two stories featuring characters from Bethlehem: the story of Micah's idol and the migration of the tribe of Dan (chapters 17-18),

---

29. On the verb "leave," *' zb*, as a play on Boaz's name see page 66, note 22.

30. The exact volume of an ephah is uncertain. "An ephah was a dry-measure equivalent to one tenth of a homer, the homer (חֹמֶר *ḥōmer*) being the amount that one donkey (חֲמוֹר *ḥămôr*) could carry." Bush, *Ruth, Esther*, 133.

(Re)reading Ruth

and the story of an unnamed Levite, his concubine, and the destruction of the tribe of Benjamin (chapters 19–21). This latter story has many similarities to Ruth, including its central theme: *foreignness and risk*. I am dealing with the allusion to Judges 19–20 here because this theme is most accentuated in Act 2. I want to warn readers, though, that this *Excursus* will have to address similarities between Act 3 and Judges 19–20. Some readers may want to return to this discussion after reading the next chapter, to preserve the serendipity of the discovery reading.

A Levite from the hill country of Ephraim took a concubine[31] from Bethlehem in Judah. We are not told why, but the concubine became angry and left the Levite to return to her father's home in Bethlehem. The Levite follows her seeking reconciliation, to persuade her to return to Ephraim with him. When he arrives in Bethlehem, the concubine's father receives him warmly and plies him with food and drink to coax him to stay. After many delays, the Levite and concubine depart for Ephraim. On the way home, needing to stay somewhere for the night, the Levite's servant boy suggests that they stop in Jerusalem. The Levite replies "We will not turn aside to a town of aliens who are not of Israel but will continue to Gibeah" (19:12). They proceed to Gibeah and receive hospitality from an unnamed old man. During the night, the house is surrounded by the local men who demand that the old man send out the Levite to be raped. The Levite throws his concubine out to the crowd, who rape her until she dies. The Levite cuts up the body and sends one piece to each of the tribes of Israel with word of what happened. The other tribes demand that the men of Gibeah be handed over to be executed. When the Benjamites refuse, the other tribes of Israel declare war on Benjamin and nearly exterminate them.

This hideous story is clearly patterned on the story of Sodom and Gomorrah (Gen 19). The most obvious difference is that the evil people whose violence culminates in their own destruction are Israelite and not Canaanite. Judges 19–20 also serves to color king Saul with suspicion when we encounter him in 1 Samuel, since he is from Gibeah and the tribe of Benjamin.[32]

---

31. The Hebrew word that I have translated "concubine," *pîlegeš*, is used for a female domestic partner who is neither slave nor wife. Her relationship to her man is important enough that her father is a "father-in-law" (*hōtēn*; Judg 19:4), but she and her children are of lesser status in the household than a wife or her children (Gen 25:1–6; 1 Kgs 11:3).

32. There are many allusions to Judges 19–21 in the Saul story. To cite just one example, the Levite cuts his concubine into twelve parts and sends them out to the tribes of Israel with a message, summoning them to war (Judg 19:29–30). Saul, likewise, cuts

Act 2 ~ Ruth 2:1–23

The parallels to the Ruth story are no less prominent. The two stories share a variety of plot-elements, themes, topics, and language:[33]

- Judges 19 and Ruth 1 open in similar ways, with a Bethlehemite leaving home, and one character attempting to persuade another to go (*hlk*) and return (*šwb*) from her father's house or to her mother's house.

    > [1] A certain man of *Bethlehem in Judah went to live* in the country of Moab, he and his wife and two sons.... [2] Ephrathites from *Bethlehem in Judah*. They *went* into the country of Moab and *remained there*.... [8] But Naomi said to her two daughters-in-law, "*Go return* each to *your mother's house*." (Ruth 1:1b, 2b, 8a)

    > [1] In those days, when there was no king in Israel, a certain Levite, *residing* in the remote parts of the hill country of Ephraim, took to himself a concubine *from Bethlehem in Judah*. [2] But his concubine became angry with him, and *she went away* from him to *her father's house* at *Bethlehem in Judah*, and *was there* some four months. (Judges 19:1–2)

- Both stories are about losing and acquiring (or re-acquiring) a partner.
- Both stories include scenes of eating and drinking at the end of the day (Judg 19:6, 9, 21–22; Ruth 3:7 [cf. 2:14]). These scenes are major turning points in the plot and are punctuated with the expression "a merry heart."[34]
- The male character "speaks to the heart" of the female character:

    > Then she said, "May I continue to find favor in your sight, *my lord*, for you have comforted me and *you spoke to the heart* of your servant, even though I am not one of your *servants*." (Ruth 2:13)

---

his oxen into twelve pieces and sends them out to the tribes of Israel with a message, summoning them to war (1 Sam 11:7). For other parallels see O'Connell, *Rhetoric of the Book of Judges*.

33. This analogy is discussed by (this is just a sample): Campbell, *Ruth*, 35–36; Fischer, *Rut*, 57–58, 109, 133–34; Raskas, "Book of Ruth," 223–32; Zakovitch, "Woman of Valor," 411–14; and Ziegler, *Ruth*, 49–57; 481–83. I have not included every verbal and topical similarities between the stories in the discussion below. Some of the similarities *reinforce* a connection between the stories, but do not help *establish* the connection. Many of these reinforcing similarities are ignored here.

34. When used of drinking, the expression "to be merry" refers to intoxication, as it does, for example, in 2 Sam 13:28; Isa 22:13; Esth 1:10; 5:9. For additional details, see comments at 3:7.

(Re)reading Ruth

> Then her husband arose to go after her, *to speak to her heart* and bring her back. He had with him his *servant* and a couple of donkeys. (Judges 19:3)

- Both stories culminate in a precarious sexual event.
- Both stories occur at night, and only end with the coming of the dawn (Judg 19:27; Ruth 3:14).
- Both stories are apprehensive about a tribe or a family-line disappearing from Israel (Judg 21:3, 6, 17; Ruth 4:5, 10).[35]

In critical ways, though, Ruth is an *inversion* of Judges 19. At all the points where the Judges story is negative, moving toward abuse and death, Ruth is positive, resulting in kindness and life.

- Both entail sexually compromising scenes at night, but they are the inverse of one another. One ends in death and loss. The other ends in a new family and new life. In one, the woman is *known* (*yd'*) by all the men of the town. In the other all the people *know* (*yd'*) the woman's virtues. In one, the woman is *seized* ('*ḥz*) and *known* (*yd'*) against her will. In the other, the man protects the woman from being *known* (*yd'*), and the only *seizing* ('*ḥz*) is when she *seizes* ('*ḥz*) her own cloak to hold the gift of grain he gives her. In one, the woman falls down, with her *hands* on the threshold of the house. In the other, the woman lies down at the *feet* of the man on the threshing floor. In one, the *woman's body is put on* a donkey. In the other, a gift of grain is *put on the woman's back*.

> 11 And now, my daughter, do not be afraid, I will do for you all that you ask, for *all the assembly of my people know* that you are a strong woman. . . . 13 *Remain this night*, and *in the morning*, if he will act as next-of-kin for you, good; let him do it. If he is not willing to act as next-of-kin for you, then, as Yhwh lives, I will act

---

35. As Raskas explains ("Book of Ruth," 227; italics original):

> In the last chapter of Ruth Boaz also faces the likely disappearance of an Israelite clan since the names of his kinsmen, Naomi's husband and sons, will be lost if her field is not redeemed. Boaz meets Naomi's closest relative and asks if he will accept the responsibilities of a *go' el*, redeemer (Ruth 4:3–5). After the latter declines, Boaz proclaims before witnesses that *the name of the deceased shall not disappear from among his brethren*, performs the ritual act of redeeming the field and then marries Ruth (4:6–10). Instead of the slaughter of brethren this act of redemption ends in new life, the birth of a son.

as next-of-kin for you. *Lie down until the morning.*" **14** So *she lay at his feet until morning* but *got up* before one person could recognize another; for he said, "It *must not be known* that the woman *came to* the threshing floor." **15** Then he said, "Bring the cloak that is *on you and hold it out*." *So she held it out*, and he measured out six measures of barley, and *put it on her back*; then he went into the city. (Ruth 3:11, 13–15)

> **25** But the men would not listen to him. So the man *seized* his concubine, and put her out to them. They *knew her* and raped her *all through the night until the morning*. And as the dawn began to break, they let her go. **26** *As morning appeared*, the woman came and *fell down* at the door of the man's house where her master was, until it was light. **27** *In the morning* her master *got up*, opened the doors of the house, and when he went out to go on his way, there was his concubine *fallen at* the door of the house, with her *hands* on the threshold. **28** "*Get up*," he said to her, "we are going." But there was no answer. Then *he put her on* the donkey; and the man set out for his home. (Judg 19:25–28)

- In Judges 19, the night ends in public rape and death. In Ruth, the night ends with a secret betrothal, leading to new life.
- In Ruth, the protagonist is a foreign woman who is at risk from Israelites (Ruth 2:9, 15–16). In Judges 19, the anti-hero believes he and his concubine are at risk among foreigners, but they too are at greater risk among Israelites (Judg 19:12, 22).
- In Judges, to avoid a tribe disappearing from Israel, the other tribes allow the surviving Benjamites to kidnap virgins and force them to become their wives (Judg 21:15–24). Ruth willingly offers herself to Boaz as a bride, and he secures the marriage publicly and legally (Ruth 3:9–13).
- Judges 19 and 21 lament that there is "no king in Israel" (Judg 19:1; also 17:6; 18:1; 21:25), which leads to chaos among the tribes. Ruth ends with the birth of David (Ruth 4:17–22), who will unite the tribes (2 Sam 5:1–5).

This elaborate allusion is clearly a reversal. Despite all the similarities between the two stories' characters and circumstances, one ends in disaster, and one ends in blessing. But there is more to it than a contrast of conclusions. The protagonists from Ruth have obvious analogues in Judges 19–20: Boaz ∥ Levite and Ruth ∥ the concubine. When we compare and contrast

(Re)reading Ruth

them it not only adds depth and texture to the characters, it also adds nuance and emphasis to the theme of foreignness.

In certain particulars, Boaz and the Levite are similar. Both are seeking a partner. Boaz has servant girls, and the Levite has a servant boy (Judg 19:3, 11 ‖ Ruth 2:8, 13, 22). Both are described eating and drinking, and both become "merry of heart" (Judg 19:6, 9, 22 ‖ Ruth 3:7). If we set these incidental similarities aside, though, the two men appear to be antithetical. Boaz protects Ruth, even from threats that are not realized (Ruth 2:9, 15, 22), whereas the Levite callously throws his concubine to the men of Gibeah to protect himself (Judg 19:25). In the process, the concubine is "seized" two times (*ḥzq*; Judg 19:25, 29). In Ruth, her garment is seized ('*ḥz*) two times (Ruth 2:15)—an expression that has resonances of rape[36]—but it is only to hold a gift of food. These echoes and correspondences make Boaz and the Levite's opposites, which certainly heightens our appreciation of Boaz. Even more, it makes Boaz like Ruth. Boaz protected and cared for Ruth when there was no certain benefit to himself, just as Ruth cared for Naomi when there was no benefit to herself. If the men of Gibeah are Israelites who sank into brutality and abuse of strangers, Boaz is an Israelite who stood up, who set aside personal reward to meet the needs of others, including one who is a stranger and a foreigner.

Ruth, likewise, has incidental similarities to the concubine. The similarities between the two, like the similarities between Boaz and the Levite, present the two woman as antithetical characters. Both go on journeys, to or from a parent's house (Judg 19:2 ‖ Ruth 1:6, 8), but where the concubine does return (Judg 19:9), Ruth does not (Ruth 1:14–18). Both face personal risk, but where the concubine is cast out to be abused (Judg 19:25), Ruth is protected from abuse (Ruth 2: 9, 15, 22). The concubine is killed, her hands on the threshold of the house (Judg 19:27); Ruth is safe, lying at Boaz's feet on the threshing floor (Ruth 3:8, 14). These comparisons do little to add depth to the portrait of Ruth. After all, they are mostly things that happen *to* the women. Instead, they further distinguish Boaz from the Levite: the man who protects from the man who is craven.

This analogy also serves to contrast threats. It reminds readers that Israelites can be as wicked and dangerous as any gentile, accentuating the book's rejection of xenophobia and bigotry. The Levite fears foreigners because they are foreign. As a result, he stumbles into a far greater threat.

---

36. Seizing someone's garment is indicative of rape in Gen 39:12 and Jer 13:22 (and implied in Neh 3:5–6).

Act 2 ~ Ruth 2:1–23

Boaz protects a foreigner because she is foreign. As a result, he stumbles into a brighter future for himself and his people.

> **18** *She picked it up and came into the town, and her mother-in-law saw how much she had gleaned. Then she also took out and gave her what was left over after she herself had been satisfied.* **19** *Then her mother-in-law said to her, "Where did you glean today? Where did you work? May the one who noticed you be blessed." So she told her mother-in-law with whom she had worked, and said, "The name of the man with whom I worked today is Boaz."* **20** *Then Naomi said to her daughter-in-law, "Blessed be he by Yhwh, whose loyalty has not forsaken the living or the dead!" Naomi also said to her, "The man is close to us. He is one of our redeemers."* **21** *Then Ruth the Moabite said, "He also said to me, 'Cling to my young women until all my harvest is finished.'"* **22** *Naomi said to Ruth, her daughter-in-law, "It is better, my daughter, that you go out with his young women, so others will not molest*[37] *you in another field."* **23** *So she clung to the young women of Boaz, gleaning until the barley and the wheat harvests were finished. And she lived with her mother-in-law.*

Her labors over, Ruth returns to Naomi to report on the day's events. We are not told where the two women are living, only that Naomi was in the town. Ruth delivers the barley she has gleaned, the leftovers from her memorable midday meal with Boaz, and news of her conversation with Boaz. Naomi immediately understands that the quantity of barley Ruth has collected could only have been acquired by favoritism, and she calls down a blessing on "the one who noticed (*nkr*) you." The pun underlines the theme of foreignness (*nkr*) that has punctuated the Act's language and allusions.[38] When Ruth identifies the man who favored her as Boaz, Naomi

---

37. As Campbell observes, there is a sound-play between "touch" (*ngʻ*, 2:9) and "molest" (*pgʻ*, 2:22), encouraging us to associate them in this context. Campbell, *Ruth*, 98, 107–8.

38. See the comments on 2:6, 10, 11–12 and see *Excursus 7*.

(Re)reading Ruth

recognizes him as a relative and a potential "redeemer" (2:20). Curiously, once Naomi makes this announcement, Ruth returns to her report and the subject is dropped. Other than verse 20, the dialogue between Ruth and Naomi seems to repeat information provided earlier in the chapter. It is not mere redundancy though. The speech repeats a number of the book's keywords: notice/foreign (*nkr*), cling (*dbk*), touch/molest (*ng'*, *klm*, *pg'*), and bless (*brk*). This encourages the reader to reconsider them, should she have missed their significance previously.

On the line "Whose loyalty has not forsaken the living or the dead," see *Excursus 2*.

Despite being superfluous to the women's conversation, verse 20 provides information that will be essential for the next two Acts. The fact that Ruth stumbled upon the field of a man who is "close to us ... one of our redeemers" is seen by Naomi as a manifestation of "loyalty" (*ḥesed*), though it is not quite clear if she is attributing this loyalty to Boaz or to God.[39] The term "redeemer," *gō' ēl*, is one that is widely misunderstood. "Redeem" is not a word that is used very often in contemporary English, and it tends to be laced with religious overtones. In Hebrew, though, it is an ordinary term. To "redeem," *g' l*, means to "buy back" or "reclaim." If an Israelite has to sell part of his land-holdings to cover a debt, a close relative is expected to buy it back (*g' l*; Lev 25:25–28). If a person sells a house in a walled town, it can be bought back (*g' l*) for up to a year (Lev 25:29). If an Israelite falls into poverty and agrees to be sold as a slave to a foreigner, a relative is expected to buy him or her back (*g' l*; Lev 25:47–55).[40] When Israel are made slaves in Egypt, God says, threateningly, "I will buy you back (*gā' altî*) with an outstretched arm" (Exod 6:6; cf. 15:13).[41] In all these cases, the redeemer is physically re-securing a person or thing that belonged to the extended family, usually through an exchange of money or goods. The term *g' l* can also be used metaphorically, as in Job 3:5. Referring to the day he was born, Job says "May darkness and deep gloom reclaim (*yig' ālû*) it," by which he

---

39. Cohen, "Ḥesed," 11–38.

40. The Torah also recognizes the notion of a "redeemer (*g' l*) of blood," a person who is legally permitted to take vengeance on someone for killing a relative (Num 35:16–29; Deut 19:4–13). This use of *g' l* is akin to the English word "collect" in the sense of collecting on a debt. The debt in this case is a life that is owed.

41. In Lev 25:39–43, Israelites are prohibited from owning one another as slaves. One reason given for this is that God already owns them, having bought them in Egypt. See verse 42: "for they are *my slaves* whom I brought out of the land of Egypt" (again in verse 55).

Act 2 ~ Ruth 2:1-23

seems to mean "I wish the world had returned to darkness (Gen 1:2) before that day had come."

The use of *gō 'ēl* in Ruth 2:20 is not so clear. It is frequently interpreted as a reference to *levirate* law. According to *levirate*, it is the duty of a brother to impregnate his dead brother's wife (should she wish), if she does not have any male children from her original husband. This provides her with a close male relative who can own and inherit the family's property. We first discussed *levirate* law in Act 1 at Ruth 1:10-14. The law reads:

> **5** When brothers reside together, and one of them dies and has no son, the wife of the dead brother will not be married outside [the family] to a stranger. Her brother-in-law will go to her and take her to himself as a wife and perform the duty of a brother-in-law to her. **6** Then the firstborn whom she bears will be established in the name of his brother, the deceased one, so that his name is not blotted out of Israel. **7** But if the man is not willing to marry his brother's widow, his brother's widow will go up to the gate, to the elders, and declare, "My husband's brother refuses to establish his brother's name in Israel! He will not agree to act like a brother!" **8** Then the elders of his town will summon him and talk to him. If he insists, saying, "I do not want to marry her," **9** his brother's widow will go up to him before the elders eyes, pull the sandal off his foot, spit in his face, and declare: "This is what is done to a man who will not build his brother's household!" **10** And his name in Israel will be called "house of the removed sandal." (Deut 25:5-10)

Not only is the term *g' l* not used in Deut 25:5-10, it is not used in the one story in the Hebrew Bible that is clearly about the practice of *levirate*, the story of Judah and Tamar (Gen 28). *Levirate* was not considered an act of redemption in the laws or narratives of the Torah. If it is considered an act of redemption in the Book of Ruth, as many interpreters think, then Ruth is unique in the Bible. But I do not think that Naomi is referring to *levirate* law when she labels Boaz *gō' ēl*. If Boaz or Nobody (4:1) was *obligated* to impregnate Naomi or Ruth, the woman could simply have claimed the right and entered the man's household, ending their troubles.[42]

If Naomi's description of Boaz as *gō 'ēl* does not mean that she or Ruth (it is not clear which) could claim the conjugal rights of a childless widow from Boaz, what else might it mean? The answer is provided by considering Naomi's whole description of Boaz: "The man is close to us. He is one of our

---

42. For a full discussion of *levirate* and Ruth see *Excursus 13*.

redeemers." This term "close," *qārôb*, appears alongside the term *gō'ēl* only in Ruth 2:20 and Lev 25:25–28:

> **25** If your kinsman falls into poverty and sells part of his landholding, his *redeemer (gō' ēl)*, the *nearest one (qārôb)*, will come and redeem what his kinsman has sold. **26** If a man has no redeemer, but if his work prospers and he finds enough for redemption, **27** he will calculate the years since its sale and return the balance to the man to whom he sold it, and he will return to his landholding. **28** If his [income from] work is insufficient to recover it, what he sold will remain in the hand of the purchaser until the jubilee; in the jubilee year it will be released, and he will return to his landholding.

Elimelek's land appears to be in the hands of another. He sold it before departing for Moab. Naomi does not say as much, but if Boaz could be persuaded to redeem that land on Elimelek's behalf, perhaps his generosity would extend to permitting the two women to maintain themselves from it, a landholding on which they could live and support themselves.[43] Alternatively, since the land redemption law is concerned with care for a destitute relative, it is possible Naomi is using language similar to that of Leviticus 25, but she is only referring to a cultural expectation that Boaz (or another "close" kinsman) should support them, in the spirit of Leviticus 25. Permanent security and a permanent food supply are suddenly and surprisingly in reach.[44]

But time passes. The Act closes with a note that Ruth continued to cling to Boaz's young women through the barley harvest and the wheat harvest too. There is some dispute about how long the barley and wheat harvests might have lasted in Canaan in the climate that prevailed over three-thousand years ago. Suffice to say that Ruth was with Boaz's women for at least three months. The narrator's silence leaves the impression that

---

43. There is another dimension to land redemption that has interesting implications for the Book of Ruth. In the same way that God will not allow Israelites to own one another because he owns Israel already (Lev 25:39–43), he will not allow land to be sold permanently because he is the permanent owner. Leviticus 25:23 reads "But the land must not be sold irrevocably, for the land is mine. You are but aliens and tenants with me." From this perspective, all Israelites are aliens in Canaan, like Ruth, and have no more right to be there than she does.

44. Beattie and Bush think Naomi is using *gō' ēl* in a "nontechnical sense" (Bush, *Ruth*, 137) "descriptive of Boaz in the part he has already played in the story" (Beattie, "Ruth III," 44). They must invent such a sense for the word, which it does not possess anywhere in the Hebrew Bible. The ways that the laws of *levirate* and land redemption have been intertwined in Ruth will be discussed in *Excursus 13*.

Boaz is either dithering or distracted. He has made no move to redeem Elimelek's land, to support the two women permanently, or to continue his pursuit of Ruth. With the end of harvest season, the women's food-supply is in doubt again. Naomi, unwilling to wait for Boaz to stir himself, decides to take matters into her own hands.

Excursus 8. **Ruth at the Well**

In this excursus, I return to Boaz's kind but seemingly insignificant gesture of offering Ruth access to his harvesters' water jars (2:9b). For someone hearing or reading the story in antiquity, a person who knew the biblical stories of Israel's ancestors intimately, this act of kindness would not be insignificant. It is, potentially, as significant as all the rest of Boaz's words together.

There are several stories in the Hebrew Bible of a man meeting a woman at a well. So-called "well stories" appear in Genesis 24, in Genesis 29 and in Exodus 2, and they have a common set of elements:

a. After a journey to a foreign country, a man arrives at a well

b. He meets a woman or women there

c. A question is posed, usually about the identity of one of the main characters

d. Water is drawn

e. Water is given by one character to another

f. Kinship of some sort is recognized between characters

g. The man is hosted by relatives of the female actant (usually a meal and accommodation)

h. Finally, there is a marriage that culminates in a birth

In Genesis 24, Abraham's servant, seeking a wife for Isaac, finds Rebecca at a well. In Genesis 29, Jacob, seeking his relatives, meets Rachel at a well, and in Exodus 2 Moses, fleeing Pharaoh's justice, meets his future wife at a well.[45]

---

45. Robert Alter refers to stories like these as "type scenes," a category he borrowed from the Homeric scholar Walter Arend (*Die typischen Szenen bei Homer*). As the name indicates, he suggests that certain types of stories—in this case, stories that begin with a man meeting a woman at a well and culminate with a marriage—are told in a stereotyped way, by repeating a set of plot points. As Alter says, "I should like to propose that there is

(Re)reading Ruth

The well story is what I call a "generative story." That is, it generates many variations of itself. Many stories take up elements of it, sometimes repeating them, sometimes reversing them, sometimes meeting the expectations that the pattern raises, sometimes disappointing those expectations. At times, the whole pattern is repeated. On other occasions, just enough of the elements of the pattern are repeated to remind the reader of the generating story. Four examples of well-like stories are Hagar's encounter with the messenger of God at a spring in Gen 16:7–14 (a blessing not a betrothal), Saul's encounter with women at a river in 1 Sam 9:11–26 (a disappointment), Tobit's journey to acquire Sara, his kinsman, as a bride in Tobit 4–8 (a close parallel), and Jesus' encounter with a Samaritan woman at a well in John 4:4–42 (an ironic inversion). Ruth is yet another variation on the well story. It is unique in that it employs elements of all three of the major well stories in the Torah: Genesis 24, 29, and Exodus 2. It is when Boaz mentions water and jars, the only gift he offers Ruth that is unrelated to the women's needs, that we begin to suspect a connection to the well story. Water jars are a necessary element of well stories and are particularly prominent in Genesis 24.[46]

Once we suspect that there may be a purposeful connection to one or more of the well stories, we can begin to consider other possible parallels.[47] If we begin with the Bible's first well story, the story of Abraham's servant (Gen 24–25), its similarities to Ruth—in language, plot-elements, themes, and imagery—immediately become apparent. They are conspicuous and numerous:

- Naomi invokes God's loyalty (*ḥesed*) on behalf of her daughters-in law, hoping he would be kind enough to give them new husbands (Ruth

---

a series of recurrent narrative episodes attached to the careers of biblical heroes that are analogous to Homeric type-scenes in that they are dependent on the manipulation of a fixed constellation of predetermined motifs [themes or topics]" (Alter, *Art*, 51). Alter's description is problematic. By assuming that certain stories are told in a certain way, as if the writers had little or no choice in the matter, he underlines the similarities between scenes and minimizes the differences. For him, the most essential thing about the well stories is that they are alike. For me, the fact that the stories are alike makes their differences stand out. In the case of Ruth, the reuse of the well story draws our attention to their contrasting views regarding marriage with gentiles.

46. Similar examples from English literature—cases in which one work of literature alludes to a pattern generated by multiple texts (just as the well story is generated by its clearest exemplars)—are analyzed in Riffaterre, "Intertextual Representation," 141–62.

47. To my knowledge, the most complete itemization of parallels between Ruth and the well story is in Porten, "Theme and Historiographic Background," 70–71. Porten only lists parallels between Ruth and Genesis 24. (See also Jones, *Reading Ruth*, 83–87.)

Act 2 ~ Ruth 2:1–23

1:8–9; cf. 2:20; 3:10). Abraham's servant prays that God would show Abraham loyalty (*ḥesed*), by helping him find a wife for Isaac (Gen 24:12, 14; cf. 24:27, 49).

- Ruth arrives in Bethlehem after a journey from Moab (Ruth 1:22). Abraham's servant arrives in Aram-naharaim after a journey from Canaan (Gen 24:10).

- Ruth happens by chance (*wayyēqer miqreh*) on Boaz's field (Ruth 2:3). Abraham's servant prays that God will happen (*haqrēh*) to give him success (Gen 24:12).

- "And behold, Boaz came" (Ruth 2:4). "And behold, Rebecca came" (24:15).

- Boaz asks, "whose is this young woman?" and received the answer "a young woman, she is a Moabite, the one who returned with Naomi from the land of Moab" (Ruth 2:5–6). Abraham's servant inquires "whose daughter are you?" and received the answer "I am the daughter of Bethuel son of Milcah, whom she bore to Nahor" (Gen 24:23–24).

- Unsolicited, Boaz offers Ruth water to drink (*šth*) which is kept in jars (*kēlîm*) and was drawn (*š'b*) by his young men (*nĕ'ārîm*) (Ruth 2:9). Abraham's servant waits for a young woman (*na'ărāh*) to draw (*š'b*) water with her jar (*kad*) and offer it to him to drink (*šth*; Gen 24:11–20).

- Boaz tells Ruth that he knows "how you left your father and your mother and the land of your birth and went to a people whom you did not know before" (Ruth 2:11). The servant is commanded by Abraham to "go to my country and to my kindred" and promised that he will be guided by the God who "took me from my father's house and from the land of my birth" (Gen 24:4, 7).

- Boaz comforts (*nḥm*) widowed Ruth (Ruth 2:11). Isaac is comforted (*nḥm*) after his mother's death by Rebecca (Gen 24:67).

- Boaz recognizes Ruth as an aspiring Israelite (Ruth 2:11–12). Abraham's servant recognizes Rebecca as Abraham's kin (Gen 24:21–27).

- Boaz hosts Ruth at a meal (Ruth 2:14–16). Abraham's servant is hosted at a meal by Rebecca's family (Gen 24:31–33, 54).

- "Blessed be he by Yhwh" (Ruth 2:20). "O blessed of Yhwh" (Gen 24:31).

(Re)reading Ruth

- When Ruth recounted her meeting with Boaz to Naomi, Naomi attributes it to God (Ruth 2:19–20). When Abraham's servant recounted his meeting with Rebekah to her father, he claimed that the proposed marriage has been divinely ordained (Gen 24:34–51).

- Boaz, no longer a "young man" (Ruth 3:10), marries Ruth who was still a "young woman" (Ruth 2:5). Isaac is forty (Gen 25:20) when he marries Rebecca, also a "young woman" (Gen 24:14, 16).

- Ruth chooses Boaz, and he accepts (Ruth 3:9–11). Rebecca is given the choice to marry Isaac or not, and she accepts (Gen 24:58).

- Boaz gives gifts to Ruth (Ruth 3:15). The servant gives gifts to Rebecca (Gen 24:22, 53).

- Boaz praises Ruth for not having "gone after" (*hlk* + *'aḥar*) young men (Ruth 3:10). Rebekah "went after" (*hlk* + *'aḥar*) Abraham's servant (Gen 24:61; cf. 24:5, 8, 39).

- After "eating and drinking" (*wayyōʾkal . . . wayyēšt*), Boaz lies down. When Ruth arrives, he tells her to "stay the night" (*lînî laylāh*) at the threshing floor. "In the morning" (*'ad-habbōqer*) he sends Ruth away so that no one sees she was with him (Ruth 3:7, 13–15). After "eating and drinking" (*wayyōʾkĕlû wayyištû*) with the family, Abraham's servant "stayed the night" (*lîn*) with Rebecca's family. "In the morning" (*babbōqer*), he says "send me back" (Gen 24:54).

- The people at the gate (*šaʿar*) bless (*bkr*) Boaz's and Ruth's marriage with fertility (*zeraʿ*; 4:11–12). Rebecca's family blesses (*bkr*) hers and Isaac's marriage with fertility (*zeraʿ*) and possession of the gates (*šaʿar*) of their enemies (Gen 24:60).

- Ruth bore no sons to Maḥlon. But when "Boaz took Ruth, and she became his wife (*wayyiqaḥ bōʿaz 'et-rût wattĕhî-lô lĕ'išāh*) . . . Yhwh made her conceive (*wayyittēn Yhwh lāh hērāyôt*), and she bore a son" (Ruth 4:13). When Isaac "took Rebekah, and she became his wife (*yiṣḥaq . . . wayyiqqaḥ 'et-ribqāh watthî-lô lĕ'išāh*)," she was infertile. So, "Isaac prayed to Yhwh for his wife . . . and Yhwh granted his prayer, and his wife Rebekah conceived (*Yhwh . . . wattahar ribqāh 'ištô*)," and she bore twins (Gen 24:67; 25:21).

All the major plot elements of a well story are present as well as a host of similar words and phrases and additional character and plot details (like the age of the man and the childlessness of the woman).

Act 2 ~ Ruth 2:1-23

All that being said, not everything is alike. All the similarities throw the two main differences between Genesis 24–25 and Ruth into sharp relief.[48] Perhaps most surprising is the omission of the well altogether. In its place stands the water jar. This substitution is not surprising on reflection, since the water jar is no less essential to a well story.[49] Second, Abraham was adamant that Isaac must not marry a gentile but had to be married to someone from Abraham's family (24:2–3, 37–38). Boaz does not hesitate to marry Ruth, a gentile Moabite, albeit one who was once part of a relative's household (3:10–13, 18; 1:4) and who has adopted Israel as her people (1:16–17). The importance of this theme to the Book of Ruth—relations between gentiles and Israelites—cannot be overstated. As Yair Zakovitch says, "The point of the story of Isaac and Rebekah's marriage is to emphasize the importance of pedigree and the prohibition against intermarriage with the people of Canaan. The story in Ruth, on the other hand, shows how there is no reason to reject Ruth the Moabite, who proves herself pleasing to both God and human."[50] This is a theme we will encounter many times as we travel through Ruth.

Ruth includes details from the other major well stories as well, from Genesis 29 and Exodus 2.[51] In Genesis 29, Jacob, fleeing his brother's wrath for stealing both his birthright and his blessing, arrives at a well "in the east" (29:1–3). There he asks after Laban, his uncle, and is told that, if he waits a bit Laban's daughter will be along to water her father's sheep (29:4–6, 9). When she arrives, it is Jacob who waters all the sheep in Rachel's care (29:10). He then kisses her, weeps loudly, and declares himself her kinsman (29:11–12a). Rachel runs to tell her father, who invites Jacob home and likewise declares him kin (29:13–14). The result is that Jacob falls for Rachel, marries her (eventually), and she give him two sons (also eventually; Gen 29:15—30:24). Every plot element of a well story is included in this account. There are a few additional lines and minor plot-points that are repeated in Ruth as well. The most noticeable is this one:

---

48. Some interpreters underline a third difference. In Genesis 24, the woman gives water to the man. In Ruth, the genders are reversed; it is the man who gives water to a woman (Alter, *Art*, 59; Eskenazi and Frymer-Kensky, *Ruth*, 98 n. 74). The man gives water to the woman in Genesis 29 and Exodus 2 too, so this element is not unique.

49. It is easy to think of the well as the most essential part of a well story because of the title "well story." If this plot pattern was called a "water-story" or "marriage-story," we would barely miss the well.

50. "Intermarriage," 65. See also, Beyer, *Hoffnung in Bethlehem*, 189–93.

51. Ziegler, *Ruth*, 271–82.

(Re)reading Ruth

> Then Jacob *kissed* (*wayyiššaq*) Rachel, and he *wept aloud* (*wayyiśśā' ' et qôlô wayyibkě*). (Gen 29:11)
>
> Then she *kissed* (*wattiššaq*) them, and they *wept aloud* (*wattiśśe' nāh qôlām wattibkênāh*). . . . Then they *wept aloud* (*wattiśśenāh qôlām watibkênāh*) again. Orpah *kissed* (*watiššaq*) her mother-in-law, but Ruth clung to her. (Ruth 1:9b, 14)

The main difference between Ruth and Genesis 29 is that Jacob's wife-to-be was not a gentile, she was from his extended family. It was partly for this reason that Isaac sent him to Laban, to get him a wife from "the daughters of his mother's brother" (Gen 28:1–5). In Genesis 29, like Genesis 24, emphasis is placed on choosing a correct spouse, "correct" being understood as acceptable in the eyes of family and clan. In the case of these two texts, the only acceptable spouse is one from Abraham's family.

Moses' story in Exod 2:16–23 also contains all the typical plot elements of a well story. Fleeing Pharaoh's justice, Moses arrives at a well in Midian (Exod 2:15b). At the local well he meets the seven daughters of the priest of Midian who have come to water their father's flock. When local shepherds try to drive the women off, Moses leaps to their aid and waters their sheep for them (Exod 2:16–17). They tell their father Reuel the tale, with the result that he inquires about Moses and invites him to a meal. The story then cuts to the finale: Moses marries the priest's daughter, Zipporah, and has a son, Gershom (Exod 2:18–22).[52] Once again, this well story includes details that reappear in Ruth. Three are particularly noticeable. First, Moses protects Zipporah and her sisters from the local shepherds (Exod 2:17), just as Boaz protects Ruth from the harvest workers (Ruth 2:9, 15–16). Second, Moses, unlike Isaac or Jacob, marries a gentile woman, daughter of the priest of Midian. Like Moses, Boaz will not hesitate to marry the gentile, Ruth. Moses does not share the fears of Abraham and Isaac about inter-marriage (Gen 24:2–3, 37–38; 28:1–5). This second similarity is also the principal difference between Exodus and Ruth, on the one hand, and Genesis 24 and 29, on the other. In Exodus 2 and Ruth, an emphasis on foreignness has replaced the emphasis on kinship. Moses names his son Gershom, which sounds like "alien there" (*gēr šām*) because "I have been an alien residing in a foreign (*nōkriyyāh*) land" (Exod 2:22). When Boaz is kind to Ruth, she asks, "Why have I found favor in your eyes . . . when I am a foreigner (*nōkriyyāh*)?"

---

52. In Num 12:1, Miriam and Aaron speak against Moses because he had taken a Cushite wife (that is, an Ethiopian). It is not indicated if this wife is Zipporah or another woman.

(Ruth 2:10). Further, Ruth is called "the Moabite" on six occasions, accentuating her status as an alien (1:22; 2:2, 6, 21; 4:5, 10).

While Ruth's foreignness is *overtly* emphasized, the analogy between Ruth's story and the well story *covertly* associates her and Boaz with great persons from Israel's ancestral past. Ruth is associated with the "correct" spouse of a patriarch (Rebecca, Rachel), and with the spouse of Israel's greatest prophet (Zipporah). Boaz is associated with Isaac, Jacob, and Moses. This accords with another allusion that we have already observed. When Boaz explained why he was showing kindness to Ruth, he described her using language from Abraham's covenants with God (see discussion of 2:11–12). *Ruth, then, is a foreigner and a gentile, but she is more like a Hebrew matriarch or patriarch than any other character in the book.* This is not the last time that she will be associated with Israel's ancestors. In Act 3, the writers of the book will construct an analogy between Ruth and another ancestor, Tamar, and in Act 4 the writers will associate Ruth with Leah, Jacob's first wife.

This complex analogy, between Ruth and the well stories, brings Deut 23:4–9 (English 23:3–8) to mind again.

> **4** No Ammonite or Moabite will enter into the assembly of Yhwh. Even to the tenth generation, no one from them ever will enter into the assembly of Yhwh. . . . **7** You will not promote their wellbeing or their good as long as you live. You will not promote their welfare or their prosperity for as long as you live. **8** You will not shun[53] an Edomite, for he is your kin. You will not shun an Egyptian, because you were a resident alien in his land. **9** The children born to them after the third generation, he may enter into the assembly of Yhwh.[54]

As noted earlier in this chapter, many ancient interpreters believed that Deut 23:4–9 was a restriction on marriages between Israelites and the people of four nations: Ammon, Moab, Edom, and Egypt. The critical phrase is "enter into the assembly." The word "assembly" (*qāhāl*) usually refers to the community assembled before God, to hear his words or to attend festivals at the temple (Deut 9:10; 10:4; 18:16; 1 Kgs 8:65; Ps 22:23, 26; 107:32; Neh 5:13; 2 Chr 7:8; 20:5, 14). Based on this, "enter the assembly"

---

53. In Deuteronomy, "abhor" (*t' b*) is used for anything or anyone offensive to Yhwh (see, for example, 7:25–26; 12:31). That person or thing is to be shunned.

54. Scholars dispute what the tenth and third generations refer to. For possibilities see Tooman, *The Torah Unabridged*, chap 3 (forthcoming); Hayes *Gentile Impurities*, 21–44.

(Re)reading Ruth

was used as a circumlocution for "enter the [place of] assembly." Lamentations 1:10b certainly uses the phrase in this way:

> she has seen her sanctuary invaded by the nations
> those whom you forbade to enter your assembly.[55]

This is not the only interpretation of the phrase though. Nehemiah 13:1–3 interprets Deut 23:4–9 as a prohibition against *any* Israelite marrying *any* gentile. In Nehemiah 13, when Deuteronomy 23 is read to the people, the Israelite men immediately divorce all their gentile wives:[56]

> ¹ On that day it was read in the Book of Moses in the hearing of the people, and it was found written in it that no Ammonite or Moabite should ever enter the assembly of God, ² because they did not meet the sons of Israel with bread and with water and hired against them Balaam to curse them. Yet our God turned the curse into a blessing. ³ When the people heard the instruction, they separated all [those of] mixed descent from Israel.

I do not know if the writers of Ruth had a singular view on the phrase "enter the assembly," or if they thought it could mean different things in different contexts. Whatever their views, the Book of Ruth contests both interpretations.[57] If Deuteronomy 23 prohibits Moabites from entering fully into the Israelite community, Ruth seems to have discovered a way to enter Israel that circumvents Deut 23:4–9. She unilaterally adopts Israel as her people and Israel's God as her God (Ruth 1:16–17).[58] If Deuteronomy 23

---

55. Cohen, *Beginnings of Jewishness*, 248–50. This interpretation can be found in the Dead Sea Scrolls too (for example, Florilegium 1:4; Temple Scroll 39:5; 40:6).

56. Also, Neh 13:23–27. This is the dominant interpretation in the *Mishna* and *Talmud*, two collections of Jewish law from c. 250 CE and c. 500 CE respectively. (See discussion in Cohen, *Beginnings of Jewishness*, 248–52.) This interpretation seems to have been inspired by the use of "enter" as euphemistic expression for marriage in Josh 23:12 and 1 Kgs 11:1–3.

57. Braulik, "Book of Ruth," 8–11. Compare Siquans, "Foreignness and Poverty," 443–52. One passage in the *Mishna* (c. 250 CE) attempts to reconcile Ruth with Deuteronomy 23 by distinguishing between Moabite men and Moabite women: "Ammonite and Moabite converts are prohibited from entering into the congregation and marrying a woman who was born Jewish, and their prohibition is eternal, for all generations. However, their female counterparts, even the convert herself, are permitted immediately" (*Yevamot* 8:3).

58. Rahab is a similar case. When she defects from Canaan to Israel, she become a part of Israel (Josh 6:24–25; cf. Deut 16:11; 26:11; and especially 29:10–11). According to one tradition she later married Joshua and was an ancestor of the prophet Jeremiah (*Megillah* 14b; a part of the Talmud).

prohibits marriage to Moabites, Boaz appears to ignore the law. By means of the analogy to the well story, the writers of Ruth make her as much like an Israelite as she can be without her having been born Israelite, which raises a complication not entertained by the blanket-restriction in Deut 23:4–9. What about the Moabite who strives to become Israelite, the Moabite who has more in common with Israel's ancestors than most Israelites? Can that Moabite "enter the assembly"?[59]

---

59. Simply associating Ruth with Moses, the prophet who revealed the law at Sinai, makes a powerful implicit argument against the interpretation of Deut 23:4–9 as a ban on marriage with gentiles like her.

CHAPTER 4

Act 3 ~ Ruth 3:1–18

ACT 3 IS THE crucial episode. The book's plotline reaches its apex as the two women take fate into their hands to secure a resolution to their challenges. It is also the most disputed part of the book. The Act is filled with elements that are difficult to understand. What did Naomi hope her plan would achieve? Why did it have to happen in secret? Did Ruth follow Naomi's scheme to the letter, as she promised, or did she improvise? What happened between Ruth and Boaz at the threshing floor? Why is there so much talk about feet? What, exactly, did Ruth ask Boaz? When Ruth returns home in the morning, why does Naomi not know who she is? These are just some of the questions presented by these puzzling scenes.

Answers to these questions are mostly found in one of two ways. Some are clarified when we observe how specific words, phrases, and themes that we have already encountered are deployed and developed in this Act. Others are only answered when we notice and explore several complex allusions that reach fruition in this Act. Ruth 3 is governed by allusions even more than the other three Acts. Before we will have a full picture of the events in Ruth 3 and their significances, we will need to explore allusions between Ruth 3 and Gen 19:30–38; 27:1–29; 38:1–30; and Prov 31:1–31.[1]

---

1. There are other allusions in this Act that we will not be able to explore due to space constraints, but the reader may wish to pursue them herself. Some are evoked by Ruth 3 while others allude to Ruth 3. Among them are Gen 9:20–28 (closely related to the Genesis 19 allusion); Gen 29:15–35; Gen 30:14–21; Judg 4:16–23; 1 Sam 20:1—21:1 (an allusion that spans Acts 1–3); 2 Sam 11–12 (esp. chapter 12); 2 Sam 14:1–20; Hosea 9:1–17; and much of the Book of Tobit.

Act 3 ~ Ruth 3:1-18

> ¹ *Naomi, her mother-in-law, said to her, "My daughter, should I not seek a resting-place for you, where things will be better for you?* ² *Now, is Boaz not our kinsman, whose servant-girls you were with? He is winnowing at the barley threshing floor tonight.* ³ *So bathe, anoint yourself, dress, and go down to the threshing floor. But do not reveal yourself to the man until he finishes eating and drinking.* ⁴ *When he lies down, note the place where he lies, then go, uncover his feet, and lie down. Then he will tell you what you are to do."* ⁵ *She replied, "everything you say to me, I will do."*

Verse 1 introduces the Act. Act 2 was drawn to a close with this summary verse: "So she clung to the young women of Boaz, gleaning until the barley and the wheat harvests were finished, and she lived with her mother-in-law" (2:23). Clearly time has passed between the end of Act 2 and the beginning of Act 3. Nonetheless, the plan that Naomi devises (3:1-4) is *presented* to us immediately after Ruth's report and Naomi's reply in Ruth 2:18-23. This creates the impression that the plan was devised in light of Naomi's conversation with Ruth at the end of Act 2. In her plan, Naomi returns to two topics that she has raised in the past: the women's need for security and their relationship to Boaz.

3:1-2	My daughter, should I not seek a resting place for you, where things will be better for you? Now, is Boaz not our kinsman, whose servant girls you were with?[2]
1:9	May Yhwh grant that you find a resting place, each in the house of a husband.[3]
2:20-22	The man is close to us. . . . It is better, my daughter, that you go out with his young women, so others will not molest[4] you in another field.

---

2. The repetition of "my daughter(s)" is a constant reminder of the importance of the theme of kinship and ironic reminder of Ruth's status as an outsider, a non-Israelite (1:11, 12, 13; 2:2, 8, 22; 3:1, 10, 11, 16, 18).

3. On the word "resting place" see comment at 1:9. (It is a single word in Hebrew: *mānôaḥ*.)

4. As Campbell observes, there is a sound-play between "touch" (*ngʿ*, 2:9) and

(Re)reading Ruth

Even though Naomi is raising topics she has mentioned in the past, the present plan is an entirely new proposal, and Ruth seems willing to hear her out.

Naomi's plan is obvious in most ways. Ruth is told to bathe, to dress up, and to sneak down to the threshing floor.[5] She is to remain hidden until Boaz has eaten, has drunk, and has settled down for the night.[6] Once he is settled, she is to "uncover his feet," lie down, and "he will tell you what you are to do." By any appraisal, the plan is highly compromising for Ruth. Clean and sweet-smelling, she is to join a potentially inebriated man[7] in his blankets in the middle of the night and assent to whatever he wishes. Even without the ambiguity of "uncover his feet," the situation is difficult to interpret in any way other than as a sexual encounter. In the cold light of day, Boaz readily recognizes that this is the obvious interpretation others will give to the situation (3:14).[8] What is conspicuously missing is Naomi's goal. What outcome does she hope to achieve by having Ruth spend the night with Boaz? I think the most obvious answer is the right one. She hopes that Ruth will become pregnant. As we saw at the end of Act 2, Boaz has not made any move to either support the women permanently or redeem Elimelek's land. So, Naomi turns to another possibility. According to 1:12 Naomi is too old to have a baby herself, but if Ruth becomes pregnant with his child, Boaz, having shown himself to be honorable, is likely to support the women. He might even take Ruth as a concubine or a spouse.[9] Should

---

"molest" (*pgʻ*, 2:22), encouraging us to associate them in this context. Campbell, *Ruth*, 98, 107–8.

5. Some interpreters see the instruction to "dress" as suggestive that Ruth is putting off her widow's garb (see Gen 38:12–14) or that it hints at wedding preparations (Daube, *Ancient Jewish Law*, 39; Eskenazi and Frymer-Kensky, *Ruth*, 51). The writers never make either of these claims; they leave the implications to imagination.

6. A harvest would never be left on the threshing floor overnight unguarded. Whether or not Boaz is alone at the threshing floor is never mentioned and does not require clarification for the story's purposes.

7. See comments on verse 7.

8. The ancient interpreters of *Midrash Ruth Rabbah* 6 §4 and *Midrash Ruth Zuta* 3 §6, 9 recognized this too. There is a strong impulse in the history of biblical interpretation to whitewash the scenario, to argue (implausible as it is) that Naomi is somehow looking out for Ruth's safety with this plan. The only motivation that I can detect for this impulse is a disbelief that the biblical writers would write Naomi as an opportunistic character. It is not an interpretation based on the plain sense of the story (the *pešat*).

9. We are never told if Boaz has a family apart from the one that he will eventually establish with Ruth. The book is focused exclusively on his marriage to Ruth and remains silent on this issue.

Act 3 ~ Ruth 3:1-18

things go to plan, the women will become a part of Boaz's household, and their immediate needs will be met. The most surprising thing about this plan (to me anyway) is that Ruth immediately gives it her approval. "Everything you say to me, I will do" (3:5). Considering all that we know about her so far, entrapment does not seem aligned with her character. Either there are dimensions to Ruth that we have not yet witnessed, or the writers are exploiting our expectations to surprise us somehow.

Before we can see how the plan turns out, we need to return to the thorny issue of uncovering the feet. Understanding the role that this phrase plays in the unfolding storyline requires clarification of three intertwined issues: what the word "uncover" (*glh*) means in biblical parlance; the terminology for male body parts, in general; and the meaning of "feet" (*margĕlōt*) in particular. We need a precise understanding of each of these before the threshing-floor story becomes clear.

First of all, the Hebrew verb *glh*, "uncover" or "reveal," is as generic a term as its English equivalents. It is used for opening eyes (Num 24:4), for revealing a secret (1 Sam 22:8), and for exposing the foundation of a wall (Ezek 13:14), to cite just three examples. When "uncover" is used of persons though, it usually refers to being stripped naked as, for example, when Noah "uncovered himself" in his tent (Gen 9:21). In fact, when used of persons it frequently refers to sexual situations, so much so that the expression "to uncover nakedness" (*'ervāh*) became a common euphemism for sex (Exod 20:26 [Hebrew 20:23]; Lev 18:7, 9, 10, 11, 15, 17, 18, 19; 20:17, 18; Isa 47:3; Ezek 16:36–37; 23:10). In this light, the directive to Ruth to uncover part of Boaz's body certainly seems to be a reference to undressing him, at least in part. It also insinuates (but does not yet prove) that Naomi hoped the encounter between the two would be a sexual one.

This leads to the second issue. Ruth is instructed to uncover Boaz's feet. If it is a liaison, this is a rather unexpected command. What have feet to do with sex? Although there is vocabulary for male genitals (*ḥălāṣayim*, for example) the Hebrew Bible mostly uses circumlocutions for them. Among the most common is the word "foot" (*regel*). The "foot" is the part of the body that is used to urinate (Judg 3:24; 1 Sam 24:4). Urine is "water of the feet" (2 Kgs 18:27; Isa 36:12), and pubic hair is "hair of the feet" (Isa 7:20). Judging from Deut 28:57 and Ezek 16:25, the euphemism seems to have originated as a shorthand for the part of the body that is located "between the feet."[10] (We would say "between the legs.")[11] Though many interpreters object to this understanding of "foot" in Ruth 3:4, I have not been persuaded that there is another plausible explanation of Naomi's instruction. To my eye, those who object to this reading are attempting to *explain away* Naomi's command rather than explain it. They are sanitizing the story to suit their own sensibilities.

This brings us to the third and final issue. The word for "foot" here is not the typical one. The usual word for "foot" is *regel*. The word here is the plural noun *margĕlōt*. The two are based on the same root, *rgl*, but though *regel* is a common word, *margĕlōt* is rare (only Ruth 3:4, 7, 8, 14, and Dan 10:6). Its meaning is disputed in Ruth, but in Daniel it refers to the "feet" or "legs" of an angelic being. So, what can *margĕlōt* mean here in Ruth 3:4? I understand it to be a synonym of *regel* and a euphemism. As explained above, this is the only interpretation that accords with the other details of Naomi's plan. That being said, the obvious difference between the *regel* and *margĕlōt* is the *ma-* prefix. In Hebrew, the *m-* prefix is often used to adjust a noun or verb to refer to a location.[12] For example, *gdl* means "be strong," and *migdōl* means "stronghold." The verb *rḥq* is "be far off," and *merḥāq* is a "distant place." The word *rbṣ* means "to lie down," and *marbēṣ* is a "resting place." The verb *nwḥ*, "rest," has a cognate noun *mānôaḥ*, "resting place," which we encountered in 1:9 and 3:1. This opens the possibility that *margĕlōt* might have a third meaning in addition to "foot" (literal) and "foot" (euphemism): something like "place of the feet." This is one of the possibilities frequently suggested at 3:8 and 14, "she lay at [*the place of*] *his feet*." I will argue, as we proceed, that the writers of Ruth exploit the ambiguity of the rare word *margĕlōt*. Here at 3:4 *margĕlōt* is a euphemism.[13] Naomi is instructing Ruth approach the intoxicated Boaz in the dark, expose him, lie down with him, and do "whatever he tells you to do."

---

10. Other likely cases of "foot" being used euphemistically are Exod 4:25 and Isa 6:2 (on analogy with Exod 20:26).

11. Péter-Contessa has shown that *regel* includes not just the "foot" but can extend up to the thigh, making sense of the expression "between the feet." Péter-Contesse, "Main, pied, paume." Other words for extremities are used as euphemisms for male genitals, like "hand," *yad* (Isa 57:8, 10) and "hand/palm," *kap* (Gen 32:25, 32 [Hebrew 32:26, 33]; Song 5:5; possibly Job 31:7). See Ellingworth and Mojola, "Translating Euphemisms," 139–43.

12. This type of prefix is sometimes called the "locative *mem*." See further GKC §85*f-m*; JM §88 L*d*; Holmstedt, *Ruth*, 155.

13. See Bledstein, "Female Companionships," 124–25; Carmichael, *Sex and Religion*, 48–50; Stendebach, "רגל," *TDOT* 13: 315.

But, because *marğĕlōt* is a polysemous word, we will have to reconsider its meaning each time we encounter it.

> ⁶ She went down to the threshing floor and did everything as her mother-in-law had instructed her. ⁷ Boaz ate and drank, and his heart was merry, and he went to lie down at the edge of the grain pile. Then she went in stealth and uncovered his feet and lay down.

Ruth follows Naomi's instructions to the letter, including uncovering Boaz's "feet." What, though, will Boaz tell her to do (3:4)?

The expression "to be merry" is a common enough expression for ordinary happiness (see Judg 18:20; 1 Kgs 21:7). When used of drinking, though, it usually refers to the jovial state brought on by intoxication. For example, in Esth 1:10–12 King Ahasuerus, being "merry" with wine, orders his Queen Vashti to appear before him and his drunken nobles, so that he can show off her beauty. It is possible that his instruction that Vashti wear her crown for the showing implies that she is to wear only her crown.[14] Outraged, Vashti rightly refuses, which incites Ahasuerus to replace her. (For other examples, see 2 Sam 13:28; Isa 22:13; and Esth 5:9.) There is another reason to think that Boaz is inebriated, which has to do with an allusion to Genesis 19 in this scene (see *Excursus* 9). The comment that Ruth "came in stealth" is related to the same allusion.

> ⁸ In the middle of the night, the man gave a start and turned and behold there was a woman lying at his feet! ⁹ And he said, "Who are you?" And she replied, "I am Ruth, your servant. Please spread your robe over your servant, for you are a redeemer."

Boaz wakes in the middle of the night to find Ruth lying at his feet. What startled him awake is not stated; it is left to the reader's imagination. Flustered and foggy, he finds Ruth lying *marğĕlōtāyw*, "at his feet." The writers

---

14. This is how the ancient Aramaic translations understand Esther 1:11. One of them, called Targum Sheni, renders Ahasuerus' command as follows: "Arise from your royal throne, strip naked, and place the golden crown on your head . . . and enter before me and before them . . . in order that they may see you, that you are more beautiful than all women."

(Re)reading Ruth

have begun to exploit the polysemy of *margĕlōt*. In Naomi's instructions, Ruth was to "uncover his feet," which she did in verse 7. Now, she is lying "at his feet." The former only makes sense if it refers to a part of Boaz's body; the second only makes sense as a location. How much of Boaz Ruth undressed before lying down is not indicated. It too is left to the imagination.[15]

In the dark and in his wine-soaked fog, Boaz does not recognize Ruth. He demands that she identify herself. (The reader may recall that this is the second time Boaz has asked her identity; see 2:5.) Ruth's reply is short, just three clauses, but it is packed with significance. The first clause is a repetition from Act 2. "I am Ruth, your servant" echoes 2:13 where Ruth thanked Boaz for speaking kindly to "your maidservant."[16] As we will see, the exchange between Ruth and Boaz will continually draw to mind their conversations in Act 2.

Ruth gets directly to her request. Ignoring Boaz's confusion she says, "spread your robe over your servant, for you are a redeemer." Ruth's request resonates with 2:12, where Boaz wished that God "whom you [Ruth] came to seek refuge beneath his wings" would "reward your deed." The two English words "robe" and "wing" are, in fact, two translations of the same Hebrew word *kānāp*. We saw in Act 2, that Boaz participated in the divine promise by caring for Ruth (see comments at 2:12). Here Ruth asks him to continue that participation, to be the "wing/robe" of God under which she can take refuge.[17] But, what does it mean, to "spread your robe over your maidservant"? This expression only occurs in one other place in the Hebrew Bible. In Ezek 16:8—an allegory about God's relationship with Israel—God is described as marrying Israel with the expression "I spread my robe over you."[18] Naomi sent Ruth out, hoping to entrap Boaz. Though she

---

15. Withholding details like this heightens the comedic dimension of the scene. See Jackson, *Comedy and Feminist Interpretation*, 180–97.

16. The word I have translated as "servant" (*'āmāh*) is often rendered "maid" or "handmaid" in English, but it usually refers to a female slave. See Gen 21:10, 12; Exod 20:10, 17; 21:7, 20; 26–27, 32; Lev 25:6, 44; Deut 5:14, 21; 12:12, 18; 15:17; etc. Several female characters use it hyperbolically to describe themselves when addressing God or a person in a position of power, as Ruth does here (1 Sam 1:11; 25:28, 31, 41; Nah 2:7; Ps 86:16).

17. The verb "spread" is ambiguous. It could be translated as an imperative or as a Hebrew jussive, which is like an English subjunctive: "please spread" or "may you spread."

18. Kruger, "Hem of the Garment," 79–86; Daube, *Ancient Jewish Law*, 34–35. Some interpreters of Ruth argue that Ezek 16:8 is not necessarily a reference to marriage (Beattie, "Ruth III," 43; Fewell and Gunn, *Compromising Redemption*, 102). However, the rest of Ezekiel 16 is predicated on the idea that Israel's infidelities *after* God spread his robe

has followed Naomi's instructions to the letter, Ruth had a different goal. At the pinnacle moment, when the man woke to find her in his "bed," she proposed. She asked Boaz to be like God one more time, in this case, by marrying her.[19]

Ruth's following statement "for you are a redeemer" rises an interpretive problem. Is she asking Boaz for one thing (marriage) or two (marriage and redemption of some sort)? We have no evidence of the idea of redemption-by-marriage from the Hebrew Bible. So, if the first possibility is correct, we would have to admit that Ruth is introducing a cultural practice unknown to us. If the second possibility is correct, what is she asking Boaz to do in addition to marrying her? The title "redeemer," as we saw at 2:20, is used for a person who purchases the land of a relative who fell into debt, for a person who purchases a relative who fell into debt out of debt-induced slavery, for a person who receives financial restitution due to a dead man, and for a person who acts as an avenger of blood. Since two of the four possibilities have to do with care for destitute relatives, Eskenazi and Frymer-Kensky suggest that Ruth is asking Boaz to support her and Naomi, to act like a redeemer.[20] If this is correct (we cannot be entirely sure), Ruth asks for one thing for herself (marriage) and a second thing (redemption) for her and Naomi.

Excursus 9. Ruth, Lot, and Lot's Daughters

Act 3 engages with two stories from Genesis about the main characters' ancestors. One is about Ruth's ancestors. The other is about Boaz's ancestors. Both entail a "bed trick." "Bed trick" is a phrase coined by Wendy Doniger to describe one of the best-known plot devices in literature: going to bed with someone who is mistaken for someone else.[21] This plot device is widely used in world literature, in many times and in many languages,

---

over her are acts of adultery, so the expression clearly signals the initiation of a legally bonded heterosexual relationship of one kind or another.

19. Another reason that Ruth phrases her request as she does is that *kānāp* is sometimes used euphemistically (as in Deut 23:1), and in this Act the writers have made extensive use of vocabulary that can be euphemistic. See Carmichael, *Women*, 74–75. See discussion of 3:1-5, note 6 on page 4, and note 38 on page 106.

20. Eskenazi and Frymer-Kensky, *Ruth*, 44, 64.

21. Doniger, *The Bedtrick*.

including the Hebrew Bible. Lot's daughters trick him into impregnating them (Gen 19:30–38). Jacob is tricked into taking Leah to bed rather than Rachel (Gen 29:15–30). Judah is tricked into taking his daughter-in-law Tamar to bed, instead of a sex-worker (Gen 38). Other stories flirt with the bed trick without bringing it to culmination, as when one character fails to manipulate another into bed. Because Potiphar's wife considers Joseph a mere slave, lacking the wherewithal to resist a command, she assumes that she can force him into bed with her, but she is disappointed (Gen 39). Sometimes the trick is more subtle: going to bed with someone who is ignorant of something essential about their lover's identity. Abimelech almost takes Sarah to bed (Gen 20), thinking she is Abraham's sister, not his wife. The Persian Emperor Ahasuerus takes Esther into his haram, ignorant of the fact that she is Jewish. On still other occasions, the bed trick is inverted. David attempts to get Uriah the Hittite drunk, so that he will sleep with his own wife, thereby covering up the fact that David has fallen into bed with her too (2 Sam 11). But David is foiled by Uriah's integrity.

Ruth 3 is an inverted bed trick story. Naomi intends it to be a classic bed trick, to trick Boaz into sleeping with Ruth. Ruth, though, chooses to be mistress of her own fate. She changes the plan at the critical moment, reveals her identity, and turns the scene into a betrothal story (2:9).[22] In the process, Ruth 3 engages with and inverts two bed trick stories: the story of Lot and his daughters (Gen 19), and the story of Judah and Tamar (Gen 38). This excursus and the next one deal with these two allusions.

The allusion to Gen 19:30–38 is signaled in three ways, by Ruth's ethnicity, by a series of plot-parallels between the two stories, and by a clever word play in Ruth 3:7. There are other similarities between the two stories, but these three direct readers' attention to Gen 19:30–38 especially. Genesis 13–19 contains the stories of Lot, Abraham's nephew, and Gen 19:30–38 is the story of the origin of the Moabites and the Ammonites, Lot's descendants. Ruth is a gentile, and this fact is important to the book's purposes (see *Excursus 8*). But, again and again the book's writers stress that she is ethnically *Moabite*.[23] At an initial reading, this repetition appears unnecessary, but it serves as a hint that some story about Moab or Moabites lies in the background of Ruth's story. What encourages a reader to focus attention

---

22. Doniger, *The Bedtrick*, 260.

23. The words "Moab" and "Moabite" occur no less than thirteen times in the book (1:1, 2, 6 [twice], 22; 2:2, 6 [twice], 21; 4:3, 5, 10).

Act 3 ~ Ruth 3:1-18

on the stories of Lot specifically are its plot-parallels with the Book of Ruth, especially Ruth 3. The shared elements even appear in the same order:

• The main characters (Lot, Naomi, Ruth) separate from their kin	Ruth 1:1–2, 14–19	Gen 13:8–11; 19:30
• The story features two women and one man on whom the women's hopes rest	Throughout Ruth	Throughout Gen 19:30–38
• Two sons-in-law die	Ruth 1:5	Gen 19:14, 30–38
• The older woman devises a plan to solve the women's need for children	Ruth 3:1–4	Gen 19:31–32, 34
• The man is inebriated and unaware	Ruth 3:7–8	Gen 19:33, 35
• There is a covert, nocturnal, liaison	Ruth 3:7–8	Gen 19:33, 35–36
• The liaison leads to the birth of a son	Ruth 4:11–13	Gen 19:36–38

The final element that directs readers toward the Lot stories is a wordplay that is only apparent in Hebrew. In Ruth 3:7, Ruth approaches Boaz, "Boaz ate and drank, and his heart was merry, and he went to lie down at the edge of the grain pile. Then she went in stealth and uncovered his feet and lay down." The key word is "stealth." The Hebrew word is *loṭ*. The word's origins are uncertain; it is either derived from the root *lʾt* (Judg 4:21) or the root *lwt* (1 Sam 18:22; 24:5).[24] Here in Ruth 3:7, though, it has been spelled with only two consonants, resulting on the word *loṭ*, "stealth." I suggest that the word was spelled this way to make it identical to the name "Lot" (*loṭ*) both in sound and in spelling. When Ruth begins to mimic the actions of her ancestor, Lot's daughter, the writers attempt to direct attention to the stories' similarities by means of this clever aural and graphic wordplay.[25]

The allusion to the Lot story affects the interpretation of Ruth significantly. It contributes to two of its themes, and it contributes to the

---

24. Joüon, *Ruth*, 71.

25. This play on words is discussed by Linafelt, *Ruth*, 52, and Schipper, "Use of *blṭ*," 595–602. The allusion to Genesis 19 provides another reason for Boaz to call Ruth "my daughter" in 3:10 and 11 (see, esp., Gen 19:30, 36).

characterisation of its three main characters. Most obviously, both stories are about the need for children (especially male children) and the lack of suitable men who might help provide them (see Ruth 1:11–13). There are three critical differences between the characters in the two stories though. As Yair Zakovitch observes,

> In the book of Ruth, the crisis of continuity is immediate: Naomi and her household have no hope of redemption except through Ruth's marriage. In Genesis 19, on the other hand, the crisis of continuity is false. Lot's daughters assume (incorrectly) that "there is no man on earth to come to bed with us like the way of the earth" (v. 31).[26]

Ruth is the opposite of Lot's daughters. The daughters are dishonest and mistaken about their situation, whereas Ruth is honest and has a clear understanding of her situation. In addition, Lot's daughters sleep with him just to become pregnant. They only seek progeny. Naomi instructs Ruth to sleep with Boaz too, and, in this respect, her motives are the same as theirs. Ruth, though, asks Boaz for marriage. She seeks more than a child; she sees long-term security for herself and for Naomi. Boaz is Lot's equivalent in this allusion, but whereas Lot in his drunkenness participates in multiple acts of incest, Boaz collects his wits and lays plans with her for a legal and public marriage (3:10–13). The virtues and vices of Ruth, Naomi, and Boaz are highlighted when compared with Lot and his daughters.

The story of Lot's demise begins in Gen 13:5–15, when Lot chose to separate from Abraham and live near Sodom. Though we did not discuss it in Act 1, there was already a subtle allusion to this scene in Ruth 1:17. The allusion in Ruth 1:17 is predicated on the repetition of a keyword from Genesis 13 and on an understanding of Lot's lineage. "Separate," *prd*, is a keyword in Genesis 13. It is repeated in Gen 13:9, 11, and 14, and in Ruth 1:17. Lot separated (*prd*) from Abraham, but Ruth vowed to never separate (*prd*) from Naomi. The connection to Lot's lineage is more complex. Terah had three sons: Abraham, Nahor, and Haran. The promise that God made to Abraham in Gen 12:1–4, 7 was only extended to Abraham and his descendants, and Abraham separated from his brothers when he obeyed God and moved to Canaan. Later in Abraham's story, though, two descendants of Abraham married women descended from his brother Nahor. Isaac married Rebecca, and Jacob married Rachel and Leah. So, in the Book of Genesis, the lines of two of Terah's sons were reunified. Lot, though, was

26. Zakovitch, "Intermarriage," 61–62.

the son of Haran. Haran's and Lot's line disappeared from the storyline after Genesis 19.[27] Ruth, being a woman of Moab, was a descendant of Lot. When Ruth refuses to be "separated" from Naomi, she is the first to bridge the divide between the offspring of Haran and those of Abraham/Nahor. When she married a man of Judah, Boaz, she became the first descendant of Haran to be integrated into the line of Abraham. With Ruth, descendants of all three of Terah's sons have been brought safely under the promise.[28] Bezalel Porten sums up the connection between the keyword *prd*, Lot's lineage, and the Book of Ruth in this way: Ruth's "refusal to be 'separated' [*prd*] from Naomi even in death (Ru. 1:17) marks a reunion of the lines of Lot and Abraham which 'separated' earlier (Gen 13:9, 11)," just as "the marriages of Isaac with Rebekah and of Jacob with Rachel and Leah were unions of Abraham's descendants with those of Nahor (Gen 24:24, 29:10)."[29] So, Ruth's commitment to Naomi and her marriage to Boaz signals that none of Terah's descendants, no matter how their line originated, stand permanently outside of God's promises.

There remains a third effect of the allusion to Lot and his daughters. That Ruth was a descendant of incest could be viewed by some as a blemish, a defect carried by her and all Moabites. When the description of the threshing floor scene is cast as repetition of the scene from Gen 19:30–38 but omits the female character compromising herself, it effectively cleanses the blemish. The logic underpinning this aspect of the allusion will be discussed in the next excursus, where the same reasoning is at work to remedy a flaw in Boaz's heritage.[30]

---

27. After Genesis 19, Lot is only mentioned in the Torah in Deut 2:9 and 19.

28. As Harold Fisch puts it, "Lot is the father of Moab and thus the ancestor of Ruth, whilst Judah is the father of Perez and thus the ancestor of Boaz. . . . [W]e have here the story of a single clan (that of Abraham and his nephew Lot) which separates (Gen. xiii 11) at an early stage and is then reunited in the persons of Ruth and Boaz." ("Structure of Covenant History," 425–37, quote at 427.)

29. Porten, "Structure, Style, and Theme," 15–16. For Porten, this also explains how Ruth can be said to have "returned" to Israel (Ruth 1:22), when she had never been there (see also "Scroll of Ruth," 26). On this allusion, see also Eskenazi and Frymer-Kensky, *Ruth*, xxi-xxiii; Schipper, "Use of *blt*," 598–99.

30. For additional discussion of the allusion between Ruth and Lot's daughters, see (alphabetically): Beyer, *Hoffnung in Bethlehem*, 184; Ebach, "Fremde in Moab—Fremde aus Moab," 277–304; Fischer, *Rut*, 39, 207–8; Gage, "Ruth upon the Threshing Floor," 369–75; Jones, *Reading Ruth*, 99–103; *Midrash Ruth Rabba* 5 §14–15; Schipper, "Use of *blt*"; Wenin, "La Stratégie Déjouée," 179–99; von Wolde, "Texts in Dialogue with Texts," 1–28; Zakovitch, *Ruth*, 28; Zakovitch, "Intermarriage," 61–62; Ziegler, *Ruth*, 297–300.

Excursus 10. Boaz, Judah, and Tamar

The threshing floor scene includes an allusion to a bed trick story regarding Ruth's ancestors, but it also includes an allusion to a bed trick story regarding Boaz's ancestors. In this case, the allusion is to the story of Judah and Tamar in Genesis 38. The writers of Ruth have signalled the allusion in four ways: by creating similarities between the plot of Genesis 38 and Ruth 3, by including many similar story elements (characters, items, and so forth), by repeating words and phrases from Genesis 38, which make the two stories sound similar, and by mentioning Judah and Tamar explicitly in 4:12: "May your house be like the house of Perez whom Tamar bore to Judah, through the offspring which Yhwh will give you by this young woman." The writers, having made explicit reference to Genesis 38, implicitly encourage readers to seek parallels to that story in Ruth, and that, in turn, is what draws attention to Ruth 3. Both Genesis 38 and Ruth 3 are stories about woman in need of husbands and male children. Both women seek those children from a male relative. Both involve a bed trick, and both end with the birth of an ancestor of David's.

In Genesis 38, Judah separates from his father's household to live near a friend, an Adullamite named Hirah. He marries a Canaanite woman, and she bears him three sons: Er, Onan, and Shelah. When Judah's oldest son Er becomes a man, Judah marries him to a woman named Tamar. Er, though, was "bad" in God's eyes, so God killed him. (In Hebrew, "Er" is "bad" spelled backward.) In the biblical storyline, Judah lived centuries before the law was given at Sinai. Despite this, he knows the law of *levirate*, and he practices *levirate* marriage in his household. (*Levirate* is discussed at 1:10–14 and in *Excursus 13*.) He tells his second son Onan to "do his duty as a brother-in-law" and impregnate Tamar. If she has a son, he will inherit Er's share of Judah's wealth and be able to provide for Tamar in her old age. But God kills Onan too, leaving only one of Judah's three sons alive, Shelah. Judah promises Tamar that Shelah will give her a son, as soon as he is old enough, so Tamar waits "in the house of her father" (Gen 38:11). Judah, though, does not do so. He fears for Shelah's life, thinking that any man who sleeps with Tamar will die. Tamar, not to be denied, takes matters into her own hands. During the time of sheep shearing, she disguises herself as a sex-worker and waits by the road for Judah. Sure enough, Judah asks to

Act 3 ~ Ruth 3:1–18

have sex with her, but because he has no payment with him, she insists that he leave his seal and cord with her as collateral. He does so. They have sex, and Tamar gets pregnant. When he sends his friend Hirah back with the payment, the "sex-worker" cannot be found. In time, Tamar is discovered to be pregnant. Judah, in a rage, commands that she be burned to death.[31] When she reveals the seal and cord, and declares the child's father to be their owner, he relents and declares her "more right than I." Tamar eventually gives birth to twins, Perez and Zerah. Perez was ancestor to both Boaz and king David. Laid out in parallel, the commonalities of Ruth and Genesis 38 are remarkable, particularly the shared plot points and story elements.[32] (I do not list the shared language here.)

- A Judean leaves his kin to live among gentiles | Ruth 1:1–2 | Gen 38:1

- The sons marry gentile woman (as do Judah and Boaz)[33] | Ruth 1:4; 4:9–10, 13 | Gen 38:2, 6

- Two sons die | Ruth 1:4–5 | Gen 38:7–10

- The daughter-in-law is sent back to her parents' household | Ruth 1:8 | Gen 38:11

- The daughter-in-law has no one to marry, because the third son is (or would be) too young | Ruth 1:11–13 | Gen 38:11

---

31. The charge, presumably, was adultery not prostitution. Adultery, in the Hebrew Bible applies to betrothed persons as well as married ones (Deut 22:23–24). Tamar, though a widow and no longer living in Judah's household, is like an affianced or married woman in Judah's eyes, because one of his sons is to be her *levir*.

32. For additional discussion of this allusion, see, for example (listed alphabetically): Adelman, "Seduction and Recognition," 87–109; Beyer, *Hoffnung in Bethlehem*, 185–88; Bos, "Out of the Shadows," 37–67; Carmichael, *Women*, 83–93; Claassens, "Resisting Dehumanization," 659–74; Fisch, "Structure," 425–37; Fischer, *Rut*, 51, 198, 247–48; *Midrash Ruth Zuta* 1 §12; *Midrash Ruth Rabba* 5 §14; von Wolde, "Dialogue," 1–28; Ziegler, *Ruth*, 300–302, 311–14; Doniger, *Bedtrick*, 255–63.

33. The ethnicity of Tamar is not mentioned in Genesis, but according to ancient Jewish tradition she was a gentile. This makes sense in the context since Judah is living among gentiles and marries a gentile himself. *Jubilees* 41:1 (written before 100 BCE) says, "Judah took a wife for Er, his firstborn, from the daughters of Aram and her name was Tamar." *The Testament of Judah* 10:1 (written before the second century CE) agrees, saying: "Judah brought Tamar, a daughter of Aram, from Mesopotamia."

• The daughter-in-law carries out a bed trick on an older man to get a baby (Naomi's intention)	Ruth 3:3–4, 6–7	Gen 38:15–19, 24
• The bed trick involves a change of clothing / disguise	Ruth 3:3–4, 7	Gen 38:14–19
• The liaison is clandestine & woman's identity is unknown[34]	Ruth 3:3, 7–9, 14	Gen 38:16
• The story takes place during barley harvest/sheepshearing	Ruth 2:23; 3:2	Gen 38:12–13
• A relative of the woman takes/ does not take responsibility to carry on the family and provide her with security	Ruth 3:13; 4:9–10	Gen 38:11, 14
• Names: Perez, Tamar, Judah	Ruth 4:12	Gen 38:29 (Perez); 38:6, 11, 13, 24 (Tamar); 38:6, 7, 8, 11, 12, 15, 20, 22, 23, 24, 26 (Judah)
• Birth of an ancestor of David	Ruth 4:17–22	Gen 38:27–29

Since Ruth's story is an inversion of a bed trick, some of the elements that are fulfilled in Tamar's case are not in Ruth's. Ruth does not complete the bed trick. She reveals her identity to Boaz and proposes to him. Boaz does take responsibility to provide for Ruth's and Naomi's needs, while Judah does not willingly meet his obligation to Tamar.

What effect does this allusion have on our interpretation of the Ruth story? The first effect is also the most important one. We have observed at several points that Ruth is depicted as being like or superior to several of Israel's venerated ancestors (see comments at 1:16–18; 2:11–12; *Excursus* 9). The allusion to Genesis 38 depicts Boaz as Judah's superior too. This is

---

34. In both stories there is a play on the word "know," *yd'*. Naomi tells Ruth not to make herself *known* to Boaz (Ruth 3:3), while he is concerned for her reputation saying, "it must not be *known* that the woman came to the threshing floor" (Ruth 3:14). Judah does not *know* he slept with his daughter-in-law (Gen 38:16), and once he finds out she is pregnant with his child he "did not *know* her again" (Gen 38:26).

Act 3 ~ Ruth 3:1-18

important because Ruth and Boaz have been carefully presented as a perfect match, as the "strong man" and the "strong woman" (see comments at 2:1; 3:11; and *Excursus 11*). Since Ruth is equal or superior to several of Israel's ancestors, Boaz needs to be her match in this way too.

Second, Tamar was a gentile (like Ruth) who became pregnant through an incestuous liaison (like Lot's daughters), and Tamar is among Boaz's ancestors.[35] Re-enacting the compromising scene between Judah and Tamar allowed a descendant of Judah to do better. If Boaz could deal with a bed trick episode in an upright and legal manner, he might be able to expunge the shame associated with Judah's treatment of Tamar. The logic of this effect is predicated on the notion of *transfer of (de)merit*. In the Hebrew Bible, the credit or blame for one's actions can be transferred from one person or generation to the next, much like moving debits and credits from one column to another in an accounting ledger. So, for example, in Exod 20:5-6 God says, "For I, Yhwh your God am a jealous God, visiting the guilt of parents on the children, to the third and fourth generations of those who reject me, but showing *ḥesed* to the thousandth generation of those who love me and keep my commandments" (repeated in Deut 7:9-10). A similar idea underpins texts like Deut 4:37-38 and 10:14-17, in which God says he shows favor to the Israelites not because of their merit but because of his love for their ancestors, Abraham, Isaac, and Jacob. Based on the idea of transferred merit, a person can ask that the credit of an ancestor be applied to themselves. In Psalm 132, for example, an unnamed king of Israel asks God to accept him based on David's accumulated credit (132:1, 10; cf. Ps 89:49-52 [Hebrew 89:50-53]). This logic works for forgiveness too. A person can beg God's forgiveness for other persons, even persons from prior generations. When Ezra prays for forgiveness in Ezra 9, he assumes that the guilt for the sins of his forbearers persists into the present. He confesses "our" sins, hoping to secure God's mercy. Since he shoulders the guilt of his ancestors' sins, he assumes that his remorse can be credited to them. When Ezra prays for forgiveness, he is, in fact, praying for an end to the cycle of transferred guilt, for all generations to be freed from the guilt of his ancestors' sins. Judah himself recognizes the principle of transferred (de)merit. When Jacob does not want to let Benjamin go to Egypt, for fear that the unknown Egyptian official (Joseph in disguise) will kill him

---

35. Sleeping with one's father-in-law/daughter-in-law is considered incest in the Hebrew Bible, the punishment for which is being "cut off" from kin and community (Lev 18:15, 29).

(Re)reading Ruth

(Gen 42:35–38), Judah volunteers to bear the blame if Benjamin does not return (Gen 43:8–10). Though Judah would not be the one who harmed Benjamin, he offers to bear the guilt *as if he had killed Benjamin himself.* He openly offers his own life in exchange for Benjamin's (Gen 43:9). When Joseph does attempt to take Benjamin from his brothers, Judah, true to his word, offers himself to Joseph in exchange (Gen 44:30–34).

Transfer of (de)merit applies not just to guilt for wrongdoing but for shame too. At the end of the *levirate* law in Deut 25:5–10, a man who is unwilling to act as *levir* is publicly disgraced, "his brother's widow will go up to him in the presence of the elders, pull the sandal off his foot, spit in his face, and make this declaration: 'Thus will be done to the man who will not build up his brother's house.' So, in Israel he will go by the name 'the family of the unsandaled one'" (verses 9–10). The shame of the failed *levir*'s action is carried by everyone in his household, and everyone who bears his name.[36] Judah was not a reluctant *levir*, but he did interfere with Tamar's *levirate* rights. As a result, his line bears the shame. By dealing well with Ruth, Boaz effectively cancels out the shame that adheres to Judah's descendants for his dealings with Tamar. Boaz's actions expunge the shame of his forbearer Judah.[37]

---

10 He exclaimed, "Blessed are you to Yhwh, my daughter! Your latest kindness is greater than the first, in that you did not go after young men, whether poor or rich. **11** And now, my daughter, have no fear. Everything that you say, I will do for you, for all the gate of my people knows that you are a strong woman. **12** Now, though it is true that I am a redeemer, there is another redeemer closer than I.[38] **13** Stay for

---

36. Morgenstern, "Book of the Covenant II," 169.

37. For a different and complimentary analysis of this allusion, see Adelman, "Seduction and Recognition," 87–109.

38. Many words in the threshing floor episode are regularly employed as double entendres, including the word "(come) close" (*qrb*) here in verse 12 (compare Gen 20:4; Lev 18:6, 14, 19; Deut 22:14; Isa 8:3; Ezek 18:6). It can be added to a list including "come" (*bw'*), 3:4a, 14; "lie" (*škb*), 3:4 (three times), 7 (twice), 8, 14; "know" (*yd'*), 3:3, 14; "feet" (*rgl*) 3:4, 7, 8, 14; "uncover" (*glh*), 3:4, 7; and "seize/hold" (*'ḥz*), 3:15 (three times). See Zakovitch, "Threshing Floor Scene," 29–33 (Hebrew); Harm, "Function of Double Entendre," 19–27.

Act 3 ~ Ruth 3:1-18

> *the night. Then in the morning, if he will act as a redeemer, good; let him redeem. But if he is not willing to redeem you, I will redeem you, as Yhwh lives. Lie down until morning."*

Boaz's instinctive response to the revelation of Ruth's identity and proposal is not shock at her boldness, or outrage at her presumption. He is bowled over. The first words out of his mouth are a blessing (again, echoing Act 2; cf. 2:8, 12). He blesses her because she has, once again, shown ḥesed, ḥesed toward him, which he declares to be "greater than" her first act of ḥesed when she remained loyal to Naomi (2:11-12). To Boaz, the fact that Ruth did not pursue a man closer to her age but chose him, shows that her ḥesed has no bounds. It is a part of her character, through and through.

We could understand this act of ḥesed in a couple of ways. It might simply refer to Ruth's "kindness" in choosing Boaz. It also could be understood as a further act of "loyalty" to Naomi. Boaz implies that Ruth has sacrificed her natural preference for a younger man on the altar of loyalty to her adopted family: Naomi. The writers do not clarify. They leave the nuances of Boaz's compliment unexplained. Perhaps he is just happy at his extraordinary luck. Perhaps, he is feeling self-conscious about Ruth's choice but is happy to seize it anyway.

If there is a single line in Act 3, that shows that Ruth has taken control of the story's events, determining to resolve the women's persistent worries in her own way, it is Boaz's next line. Naomi instructed Ruth that, following the stealth, the undressing, and the snuggling up to Boaz, "he will tell you what to do" (2:4). Instead, Ruth told Boaz what *she* wanted *him* to do, and he replied with a mirror of Naomi's words: "Everything that you say, I will do for you." Indeed, the rest of the book's plot is an unbroken sequence of actions, almost all of them by Boaz, to accomplish what Ruth asked. Ruth will take few actions from this point on, but everything that does happen will fall out according to her plan. There is an irony in the fact that the woman who characterized herself as a servant three times (2:13; 3:9) is the person who is now determining events.[39]

The reason that Boaz has no hesitation doing as Ruth asked is that "all the gate of my people knows that you are a strong woman." This might seem a strange reason to us, but it is another of the book's symmetries, in this case casting Boaz and Ruth as equals. Boaz was introduced in 2:1 as an *'îš gibbôr ḥayil*, a "mighty man of strength." Boaz now acknowledges

---

39. Trible, *Sexuality*, 195-96.

that she is a woman of strength. His compliment is also a key part of an extended allusion to Prov 31:10–31, a poem that describes how to choose a wife and extols the choice of a "strong woman." (This allusion is described in *Excursus 11*.)

Boaz, though eager to comply with Ruth's request, raises a sticky issue. He says, "though it is true that I am a redeemer, there is another redeemer closer than I . . . if he will act as a redeemer, good, let him redeem, but if he is not willing to redeem you, I will redeem you, as Yhwh lives." The issue of redemption was discussed at 2:18–23, but Boaz adds a new twist. Somehow, Ruth herself is entangled in the redemption. What is unclear is whether Boaz is talking about one issue or two. Does the nearer redeemer have priority over Boaz when it comes to redeeming *and* marrying Elimelek's daughter-in-law? Or is Boaz simply referring to the near redeemer's obligation to support the two widows? (See comments at 3:9.) Put differently, does "redeem you" mean "marry you"; does it mean "support you," or does it mean both? This issue will be discussed in the next chapter where it is central to the conversation between Boaz and Nobody (see Redemption of Ruth in *Excursus 13*). For now, the writers have chosen not to explain the connection between redemption and Ruth's hand, so we too will wait for its resolution.[40]

> **14** *So she lay at his feet until dawn. She got up and, before one person could recognize another, he thought, "Let it not be known that the woman came to the threshing floor."* **15** *And he said, "Take the cloak on you and hold it firmly." So, she held it while he measured out six barley, and he put it on her, and he came to the town.*

---

40. Some interpreters take the double instruction "stay the night" and "lie down until morning" as clues that Ruth and Boaz consummated their tentative betrothal at the threshing floor (so, Doniger, *Bedtrick*, 262–63). This seems an unlikely reading to me for two reasons. As Moshe Bernstein points out, the line "she lay at his feet" probably precludes this interpretation ("Two Multivalent Readings," 16). Second, such a reading creates problems with the story's logic. In a culture with acute standards of men's prerogatives over women, especially sexual prerogatives, and strong punishments for those who disregarded them (compare Exod 22:26–27 [Hebrew 22:15–16]; Deut 21:10–14; 22:13–14, 23–24, 28–29; 24:1–4), would Boaz, who has always and only been depicted as a man of stature and virtue (2:1, 8–9, 11–12, 15–16, 20; 3:10–11, 14–15) have blithely slept with Ruth when a closer relative had priority? Would he have casually slept with Ruth and then suggested that the relative marry her? If he did, the scene at the city gate in chapter 4 would be a "sham" (ibid., 17).

The notation that Ruth stayed until morning, and that Boaz took steps to protect Ruth's reputation (and his own) concludes the threshing-floor scene. Either Boaz did not want Ruth to return to Naomi in the middle of the night, for her physical safety, or the town gates were shut, and Ruth could not enter until dawn. Whatever the case, for the safety of her reputation, he does not wish her to stay until the sun is fully up.

Verse 15 is both awkward (especially in Hebrew) and seems unnecessary, but it is not. Its main purpose is to create another symmetry with Act 2. At the close of Ruth 2, after the very fruitful exchange between Ruth and Boaz (2:8–13) and the memorable daytime meal that they shared (2:14), Boaz gifted Ruth with an abundance of grain (2:14b and 2:16). Here, after an even more fruitful exchange and an unforgettable nighttime liaison, Boaz again gifts Ruth with an abundance of grain. Many interpreters detect a play on the theme of seed in the book, which is most obvious here in 3:9–15. Boaz provides grain seed to preserve life, and Boaz will provide human seed to create life (see 4:12). At the threshing floor Boaz gave the former, and he promised the latter.[41]

Excursus 11. Ruth & Boaz, the Strong Woman & Strong Man

At the pinnacle of not just Act 3 but the whole of Ruth, Boaz announces Ruth's greatest virtue. Freshly struck by her initiative, he proclaims "the whole gate of my people knows that you are a strong woman (*ʾēšet ḥayil*)" (Ruth 3:11).[42] It is a rare compliment in the Hebrew Bible, occurring only three times (Prov 12:4; 31:10; Ruth 3:11). Boaz's compliment is not the pinnacle of the book just because he admits that he wants to marry Ruth. It is also the book's pinnacle because—once we recognize the source of the phrase *ʾēšet ḥayil*—it is apparent that Proverbs 31 has determined many of the book's topics, events, and arguments, as well as shaping characterization of Ruth and Boaz.[43]

---

41. See, for example, Green, "Field and Seed Symbolism"; Nielsen, *Ruth*, 80; Porten, "Scroll of Ruth," 40; Stone, "Six Measures of Barley," 189–99; Sutskover, "Themes of Land and Fertility," 283–94.

42. "Gate of my people" is an idiom for the judges and elders (Deut 21:19; Amos 5:12; Prov 31:23; Ruth 4:2).

43. This allusion has been explored by many interpreters, including, but not limited to, Beyer, *Hoffnung in Bethlehem*, 160–70; Dell, "Didactic Intertextuality," 103–14;

(Re)reading Ruth

Proverbs concludes with two poems attributed to gentiles: "the words of Agur son of Jakeh" (30:1–33) and "the words of Lemuel, king of Massa, with which his mother admonished him" (31:1–31). Lemuel's mother, who is never named, is concerned about her son's choices. In particular, she is worried about who he might choose as his wife and queen. The greater part of her admonition (verses 10–31) extols the choice of an ʾēšet ḥayil, a "strong woman" (31:10). Lemuel should not waste his own strength (ḥayil) chasing after many women (31:3). He should choose the woman who brings strength to the partnership. A strong woman, according to Lemuel's mother, is one a husband can confide in, who works hard, tends his property, plans for adverse times, and gives openhandedly to the poor. What *he* gains from this choice is reputation as a wise man and time to serve the community, to "sit among the elders of the land" (31:23).

Once a memory of Proverbs 31 is triggered by the rare phrase "strong woman" in Ruth 3:4, many other similarities between Ruth and Proverbs 31 then stand out. There are obvious correspondences between the strong woman and Ruth. For example, Ruth works from dawn to dusk (Ruth 2:7, 17), as does the strong woman (Prov 31:15, 18). Both Ruth and the strong woman display *ḥesed* (Ruth 3:10; Prov 31:26). Ruth is a gentile like Lemuel, his mother, and (presumably) whomever he will marry. Ruth is "good" (*twb*; Ruth 3:10; 4:15), and the strong woman brings "good" to her husband (*twb*; Prov 31:12). The strong woman "looks to the ways of her household (*bayit*) and does not eat the bread (*leḥem*) of idleness" (31:27). Ruth, likewise, tirelessly pursues bread and a new household in Bethlehem (*bēyt-leḥem*). The strong woman sets tasks for her servant girls (31:15). Boaz's servant girls (Ruth 2:8, 13) become Ruth's servant girls when the two marry, placing them under her authority. The strong woman is praised "in the gates" (Prov 31:31), and Ruth is praised by the people at the gates (Ruth 4:11–15). Of the strong woman, Lemuel's mother says, "many daughters (*bānôt*) act with strength (*ḥayil*), but you surpass them all" (Prov 31:29). Boaz says of Ruth "blessed are you my daughter (*bittî*) . . . you are a strong (*ḥayil*) woman" (Ruth 3:10–11). In other words, what Proverbs extols in the abstract, Ruth depicts. She is neither rich, nor well connected, nor Israelite, but she is a strong woman. As far as Lemuel's mother and the writers of Ruth are concerned, that is the most important criterion for choosing a partner.

Fischer, "Von der *Vor*geschichte zur *Nach*geschichte," 143–60; Goh, "Ruth as a Superior Woman," 487–500; McCreesh, "Wisdom as Wife," 25–46; Quick, "Ruth and the Limits of Proverbial Wisdom," 47–66; Zakovitch, "A Woman of Valor," 401–13; and, most notably, Agenthe Siquans, "Männer und Frauen," 20–38.

Act 3 ~ Ruth 3:1-18

The allusion between the Book of Ruth and Proverbs 31 does more than reveal Ruth to be a model of the strong woman. There are also correspondences between the strong woman and Boaz (or Ruth and Boaz together). The strong woman is open handed with the poor and needy (Prov 31:20). Boaz allows the poor to glean in his fields (Ruth 2:3), and he gives gifts of food to Naomi and Ruth (2:15-19; 3:15).[44] Lemuel's mother urged him not to choose a beautiful young woman over a strong woman (Prov 31:30-31). At the threshing floor, when Ruth asks Boaz to marry her, he praises Ruth for making the same choice: "blessed are you to Yhwh, my daughter! ...[Y]ou did not go after young men" (Ruth 3:12). Boaz sits in the gate with the elders (4:1-2) to *gain* the strong woman, who will in turn enable him to keep his place there (Prov 31:23). Finally, Boaz acquires Elimelek's fields (Ruth 4:5). The strong woman also "considers a *field* and *acquires* it" (Prov 31:16a).

Ruth and Boaz correspond to the strong woman of Proverbs 31 and correspond to one another. The writers go to great lengths to show that all three are alike by repeating "strong" again and again (using both *ḥayil* and *'ōz*). Boaz is introduced as a strong man, as *'îš gibbôr ḥayil*" (Ruth 2:1). Ruth is recognized by everyone as a strong woman, as *'ēšet ḥayil*" (3:11). The people at the gate bless the new pair at their betrothal, by wishing them children who will also be strong: "may you make strong children (*ḥayil*) in Ephrata" (4:11).[45] Boaz's name (*bō' az*) means "in strength" (2:1). Not only does this cast him as Ruth's equal, but it may also be a clever allusion to Prov 31:17: "She girds herself with strength (*bĕ' ōz*)."[46] If so, by attaining Boaz Ruth has "girded herself" with him and his strength. (This would make Boaz, metaphorically speaking, Ruth's accessory, her trophy husband.) Similarly, Prov 12:4, the only other text to mention the strong woman, says "a strong woman (*'ēšet ḥayil*) is the crown of her husband (*ba' al*)." I cannot prove but suspect that Boaz's name was chosen not just to echo Prov 31:17 but also as a pun on "husband" from Prov 12:4 (*ba' al* ‖ *bō' az*). The purpose of all these correspondences is to present the two as the perfect match. Boaz recognizes Ruth's strength and is attracted

---

44. As Siquans ("Männer und Frauen," 38) says, "While the man there [Proverbs 31] profits from the tireless work of his wife, in Ruth the pair work on the same project. Both take responsibility for their people and, as *'ēšet ḥayil* and *'îš gibbôr ḥayil*, contribute to their [people's] continued existence and well-being."

45. Many English translations obscure the strength-theme with translations like, "may you produce children in Ephrata" (NRSV), or "may you prosper in Ephrata" (NJPS).

46. See *Excursus 1* and *Midrash Ruth Rabba* 7 §15.

to it. Ruth sees in Boaz a man who is her equal and pursues him. Ruth is like the strong woman whom Lemuel is encouraged to choose, but she is also wise enough to pursue a strong partner for herself. Boaz too behaves with the insight Lemuel's mother encourages; he sees the wisdom of having a strong partner, and when the opportunity arises he does not hesitate.

The extent to which the whole Ruth story is aligned with Proverbs 31 is remarkable. *It looks for all the world like the writers of Ruth have shaped the story around elements from the poem: fields, bread, home, gates, strength, kindness, and (not least) marriage.*[47] But there are also key differences between the strong woman of Proverbs 31 and the strong woman of Ruth. The main difference is that the woman of Proverbs 31 is wealthy, whereas Ruth is poor. This distinction is crucial. The following, adopted from Agenthe Siquans,[48] illustrates some of the major differences:

- In Proverbs 31, the benefits of marrying a strong woman are that she is trustworthy and brings her husband economic benefits (esp. 31:11). While the first could be said of Ruth, the second could not. As Siquans put it, "she [Ruth] is by no means wealthy, and she is economically dependent on Boaz. As a foreign and poor woman, Ruth is nevertheless a 'strong woman'—that is the answer in the Book of Ruth to ... Proverbs."[49]

- In Ruth, the "good man" (implied in Ruth 2:22; 3:1) and the "good woman" (3:10; 4:15) do what is good for Naomi (4:14–15), whereas in Proverbs 31, the good flows one way: the strong woman does what is good for her husband.

- In Prov 31:11 the woman provides for the man; in Ruth 2:16 it is the opposite.

---

47. Some interpreters see Proverbs 31 as modelled on Ruth and not vice versa. Zakovitch, for example, dates Ruth to the Second Temple period (early sixth to fourth centuries BCE) and Proverbs 31 to the Hellenistic period (late fourth century BCE; *Rut*, 62–64). For the purposes of this study, it does not much matter. Readers of the completed Hebrew Bible—which is our focus—will think of Ruth when reading Proverbs and will think of Proverbs when reading Ruth. They will be encouraged to do so by the fact that Ruth often follows immediately after Proverbs in the Hebrew Bible. See the Appendix on the different arrangements of the Jewish and Christian Bibles.

48. Siquans, "Männer und Frauen," 21–26.

49. Siquans, "Männer und Frauen," 21.

Act 3 ~ Ruth 3:1-18

- In Proverbs 31, the woman commands her servant girls, but in Ruth, the "young women" are Boaz's, and Ruth is a "young woman" who belongs to no one.

- It is Boaz who provides charity for the poor in general and for Ruth and Naomi in particular, whereas in Proverbs 31 the strong woman is charitable to the poor.

These differences are not incidental. For the reader who encounters Proverbs 31 first and Ruth second (as the two books appear in most Jewish Bibles),[50] Ruth clarifies the wisdom of Proverbs 31. A "strong woman" is not just a trustworthy, hard-working, and *wealthy* woman. *Any* trustworthy, hard-working woman is a "strong woman." Ruth effectively eliminates wealth as a consideration when choosing a partner. It is character that matters, not class.

In addition to eliminating class from consideration when choosing a spouse, Ruth eliminates ethnicity as a concern. As many readers will know, Proverbs has a series of mini-lectures, cautioning "my son"—the notional recipient of the book's wisdom—away from the "strange woman" (Prov 2:16-29; 5:1-23; 6:20-35; 7:1-27).[51] The "strange woman," as she is often called in English Bibles, is a caricature of a dangerous woman. She is dangerous mainly because she leads young men into adultery and death. She is such a threat to the wise life that elements of the "strange woman" are used to assemble the character of personified foolishness, "Lady Folly" (Prov 9:13-18), who stands in contrast to "Lady Wisdom" (Prov 1:20-33; 8:1-36; 9:1-12). In several ways, the strong woman of Proverbs 31 has been deliberately contrasted with the strange woman. For example, the strange woman leaves home to stalk the streets (Prov 7:11-27) while the strong woman conducts her work within the household (Prov 31:23). The strange woman is beautiful (Prov 6:25), while Proverbs 31 declares beauty ephemeral and deceptive (Prov 31:30). The strange woman deceives her husband to take secret lovers (Prov 7:19-20), while the strong woman maintains her partner's trust (Prov 31:11).[52]

So, what does this have to do with Ruth? The so-called "strange woman" goes by more than one name. She is called "strange" (*zārāh*) and "bad" (*ra'*), but she is also called *nokriyyāh* no less than ten times in

---

50. See Appendix.
51. She also appears in passing in 22:14; 23:27.
52. Zakovitch, "Woman of Valor," 402; Fox, *Proverbs 10-31*, 411.

Proverbs (2:16; 5:10, 20; 6:24; 7:5; 20:16; 23:27; 27:2, 13). Ruth, we will recall, calls herself *nokriyyāh*, "foreign," in 2:10, and she is referred to as "the Moabite" more often than she is called by her name. It is important to understand that the word *nokriyyāh* can mean either "unknown" or "foreign." There is no reason to think that it must mean "foreign" in Proverbs. As Michael Fox says, "Nothing whatsoever in any of the lectures indicates that the strange woman is a foreigner or even a social outsider. The antithesis of the *zārāh-nokriyyāh* is not an Israelite woman or a woman of proper social standing, but rather one's own wife (5:15–20)."[53] Nonetheless, there are interpreters, both ancient and modern, who have been tempted to interpret Proverbs as cautioning good Israelites away from mixed marriages. Considering its elaborate engagement with Proverbs 31, Ruth appears to be deliberately contesting this interpretation. Not only is it acceptable to marry a gentile, but a gentile can be the paragon of wisdom; she can be the strong woman.[54]

---

16 *And she came to her mother-in-law, and she [Naomi] said, "Who are you, my daughter?" She reported to her everything that the man had done for her.* 17 *And she said, "These are six barley he gave to me, because he said to me, 'You should not come to your mother-in-law*

---

53. Fox, *Proverbs 10–31*, 140.

54. In the Jewish Bible, the Book of Ruth typically follows Proverbs rather than Judges. Zakovitch ("Woman of Valor," 412) includes the following telling extract from the end of *Midrash Lekaḥ Tov* (an eleventh-century commentary), which recognizes the importance of Proverbs 31 for the interpretation of Ruth and associates it with the order of books in the Jewish canon:

> ... for Solomon who spoke in Proverbs ... juxtaposed [Ruth's] book to his book, and Solomon said at the end of his book, "A woman of valor [*ḥayil*], who will find?" (Prov 31:10), and he praised and glorified the woman of valor a great deal ... and he ended his book "grace is deceptive, beauty is illusory" (31:30) and "extol her for the fruit of her hands" (31:31). Since Naomi was a god-fearing woman and Ruth a woman of valor, for it says, "for all the elders at the gate know what a woman of valor you are" (Ruth 3:11), that is why he [Solomon] mentioned them and juxtaposed them to the book of Proverbs, teaching us that everything that Solomon said about the woman of valor refers to such as them, Naomi and her daughter-in-law ....

For details about the order of books in the Jewish canon see the Appendix.

Act 3 ~ Ruth 3:1-18

> *empty handed."'* ¹⁸ *And Naomi said, "Sit, my daughter, until you learn how the matter turns out. For the man will not rest, but he will finish the matter today."*

This paragraph is an apt conclusion to the Act. Like Act 2, Act 3 closes with Ruth reporting events to Naomi. The line "everything the man had done for her" helps round-off the scene. It is pair to the line "everything you say to me I will do," in the opening paragraph. Ruth's one addition to the story—"he said to me, 'You should not come to your mother-in-law empty handed'"—reminds us of the emptiness-fullness theme and signals that we are reaching its pinnacle. All of Naomi's emptinesses are (potentially anyway) about to be filled. Her empty belly, in both senses, looks to be memory. The concluding verse is a transition to the next Act, where we will watch as Boaz strives to "finish the matter."

The one puzzling element of this paragraph is Naomi's question "who are you, my daughter?" Who else is Naomi expecting to arrive early in the morning but Ruth? More confusing yet, the question is self-contradictory. Naomi asks who it is but then names the arrival as "my daughter." Who else would she call "my daughter" but Ruth? Translators and interpreters have spent a lot of energy trying to resolve these issues. Some consider the question to be a mistake and eliminate it.[55] Some rewrite the question. Popular attempts include: "who are you now, my daughter?" (meaning, "do you belong to a different household now?"); "is that you, my daughter?"; and "how did things go, my daughter?" Others consider it an awkward attempt to contribute to the theme of Ruth's identity. Who is she? Moabite or Israelite? Impoverished widow or mistress of a householder? Pagan or Jew?[56]

Very often, when a line or a paragraph in a biblical story does not seem to fit and leaves the reader scratching her head it is because it has an important literary function, a function that is important enough for the writers to risk some confusion by including it. In this case, I believe that the question "who are you, my daughter?" has a double function. First, and most obviously, the two parts of Naomi's question are both found on Boaz's lips in 3:9-10 ("who are you?" and "my daughter"). Having Naomi repeat

---

55. Many Septuagint manuscripts (the ancient Greek translations of the Hebrew Bible) eliminate the question.

56. See, for example, LaCocque, *Ruth*, 3; Koosed, *Gleaning*, throughout and especially page 93.

Boaz's words invites a comparison between the two. In what other ways are Boaz and Naomi alike or different in Act 3? Naomi sent Ruth out into the night to deceive Boaz, and she did so with no regard for Ruth's safety or reputation. She did it to secure his seed, to steal offspring from him. Boaz, however, protected Ruth and returned her to Naomi with her reputation intact. More than this, when approached openly by Ruth, he freely offered her everything she needed: food, offspring, and a household of her own. Because she spoke truthfully, Ruth was offered a bounty that far exceeded the one Naomi sent her to steal.

Second, Naomi's question appears to be part of an allusion to Genesis 27 that runs through the Act, and that establishes a second comparison. Naomi asked Ruth to behave like Jacob when Rebecca sent him to steal his brother's blessing. In both stories, it is the mother who devised the plan (Gen 27:6–17; Ruth 3:1–4) and sent her son/daughter to execute it (Gen 27:10, 17–18; Ruth 3:5). The plan involved a lie, deceiving the sucker (Isaac or Boaz) into giving away something that he did not intend to give (Gen 27:12, 19; Ruth 3:4). The target of the deception in both stories was much older than the trickster. In both, he was vulnerable to manipulation because he could not see (Gen 27:1; Ruth 3:9–10).[57] Both stories involve a blessing (Gen 27:4 and throughout; Ruth 3:10) and the themes of grain and fertility (Ruth 3:2, 9, 15; Gen 27:28). Most importantly of all, both Isaac and Boaz ask the question, "who are you, my son/daughter?" (Ruth 3:9–10; Gen 27:18). The comparison established by this allusion is between Ruth and Jacob, on the one hand, and Naomi and Rebecca, on the other. Naomi is like Rebecca. She initiated a deceit, attempting to steal what was not hers (or Ruth's) by right, and she attempted to exploit Boaz when he was defenseless. Ruth, though, was not like Jacob. Though she obeyed all her mother-in-law's specific instructions, at the critical moment she decided to deal openly with Boaz. She did not keep her identity hidden, and she asked for what she wanted. Naomi is Rebecca's equal, but Ruth is Jacob's superior. Sure enough, in both stories the characters reap what they sow. Ruth speaks truthfully to get what she wants, and her hope is fulfilled. Jacob lies to get what he wants, and it results in fear and flight. Ruth's truth builds a new household. Jacob's lie fractures a household. Ruth reaps the reward of her truth almost immediately. Jacob spends years unravelling the consequences of his lie.

---

57. Jones, *Reading Ruth*, 77–82.

Act 3 ~ Ruth 3:1-18

Excursus 12. Act 2 ‖ Act 3

As I described in chapter 1, the structure of Ruth invites certain comparisons, particularly between Acts 2 and 3 and between Acts 1 and 4.[58] The invitation is extended by means of a complex set of similarities between the Acts. In broad strokes, the similarities between Act 2 and Act 3 are the following. Acts 2 and 3 both happen on Boaz's property. The main characters in the frame segments (2:1-3 ‖ 3:1-4 and 2:18-23 ‖ 3:15b-18) are Ruth and Naomi. The main characters in the heart of each Act (2:4-17 ‖ 3:6-15a) are Ruth and Boaz. At the beginning of each act a plan is proposed and accepted (2:1-3 ‖ 3:1-4). The body of each act is dominated by conversation between Ruth and Boaz. At the end of each Act, Ruth receives a gift of grain from Boaz and makes a report to Naomi (2:18-23 ‖ 3:16-18). In Act 2, Boaz is blessed (2:20). In Act 3 Ruth is blessed (3:10). In Act 2, Boaz says Ruth sought shelter under God's wing (*kānāp*). In Act 3, Ruth asks Boaz to extend his robe (*kānāp*) over her. In both Acts, Boaz takes action to protect Ruth, her physical safety in Act 2 and her reputation in Act 3. In addition, there are elements that are antithetical. Act 2 occurs in the daytime, while Act 3 occurs at night. Ruth devises the plan and Naomi agrees in Act 2. Naomi devises the plan and Ruth agrees in Act 3. Boaz delays acting at the end of Act 2. At the end of Act 3, he acts quickly and decisively. There are many other similarities and antitheses between the Acts on matters of detail and language. Laid out in parallel, the major points of comparison look like this:

---

58. Select parallels between Acts 2 and 3 are mentioned by Bertman, "Symmetrical Design," 165-66; Porten, "Rhetorical," 23; and Ziegler, *Ruth*, 285-89.

(Re)reading Ruth

	Act 2		**Act 3**
2$^{1-3}$	Ruth proposes a plan Naomi agrees to the plan	3$^{1-4}$	Naomi proposes a plan Ruth agrees to the plan
2$^{4-7}$	Boaz arrives & inquires about Ruth's identity Boaz's foreman replies	3$^{6-9}$	Ruth arrives & Boaz inquires about her identity Ruth replies (*kānāp*)
2$^{8-13}$	Boaz speaks with Ruth, offers protection and water Ruth questions Boaz's offer Boaz gives his reasons (*kānāp*) Ruth responds with gratitude	3^{10-14a}	Boaz blesses Ruth, offers to do whatever she instructs Boaz gives instructions to Ruth Ruth follows his instructions
2^{14}	Boaz invites Ruth to eat and gives her a gift of grain	3$^{14b-15a}$	Boaz protects Ruth's reputation and gives her a gift of grain
2$^{15-17}$	Boaz instructs harvesters, offers more grain and protection		
2$^{18-22}$	Ruth reports to Naomi Naomi blesses Boaz Naomi advises Ruth to stay with Boaz's workers Boaz delays acting	3^{15b-18}	Ruth reports to Naomi Naomi advises Ruth to stay at home and wait for Boaz to act Boaz springs into action

It is obvious that each Act has its own contours. Not every action is mirrored in the opposite Act. Nor do the comparable elements always occur in the same order. Nonetheless, there are so many similar story-elements that it is difficult to avoid the conclusion that the two Acts are meant to be mutually informing.

In this case, the comparisons shed more light on the characters than on the events (the contrast between Boaz's actions and Naomi's being clear). The

Act 3 ~ Ruth 3:1-18

comparison does not reveal a lot of new information about the characters though. In the case of Naomi and Boaz, it underlines, and highlights features of their personalities and behavior that we have already witnessed. Naomi, after recognizing Boaz's kindness and blessing him in Act 2 (2:20) attempts to cheat him in Act 3. This is certainly concordant with her character to this point. So far, she has disregarded the pain of her daughters-in-law, claiming that hers is greater (1:13), voiced her bitterness against God (1:20-21), passively allowed Ruth to attempt to support them alone (2:1-3), and demonstrated a profound lack of concern for the safety and reputation of her daughter-in-law (3:13). Surely, if we lived alongside her, we would feel that Naomi's had legitimate grievances. As a character in a story, though, the writers of the book have chosen to present her in a poor light and expect us to adopt a low opinion of her. Boaz, in contrast, is the same positive character throughout. He is kind. He looks out for Ruth's safety and reputation. He looks out for both women's food. He recognizes Ruth's virtues and values them. He responds to her proposal with delight and action. Apart from Boaz's failure to act decisively at the end of Act 2 (which was a plot-requirement, in any case), the writers do not allow us to see any flaws in his character.

Ruth is a different case. She changes between Act 2 and Act 3. In Act 2 she is active and finds a way to support Naomi and herself, at least for the harvest season. But she is not directing events. It is only by chance that she happens to glean in Boaz's field (2:3). Once Boaz sees her, he begins to direct events. He deals kindly with her. He directs his harvesters how to engage with her (or not). He feeds her and flatters her. In Act 3, though, she takes control. In an instant, when she reveals her identity and proposes to Boaz, she seizes control of the storyline (3:9). In that very brief speech, she both deviates from Naomi's directions and begins to direct Boaz's plans and movements. She never speaks in the story again. She never acts in the story again. But her influence is omnipresent. Everything that happened from 3:9 to 4:22 happens because of Ruth's words in 3:9b, "Please spread your robe over your servant, for you are a redeemer."

CHAPTER 5

Act 4 ~ Ruth 4:1–22

Note: I expect that certain readers will not find detailed issues of ancient Israelite law particularly engaging. For those readers, I have attempted to write this chapter in such a way that it can be navigated (more or less) without fully comprehending the legal issues presented by the chapter. The understanding that results will be incomplete, of course, but not inaccurate. For those who want to understand the bearing of *levirate*, land redemption, and inheritance law on Act 4, I have provided an extensive *excursus* at the end of the chapter (*Excursus 13*).

ACT 4 TIES UP loose threads. Ruth's and Naomi's needs will be met. Boaz will resolve the issue of Elimelek's land and marry the woman he desires, and the destiny of his and Ruth's household will be unveiled. This does not mean that the Act is without any drama or surprises of its own. The conversation between Boaz and Nobody is a masterpiece of ambiguity and persuasion. The legal implications of their conversation are puzzling, as is the focus on Naomi at the end. Also, the purpose of the closing genealogy is disputed.

> *¹ And Boaz went up to the gate, and he sat down there. And behold the redeemer was passing by (the one Boaz had spoken about). And he said, "Turn aside, sit down here Nobody." So, he turned, and he sat. ² Then he took ten men from the elders of the town, and he said, "Sit here." So, they sat.*

Act 4 ~ Ruth 4:1-22

Act 3 closed with Naomi assuring Ruth that "the man will not rest, but he will finish the matter today" (3:18). When we next see Boaz, he is already at the gate of Bethlehem seeking the relative with the greater right to redeem Elimelek's land. Most of the Act will occur in the gateway. The gateway was not only a logical place to wait for someone to pass, there being so few entrances and exits to any walled town, but it was where the town elders could often be found, holding court as it were. Should the redeemer pass by, Boaz could turn to them immediately.

Regarding the term "redeemer" see comments at 2:18-23.

"Nobody" is my translation of a compound title, *pĕlōnî ' almōnî*, which is derived from *pl'*, "hidden" or "mysterious," and *' lm*, "silent" or "mute." Taken together, it means something like "unknown and unspoken." Used of places it means "such-and-such a place," that is, an unnamed or unknown locale (1 Sam 21:3; 2 Kgs 6:8). When used of people it means something like "so-and-so" or "nobody." The writers of Ruth use the phrase *pĕlōnî ' almōnî* rather than the man's name as a way of foreshadowing what will happen in the Act. According to Deut 25:10, the man who will not act as a *levir* loses his family name. From that point forward, his household is called "the family of the unsandaled one." Of course, the writers of Ruth have led us to *wish* Ruth to be with Boaz rather than any other man, but they still disapprove of the man's unwillingness to redeem Elimelek's land (4:6). So, in keeping with Deut 25:10, they deny him a name.[1] As will be explained in *Excursus 13*, Boaz's marriage to Ruth does not correspond with *levirate* marriage as it is described in the Hebrew Bible (especially at Deut 25:5-10). Nonetheless, the writers of Ruth interact playfully with several elements of the *levirate* law in this Act, including removing the reluctant man's sandal and name.[2]

> **3** *He said to the redeemer, "Naomi—the one who returned from the fields of Moab—is selling the allotment of farm-field[3] that belonged to our brother, Elimelek,* **4** *and I thought*

---

1. Demsky, "Names," 35, derived from Rashi. See also *Midrash Ruth Rabba* 7 §7.
2. See discussion in Beyer, *Hoffnung in Bethlehem*, 114-20.
3. The phrase that I have rendered "allotment of farm-field" has attracted the attention of some interpreters, who think it refers to a portion of Elimelek's land. (See, for example, Jackson, "Nature of Biblical Law," 100-104.) This leads to speculation about the remainder of Elimelek's land. The whole phrase, *ḥelqat haśśādeh*, is employed as a synonym for "field" or "land (owned by a particular person)" in Gen 33:19; Josh 24:32; 2 Sam 23:11; Ruth 2:3. The interpretation that it is just a part of Elimelek's fields conflates

> *I should bend your ear.*[4] *Acquire it in the presence of those sitting here, and in the presence of the elders of my people. If you will redeem it, redeem. But if you will not redeem it, tell me so I may know. For there is no one before you to redeem it, and I come after you." And he said, "I will redeem it."*

Boaz presents Nobody with an opportunity and a choice. He can redeem Elimelek's land from the unnamed person who holds it. In accordance with the land redemption law in Leviticus 25, Nobody has the right to buy back (redeem) Elimelek's land at any time.[5] As the redeemer, Nobody could then profit from its use until the Jubilee year when it would return to Elimelek's heirs. As we know, Elimelek has no heirs. As his closest living relative, Nobody is both redeemer and heir. This means that should he choose to redeem Elimelek's land, it would become his permanently. Boaz offers to redeem it himself, being next in the line of potential redeemers, but Nobody is quick to jump at the opportunity.[6]

Before we observe how Boaz responds, there is a legal issue that requires clarification. If widows do not inherit their husband's property (see comments at 1:1–5), why does Boaz say that *Naomi* is "selling" Elimelek's land? The verb translated "sell" in most English Bibles can refer to different activities.[7] In this case, the only sense in which Naomi is "selling" Elimelek's land is that she wants her relative Nobody to buy it by redeeming it. Boaz is employing an imprecise and non-technical way of talking about the ownership of Elimelek's land, similar to what we see in Jer 25:9. (See *Excursus 13* for explanation.)

> [5] *Boaz said, "On the day that you acquire the field from the hand of Naomi and from Ruth the Moabite, I acquire the*

---

two meanings of *ḥlq*: "portion" or "share" of something (Gen 14:24; Deut 18:18; Eccl 11:2), and "plot of land" (Gen 33;19; 2 Sam 14:30–31; 2 Kgs 9:25–26; Amos 4:7). See Tsevat, "חלקII," *TDOT* 4:447–48.

4. The expression "bend your ear" is my equivalent for the Hebrew idiom "uncover your ear," which means "tell you something [that you don't already know]."

5. Leviticus 25 was discussed at 2:18–23.

6. Sasson, *Ruth*, 139–40.

7. The verb translated "sell" is *mkr*, which is used for (1) trading one thing for another (Gen 25:31, 33; 47:20), or (2) selling for money (Gen 37:27–28, 36; 45:4; Exod 21:7–8, 16, 35; 22:2; Lev 25:47). When selling for money, some things can be "sold" while still retaining a "right of redemption," a buy-back clause in modern parlance.

wife of the dead man, in order to perpetuate the name of the dead over his inheritance." **6** *The redeemer replied, "I am not able to redeem it myself, lest I ruin my inheritance! You redeem my redemption-right, for I am unable to redeem."*

Verses 5 and 6 are the most difficult in the Act. The first interpretive challenge is a textual variant in the Hebrew, called a *ketiv-qere*. With a *ketiv-qere*, the scribes who produced our manuscript (B19a) wrote the consonants of one word (the *ketiv*) but gave it the vowels of another word (the *qere*).[8] This results in two reading possibilities. If we read the consonants, Boaz says, "on the day you acquire the field ... *I acquire (qnyty)* the wife of the dead man." If we read the vowels (deducing the consonants that they match), Boaz says, "on the day you acquire the field ... *you acquire (qānîtā)* the wife of the dead man." The second interpretive challenge is that Boaz now says that the field belongs to Naomi *and* Ruth. So, when he follows this with "you/I acquire the wife of the dead man," which woman is he referring to, Naomi or Ruth? And which "dead man" is he discussing, Maḥlon or Elimelek?[9] Finally, how does marriage affect Nobody's inheritance? If we follow the *qere*, his marrying one of the widows will ruin his inheritance. If we follow the *ketiv*, Boaz marrying her will ruin his inheritance.

Our choice regarding the *ketiv-qere* determines our answers to all these questions. We have no evidence that a redeemer would be required to marry anyone when redeeming land. There is no connection between land redemption and *levirate* marriage in biblical law. Nonetheless, according to the *qere*, Boaz asserts that the redeemer must marry "the wife of the dead man" to "perpetuate the name of the dead over his inheritance," in accordance with Deut 25:6, "the first son whom she bears will be established in the name of his brother, the deceased one, so that his name is not blotted out of Israel."[10] Although Nobody seems surprised by this, he does

---

8. The reasons for *ketiv-qere* readings are disputed. Some scholars think they are variant readings (two legitimate reading possibilities), and some think the *qere* is a correction of the *ketiv*. For a short description, see Kahn, "*Ketiv* and *Qere*."

9. Some English translations resolve the ambiguity of the woman in question like the NRSV does: "The day you acquire the field from the hand of Naomi, *you are also acquiring Ruth the Moabite*, the widow of the dead man." This translation was adopted from the Old Latin versions (produced before the Vulgate was in the fourth century CE) rather than the Hebrew.

10. For Deut 25:6 to apply to Nobody and Boaz, *levirate* law would have to apply to men who are more distantly related than full brothers. On this possibility, see *Excursus 13*.

(Re)reading Ruth

not contest the claim. The "wife of the dead man" whom Nobody must marry would have to be Naomi, of course, since it is Elimelek's land that is in question.[11] If Nobody followed through and married Naomi, one of two things would happen. Either Naomi would give birth to a son who would inherit Elimelek's land, or she would not, and Nobody would inherit. Nobody's claim that marrying the dead man's wife would "ruin my inheritance" makes sense in the first scenario. Should he give Naomi a son, the son would "be established" in Elimelek's name and inherit Elimelek's land.[12] So, if we follow the *qere* reading, we must conclude that Boaz is deliberately misleading Nobody about his legal obligations.

If we follow the *ketiv* reading, the legal logic is similar, but Nobody's reasons for declining are different. Nobody makes an about face when Boaz announces that, no matter what Nobody does, he, Boaz, will marry the dead man's wife. If Boaz were to impregnate Naomi with a son, that son would have the stronger claim to Elimelek's property. In effect, Boaz says to Nobody, "go ahead and redeem, but I am going to marry the dead man's widow, so you are unlikely to inherit." Boaz never claims that he is following *levirate* law, and he never specifies which widow he plans to marry. Boaz is intentionally vague, never specifying whether he has Naomi or Ruth in mind. He allows Nobody to draw his own inference, and Nobody concludes that Boaz's actions will ruin his chance at the inheritance. So, if we follow the *ketiv* reading, Boaz never claims that Nobody must marry. He only claims that he is marrying the dead man's widow himself. It sounds like Boaz is misleading Nobody in this interpretation too. However, there is one way that Boaz could be speaking plain truth, even though *levirate* is not applicable in this situation. We will have to see how this can be.

Since Jack Sasson asserted in 1979 that Boaz was freely innovating with redemption and *levirate* law to manipulate Nobody, his has become a commonplace interpretation (*qere*).[13] I prefer to think that Boaz was deliberately vague about his intentions and allowed Nobody to draw unconfirmed assumptions (*ketiv*), which corresponds better with the writers'

---

11. Elimelek is the only deceased person mentioned in the conversation. Maḥlon has not been mentioned at all. So, without our prior knowledge that Boaz intends to marry Ruth (which Nobody does not share), Elimelek is the natural referent of the phrase "the dead man."

12. In this interpretation, either Nobody does not know that Naomi is too old to have sons (1:15), or he is not willing to risk that she might have a son late in life.

13. Sasson, *Ruth*, throughout (esp. 228–30), followed, for example, by Hawk, *Ruth*, 122–29; Wojcik, "Improvising Rules," 145–53.

Act 4 ~ Ruth 4:1–22

characterization of Boaz so far. Whatever the case, Boaz's vow that we will encounter in 4:10 will further affect the legal situation.

> (⁷ *Now this was formerly done in Israel in cases of redemption and payment: to settle a transaction, one man would take off his sandal and gave it to the other. This was an act of confirmation in Israel.*) ⁸ *When the redeemer said to Boaz, "Acquire for yourself," he took off his sandal.* ⁹ *And Boaz said to the elders and to all the people, "You are witnesses today that I am acquiring all that belonged to Elimelek and all that belonged to Kilyon and Maḥlon from the hand of Naomi.* ¹⁰ *And also Ruth the Moabite, the wife of Maḥlon, I am acquiring as my wife, to perpetuate the name of the dead man over his inheritance, that the name of the dead man may not be cut off from among his kinsmen and from the gate of his place.*¹⁴ *You are witnesses today."*

Verses 7–8 sound like Deut 25:9, "his [the reluctant *levir*] brother's widow will go up to him in the presence of the elders, pull the sandal off his foot, spit in his face, and make this declaration: 'Thus will be done to the man who will not build up his brother's house.'" In this case though, the writers identify it as a ritual related to "redemption and payment." It has nothing to do with *levirate* practice. The sandal seems to function like a signed contract does today. It was evidence held by the purchaser that the sale had been performed with the full consent of the seller. With the act of surrendering his sandal, Nobody surrenders his right of redemption over Elimelek's land. The right passes irrevocably to Boaz, and Nobody is no longer counted among Elimelek's heirs (4:6; compare 3:13). In this scenario, the elders are not judges, arbitrating the legality of the sale. They are witnesses of the transfer of rights.

Once the issue of the redemption right is settled, Boaz reveals that he will marry Ruth, not Naomi. He could have stopped there. He has Elimelek's land, and he is free to marry Ruth. He chooses, instead, to make a grand gesture in the presence of the elders and "all the people." He vows that he will, in fact, perpetuate the name of the dead man over his inheritance.

---

14. A person's "place" could be her or his town, country, or property. Considering the themes of Ruth, I suspect that the writers have the latter in mind.

(Re)reading Ruth

Since this is not *levirate*, he is not obligated to name his first son Elimelek, but he still vows that his first son will inherit in Elimelek's place and preserve Elimelek's line. Boaz acts of his own free will; none of this is legally required. A cynical reading might interpret this as an attempt to save face in public, since he intimated to Nobody that the land's redeemer would have to marry the dead man's widow and perpetuate the man's line (4:5). Whether or not this is true (we have no way of knowing), generosity *is* in Boaz's character. He has given gifts to Ruth and Naomi on several occasions already (2:14–16; 3:15, 17). This is his largest gift, to be sure, but it is like him to give it.

In verse 10, Boaz makes a new pun on Maḥlon's name. His name is no longer associated with "sickness" (ḥlh; see *Excursus 1*). It is now associated with "inheritance" (nḥl). Though he died without sons, leaving no one to inherit his portion of Elimelek's land, Boaz has promised to graft his first son onto Elimelek's line, "to perpetuate the name of the dead man over his inheritance."[15]

On the legality of an Israelite marrying a Moabite, see the discussion in *Excursus 8*.

> 11 *And all the people who were at the gate and the elders said, "We are witnesses. May Yhwh make the woman who is coming into your house like Rachel and Leah, who built the house of Israel, the two of them. Make strong children in Ephrathah and perpetuate a name in Bethlehem.* 12 *And may your house be like the house of Perez whom Tamar bore to Judah through the seed which Yhwh will give you from this young woman."*
>
> 13 *So Boaz married Ruth; she became his wife, and he came into her, and Yhwh gave her a pregnancy, and she bore a son.*[16] 14 *Then the women said to Naomi, "Blessed be Yhwh, who has not withheld a redeemer from you today. May his name be spoken in Israel.* 15 *He will restore your life and*

---

15. Garsiel, *Biblical Names*, 251. Since we know that the child will be named Obed not Elimelek, the name to be perpetuated must be the family name "Ephrathite" (see comments at 1:1–5).

16. A literal rendering of the Hebrew would be "Yhwh gave her a pregnancy" (Holmstedt, *Ruth*, 205).

Act 4 ~ Ruth 4:1-22

sustain your old age. Because your daughter-in-law who loves you bore him. She is better to you than seven sons."

In verses 11–15, the writers begin to tie up several intertwined themes: the similarities of Ruth to the matriarchs and patriarchs of Israel's past, the "strength" theme, the emptiness-and-fullness theme, and the redemption theme.

The elders and people at the gate now pronounce a blessing on Boaz. They bless him with the hope of a household brimming over with strong children, a household like Jacob's or Judah's. The details of the blessing are significant. We have seen in the previous Acts that Ruth is analogous to founding figures from the patriarchal age, Abraham, Jacob, and Tamar. She is now associated with Jacob's two wives, Rachel and Leah, mothers of the twelve sons who founded the tribes of Israel. Wojcik notes that Ruth is already like Rachel and Leah: "She is the beloved, like Rachel, and at the same time a woman he [Jacob] is somewhat pressured into marrying, like Leah."[17] Also like Leah, she will be given a pregnancy by God (Ruth 4:13 ‖ Gen 29:31–35). This blessing entails a measure-for-measure component. That is, both Boaz and Ruth have shown themselves to be strong people, rather like the strong woman of Prov 31:10–31 (see *Excursus 11*). Like a reward-in-kind, the elders and people now wish strong children for them, saying, in effect, "may your children be like you."[18] (Regarding the analogy between Ruth and Tamar in verse 12, see *Excursus 10*.)

The emptiness-and-fullness theme is now reaching its natural conclusion. Its fulfillment is signaled not by the word "full" but by the word "return." In Act 1, when Naomi arrived in Bethlehem, grieved at the deaths of her husband and sons, she said "God returned (*šwb*) me empty" (1:21). Here, as new life enters the family, the child is called "restorer (*šwb*) of life" (literally "returner of life"). We noted at the end of Act 1 that Naomi was blind to the gift of Ruth. Though she declared herself empty, she still had Ruth, the progenitor of all her future happiness. The writers of Ruth, while celebrating the arrival of the boy Obed, also want to remind us how pivotal

---

17. Wojcik, "Improvising Rules," 151. See also Klagsbrun, "Ruth and Naomi, Rachel and Leah," 261–72.

18. The Hebrew expression is, literally, "make/do strength in Ephrata." Most English versions and commentaries interpret "do strength" as a metaphor for "be prosperous" or the like. However, the immediate context (4:11–17) is focussed on *offspring*, and the strength theme is about strong *people*, intimating that "make strength" refers to children.

Ruth has been to Naomi's life. Ruth's son is named "returner of life," but Ruth herself is declared "better than seven sons."[19]

Finally, there is one last twist in the redemption theme. The women declare Obed to be Naomi's redeemer. Naomi saw Boaz as a potential redeemer (2:20; 3:1–4), Boaz presented Nobody as the closest redeemer (3:12), and Boaz convinced Nobody to let him be the redeemer by purchasing Elimelek's land (4:1–6). The last word on the subject, though, is given to the unnamed women at the gate. They pronounce Ruth's child to be Naomi's redeemer. Because of Boaz's vow in 4:10, the child will inherit Elimelek's land. When he is born, Boaz's role as redeemer ends. The child takes over that role. He will support Naomi in her old age. Appropriately, the child is named Obed, which means "serving one" or just "servant." He will be like a faithful servant, caring for Naomi's needs and easing her twilight years.

> **16** *Naomi took the child and held him to her breast and became his nurse,* **17** *and the neighbors gave him a name, saying, "A son is born to Naomi." They called his name Obed. He was the father of Jesse, father of David.*

Ruth has been associated with Israel's ancestors many times. Here at the end of the tale—her pains bound up, if not healed—Naomi too is permitted a second association with a great woman from Israel's past.[20] When Moses was born in Exodus 2, he was destined to be thrown into the Nile according to command of the Pharaoh. His mother followed the letter of the law and cast him in. She defied the law, though, by placing him in an ark, a little boat that would carry him safely through the waters.[21] When he was found and saved by the daughter of Pharaoh, Moses' sister shrewdly offered to hire a wet nurse for the baby from the Hebrew slaves:

> His sister said to Pharaoh's daughter, "Should I go and bring you a nurse from the Hebrew women to nurse the child for you?" Pharaoh's daughter said to her, "Yes." So, the girl went and collected the child's mother. Pharaoh's daughter said to her, "Take this child and nurse it for me, and I will give you your wages." So, the woman took the child and nursed it. (Exod 2:7–9)

19. Saxegaard, "More than Seven Sons," 257–75.
20. On Naomi's similarities to Rebecca, see comments on 3:16–18.
21. The floating basket Moses is placed into is called an ark (*tēbāh*) in Exod 2:3 and 5, which is just one element of a sustained analogy between him and Noah.

Act 4 ~ Ruth 4:1–22

In verse 16, Naomi is equated with Moses' mother. She becomes wet nurse to a child of her own blood, a child who "belongs" to a gentile woman, a child of destiny. No doubt this analogy hints at the child's legacy as grandfather of David, but it also reveals something significant about Naomi. Naomi is like a legendary woman too. In her case, it is not because she shares virtues with Moses' mother but because of the fortune brought to her by Ruth. It is Ruth who gives birth to the child of destiny, not Naomi. But, like Moses' mother, Naomi is permitted a role in rearing her own redeemer. Ruth's greatness, engendered by her strength and virtue, spills over to Naomi and makes her a greater woman than she otherwise would be.

The line "A son is born to Naomi" fulfills Boaz's vow in 4:10. Boaz and Ruth gift Obed to the line of Elimelek. (Similar to Hannah gifting Samuel to God in 1 Samuel 1–2.) Naomi now has a "son" to stand in Mahlon's place and inherit his land.

The second half of verse 17 closes Act 4, the book's final verses being an Epilogue. It ties off the book neatly, balancing the three deaths at the book's beginning (Elimelek, Mahlon, Kilyon) with three births at its end (Obed, Jesse, David). "The book opens with men who have no future. It ends with men who have a glorious future."[22]

Epilogue (4:18–22): From Death to Life, from Poverty to Glory

> 18 *These are the descendants of Perez: Perez fathered Hezron,* 19 *Hezron fathered Ram, Ram fathered Amminadab,* 20 *Amminadab fathered Nahshon, Nahshon fathered Salmon,* 21 *Salmon fathered Boaz, Boaz fathered Obed,* 22 *Obed fathered Jesse, and Jesse fathered David.*

The Book of Ruth ends with a recitation of the ancestors of David from Perez, son of Judah and Tamar, to David himself. Scholars have long debated why the Book of Ruth concludes with a focus on David. Does it point to the broader purpose of the whole book? Does it just serve as a bridge between the books of Ruth and Samuel? Or does it have another function?

---

22. Hawk, *Ruth*, 137.

(Re)reading Ruth

Many interpreters think that the Book of Ruth, with its ideal characters Ruth and Boaz, was written to remove a blot from David's family tree. It is biblical propaganda, making David's linage acceptable to those who might be opposed to a descendant of a Moabite sitting on the throne of Israel.[23] However, possessing dispreferred ancestors was not a bar to becoming a king in the ancient Near East. It certainly was not in ancient Israel. Solomon, after all, was less than half Israelite (1 Kgs 1:11). King Rehoboam's mother was an Ammonite (1 Kgs 14:31; 2 Chr 12:13), and King Jehoram of Israel (also called Joram) was the son of Jezebel the Sidonian princess (1 Kgs 16:31; 2 Kgs 3:1–3; 9:22). I think that the focus on David serves a different purpose. It underscores one of the major themes of *his* story: that he was a humble shepherd, elevated by God to the throne of Israel. It is a theme reiterated many times in the tales of David (1 Sam 16:19; 2 Sam 7:8; 12:7–8; Ps 78:70; 1 Chr 17:7, etc.). The Book of Samuel opens with a lengthy poem, the song of Hannah, which extols God for elevating the poor and humble in Israel, elevating one of them to the throne of the kingdom (see especially 1 Sam 2:7–10). By identifying Ruth as David's grandmother, the writers intensify the humility of his roots. He is descended from a poor, vulnerable, immigrant woman. Despite this, she rose in the world, as he will. Both Samuel and Ruth credit God with this metamorphosis, elevating the poor and glorifying the humble (see discussion in *Excursus 5*). The women of Bethlehem called a blessing over Ruth and Boaz. They were to "make strong children in Ephrathah and perpetuate a name in Bethlehem." What name is greater in Bethlehem than David's? What other character in the Hebrew Bible could be called "strong" (per *Excursus 11*), if not David?[24]

Like most genealogies in the Bible, this one has been crafted for literary effect.[25] It includes ten names, five of whom lived before the exodus and five after, which might explain why Judah was omitted.[26] It makes the list an even number. Likewise, several of the names—Hezron, Nahshon, and

---

23. See, for example, Gerleman, *Rut*, 7, 37–38; Eskenazi and Frymer-Kensky, *Ruth*, 93; Gow, *Ruth*, 183–210.

24. For all these reasons the writers choose to ignore Boaz's vow in 4:11 and regard David as a descendant of Boaz's and Ruth's, not a descendant of Maḥlon's.

25. See Plum, "Genealogy as Theology," 66–92.

26. Eskenazi proposes that the genealogy begins with Perez, whose name means "breach," because while the book validates the marriage of a Moabite and an Israelite, it also "acknowledges it as a breach." Eskenazi and Frymer-Kensky, *Ruth*, 94.

Salmon—rhyme with Maḥlon and Kilyon, linking the end of the book to its beginning in yet another way.[27]

Excursus 13. *Levirate* Law & Land Redemption

The Book of Ruth engages with *levirate* law and land redemption law. These two sets of laws entail issues of inheritance as well. All three are intertwined in Ruth, causing interpreters no end of grief attempting to unravel them. The grief arises for two reasons. Ruth refers to both legal practices but does not provide an explanation of how they relate to one another. In the laws of the Torah, the two issues are not connected with one another. In this *excursus*, I will explain the two laws as they are described in the Torah, explain how they are described in Ruth, and then offer some thoughts on the association of the two in Ruth.

Levirate Law

Because marriage created a kinship bond (Gen 1:22), it was illegal for a man to sleep with his brother's wife (Lev 20:21). To do so was considered incest. There was an exception to this law, however. *Levirate* is the fully legal practice of a living man impregnating his dead brother's wife, should the brother have died without sons. The only law regarding *levirate* in the Hebrew Bible is found in Deut 25:5–10:

> 5 When brothers reside together, and one of them dies and has no son, the wife of the dead brother will not be married outside [the family] to a stranger. Her brother-in-law will go to her and take her to himself as a wife and perform the duty of a brother-in-law to her. 6 Then the first son whom she bears will be established in the name of his brother, the deceased one, so that his name is not blotted out of Israel. 7 But if the man is not willing to marry his brother's widow, his brother's widow will appear before the elders in the gate and declare, "My husband's brother refuses to establish

---

27. Kirsten Nielsen (*Ruth*, 7) observes that opening or closing a story with a genealogy is common in Genesis. Since Ruth has been carefully associated with Abraham, Jacob, Lot's daughters, and Tamar, who are all from the Book of Genesis, this is a logical way for her story to end. Verse 18 even opens with the word *tôlĕdôt*, "descendants" or "generations," which also appears in Gen 2:4; 6:9; 36:1; 36:9; and 37:2.

a name in Israel for his brother. He will not perform the duty of a *levir*."²⁸ **8** The elders of his town will then send for him and talk to him. If he insists saying, "I do not want to marry her," **9** his brother's widow will go up to him in the presence of the elders, pull the sandal off his foot, spit in his face, and make this declaration: "Thus will be done to the man who will not build up his brother's house." **10** So, in Israel he will go by the name "the family of the unsandaled one."

Deuteronomy 25 clarifies that a widow without sons should not be married outside the family. Instead, her brother-in-law was expected to "take her to himself as a wife" and "do his duty as a brother" by giving her children. A son of a *levirate* union was given the name of the dead man, because, while the child was the son of the brother-in-law, he was legally considered to be brother of his mother's brother-in-law (his biological father).²⁹ A son born into a *levirate* union could then inherit the dead brother's property (notably his land) and provide his mother with the security of a place in his household in her old age.³⁰ From the description in Deuteronomy 25, there does not appear to be any legal punishment doled out to the man who refuses to practice *levirate*. The punishment is social. He endures a public shaming by the offended widow and his household is scorned in the community as an "unsandaled one."³¹

It will be obvious to many readers that this law is incomplete. Several issues are not explained. Was a *levirate* marriage a permanent union, or did it only last until a son was born?³² What provisions were there for wives who could not bear children? What provision was there for the widow who

---

28. *Levir* is a Latin word meaning "brother-in-law."

29. For a more robust description of *levirate*, see Weisberg, *Levirate Marriage*, 1–22. For examples of *levirate* practices in other cultures see Westermark, *History of Human Marriage*, 3:208–22; Doniger, *Bedtrick*, 179–88, 237–39, 248–63, 269–71.

30. Frederick Greenstein does not think that preserving the "name of his brother" is the principal reason for the practice, because the surviving brothers would carry on the family name. Preserving inherited property within the family and maintaining a duty of care for widows in the family were the more urgent motives. *When Brothers Dwell Together*, 53.

31. Dvora Weisberg points out that Deuteronomy 25 and Genesis 38 share the theme of "discomfort with *levirate* marriage, particularly on the part of men." This discomfort contributes to the restriction of *levirate* practice in the Rabbinic period. "The Widow of Our Discontent," 403–29, quote at 403.

32. Belkin, "Levirate and Agnate Marriage," 277–80.

had daughters but not sons?[33] The brother clearly had no free-will in the matter, but could a widow choose to abstain from *levirate*? Could the widow choose a different partner than the brother-in-law, either before or after having given birth to a son by the brother-in-law? These questions illustrate that we know little about the legal exercise of *levirate* in ancient Israel. Even Deut 25:5–10 says more about the law's breach (verses 7–10) than about its practice (verses 5–6). Some scholars assume that the practice of *levirate* as reflected in narrative texts like Genesis 38 and Ruth can be used to fill in some of the gaps in Deut 25:5–10. Other scholars are more cautious.[34]

The levirate law is also ambiguous at two points that are key for its interpretation. Who is a "brother"? In the Hebrew Bible the word "brother," ʼaḥ, is used for a wide range of relatives: biological brothers (Gen 4:2), half-brothers (Gen 37:4), nephews (Gen 14:16), male cousins (Gen 29:15), any male kinsman (Gen 13:8), or someone from the same tribe (Judg 9:18). It can also be used of a companion (2 Sam 1:26) or as a title of courtesy (Gen 29:4; 1 Kgs 9:13), just as it can in English. Many interpreters assume that the *levir* must be a biological brother, possibly extending to a half-brother.[35] But that partakes of modern cultural assumptions of what constitutes the kindred of brothers, namely, a shared progenitor or progenitors (close genetic relationship). That notion is not shared by many traditional cultures. In some societies, there is no difference between blood relatives and relatives by marriage or even relatives adopted by ritual or vow (compare Gen 15:2; 1 Sam 20:42—21:1; 2 Sam 9:1–12, especially verse 11).[36] I am not claiming that *levirate* could be applied in all these relationships. I am pointing out that the law is less clear on this point than it might be.

The second ambiguity arises from the phrase "when brothers reside together." Is this just a practical concern, stipulating that *levirate* law need not be enforced when it is unreasonable to do so, like when brothers live far apart? Or does the phrase mean, "when (and only when) brothers reside together"?[37] In the second case, the concern would be land-inheritance.

---

33. Numbers 27:8–10 allows a daughter to inherit her father's land, but this possibility is not mentioned in Deut 25:5–10 (see below). Could a widow demand her *levirate* rights from a brother-in-law even if she had a living daughter?

34. Greengus, *Laws*, is one scholar who uses biblical narratives and prophecies to fill out his descriptions of legal practices in ancient Israel. I adopt a more cautious approach.

35. So, Burrows, "Marriage of Boaz and Ruth," 445–54.

36. The term "brother-in-law," *yābām*, is only used here in Deut 25:5, 7 (the feminine form appears in Ruth 1:15), and we cannot tell if it narrows the possibilities or not.

37. For example, Davies, "Inheritance Rights," 264–66, and Rashi.

For instance, if two brothers lived together, their land joined as a common estate, and one brother died, the estate would fall to the surviving brother. But the widow of the dead man could claim her *levirate* rights, and the surviving brother would have to father a son who would become co-owner of the estate. If this is what the phrase implies, then *levirate* law is only concerned with a very special legal circumstance related to inheritance.[38]

Land Redemption Law

In Leviticus, the land redemption law is preceded by laws on the sabbatical year (Lev 25:2–7) and Jubilee (25:8–22). The law of the Sabbath year stipulates that every seventh year fields must lay fallow. The Jubilee law enforces a special sabbatical year every fiftieth year (after 7 x 7 years). The Jubilee is not just a Sabbath for the land, it is a "liberation" of all land and people (25:10). Land that has been "sold" returns to its ancestral owners. Israelite slaves are freed; debts are absolved. The rest of the chapter is dedicated to four special cases: when an Israelite sells his land (25:23–28), sells a house in a walled city (25:29–34), borrows money (25:35–38), or sells himself as an indentured servant to cover his debts (25:39–54). The context suggests that all four situations are instigated by financial difficulties, and three of the four are reversed on the Jubilee. (The house sale is not.)

The laws about an Israelite selling and redeeming land are important legal background for the Book of Ruth. Land redemption is the main issue discussed by Boaz and Nobody. The land redemption law reads as follows:

> 23 Land must not be sold irrevocably, for the [whole] land is mine. You are but aliens and tenants for me. 24 Throughout the land that you hold, you shall provide for the redemption of the land. 25 If your kinsman falls into poverty and sells part of his landholding, his redeemer, the nearest one, will come and redeem what his kinsman has sold. 26 If a man has no redeemer, but if his work prospers and he finds enough for redemption, 27 he will calculate the years since its sale and return the balance to the man to whom he sold it, and he will return to his landholding. 28 If his [income from] work is insufficient to recover it, what he sold will remain in the hand of the purchaser until the jubilee. In the jubilee year it will be released, and he will return to his landholding.

---

38. See discussions in Westbrook, *Property*, 78–79, 138–39; Thompson and Thompson, "Legal Problems," 79–99; Jackson, "Nature of Biblical Law," 96–97; and Braulik, "Book of Ruth," 16–18.

Act 4 ~ Ruth 4:1-22

A man can sell his land to another person for whatever time remains until the next Jubilee year, when it will be returned to him. The best scenario, should an Israelite find himself in a financial crisis, is that the land be retained by the family or clan. The seller's family always retains the right to "redeem" the land, so long as someone in the family is wealthy enough to do so. Redeeming land is a simple act of repaying the seller's proceeds from the sale thereby re-securing the land for the family. The land, at that point, presumably can be gifted back to the original owner (verse 27), or it can be "owned" by the purchasing family member until the Jubilee. Ordinarily, only male children inherit, but Num 27:8-10 concedes that a daughter could inherit her father's land if he died without sons. Nothing is said, anywhere in the Bible, that indicates a widow could inherit from her husband.[39]

The clearest example of land redemption in the Hebrew Bible is found in Jer 32:6-15. Jeremiah's cousin Hanamel, son of his uncle Shallum, asks Jeremiah to redeem his field at Anatoth. Hanamel has fallen into debt, cannot repay, and his land is forfeit to his creditor. If Jeremiah will step in, the land, Hanamel admits, would then be his to dispense with: "the right of possession and redemption is yours; buy it for yourself" (verse 8). So, Jeremiah redeems the land "from my cousin Hanamel." Two things about this story are potentially helpful for understanding Ruth. First, the purchase is presented as being from Hanamel to Jeremiah not from Hanamel's creditor, the person who now holds legal right to Hanamel's property. That person remains unnamed.[40] Jeremiah, though redeeming the land by paying off Hanamel's debt, is said to have purchased it "from my cousin" (verse 8). We will see in a moment how this could affect our reading of Ruth. Second, verses 9-12 provide a helpful description of the procedure Jeremiah followed:

> ⁹ So I bought the field at Anatoth from Hanamel, son of my uncle. I weighed out the silver to him, seventeen shekels of silver. ¹⁰ I signed the deed, sealed it, secured witnesses, and weighed the money on scales. ¹¹ Then I took the deed of purchase, the sealed terms and conditions, and the open copy, ¹² and I gave the deed of purchase to Baruch son of Neriah son of Mahseyah, in the presence of my cousin Hanamel, in the presence of the witnesses who

---

39. One attempt to overturn this conclusion is Osgood, "Women and the Inheritance of Land," 29-52.

40. Some interpreters see Jeremiah's purchase as preventing the imminent surrender of the property to someone outside of the family, but that defies the typical use of "redeem," *g' l*, which is to "buy back" or "re-secure" Westbrook, "Redemption of Land," 368.

signed the deed of purchase, and in the presence of all the Judeans who were sitting in the court of the guard.[41]

This procedure is more detailed than the description in Ruth, but it is similar.

The Book of Ruth

Issues of land redemption and *levirate* marriage in Ruth do not correspond seamlessly with what we observe in the Torah. There are similarities and there are differences. Some of the differences arise because Ruth deals with different circumstance than those mentioned in the Torah, and some of the differences simply remain opaque to us. In the following paragraphs, I will describe the evidence presented by Ruth, working through the book from top to bottom.

Levirate Law

In Act 1, Naomi brought up the subject of *levirate* marriage and Ruth's and Orpah's right to marry any sons Naomi might have in the future. But she declared herself too old to get pregnant and encouraged her daughters-in-law to seek husbands in Moab (Ruth 1:11–13). There is no indication in the Hebrew Bible that Naomi's *levirate* right could be "inherited" by her daughters-in-law. Even if Naomi could demand that the "near kinsman" give her a son, that right would not extend to Ruth or Orpah. When Boaz meets Nobody at the town gate and persuades him to relinquish his redemption right, the compact is sealed by removing Nobody's sandal as "was formerly done in Israel in cases of redemption and payment" (4:7). This sounds like the *levirate* law, in which the scorned widow marked and shamed a reluctant *levir* by drawing off his sandal (Deut 25:9–10). As Westbrook points out, though, in Deuteronomy the symbolic act represents "failure to perform a duty," whereas in Ruth it represents "concession of a right." The two are opposite.[42] In Act 4, when Boaz vows to "perpetuate the name of the dead man" he is being generous; he is not following *levirate* practice (see comments on 4:7–10). This is why, when Ruth's son is born,

---

41. It is not clear what or where this might be. "Court of the guard" is the proposal found in many ancient Greek translations (and several English Bibles). The ancient Aramaic translators suggested "court of the prison house."

42. Westbrook, *Property*, 83.

he is not named Maḥlon. He is named Obed, and nothing more is said of Maḥlon (4:17).⁴³

Because Naomi refers to *levirate* in Act 1, because Nobody is denied a name, because of the sandal-ritual, because Boaz vows "to perpetuate the name of the dead man over his inheritance" (4:10), and because the book alludes to the story of Judah and Tamar—a story about *levirate*—many interpreters are inclined to think that the union between Ruth and Boaz must be a *levirate* marriage. But the book's description of their marriage simply does not align with the description of *levirate* in either Deuteronomy 25 or Genesis 38. If it is a *levirate* marriage, it is not any species of *levirate* known to us.⁴⁴

Land Redemption Law

The Book of Ruth does not say as much, but Elimelek seems to have disposed of his land before he departed Bethlehem for Moab. Several clues recommend this deduction. Elimelek "sojourned" in Moab for at least a decade, and his sons married local girls. Such a long absence from Israel implies that he did not have property to tend in his hometown. When Naomi did return to Bethlehem, she had nowhere to go and declared herself "empty" (1:21-22). She seemed to consider Elimelek's land as beyond reach. As a result, the two women were reduced to gleaning, further indicating that Elimelek's land was inaccessible to them. This suspicion was confirmed when we learned that the land was eligible for redemption, in accordance with Lev 25:25. Why Elimelek disposed of his land in the first place is never indicated, but it is no longer in the possession of a relative.

When Elimelek died, his land normally would have been inherited jointly by his sons, Maḥlon and Kilyon.⁴⁵ Since it was sold, they would not receive it until the Jubilee, when it should be restored to the family. This may explain why they too made no effort to return to Bethlehem. When Maḥlon and Kilyon die, the inheritance right passed to Nobody, Elimelek's closest male relative. Nobody already held the right of redemption as "near

---

43. Regarding Boaz's claim that he will "perpetuate the name of the dead man over his inheritance" (4:5, 10) see comments at 4:5-6 above.

44. For an alternative proposal, see Jones, *Reading Ruth*, 129-35.

45. Daube, "Consortium in Roman and Hebrew Law," 71-91.

(Re)reading Ruth

kinsman." As a result, if Nobody were to redeem the land, it would be his forever. This explains why he is so eager to do so (4:4).[46]

A complicating factor in all this is Boaz's comment in 4:3. He says, "Naomi—the one who returned from the fields of Moab—is selling the allotment of farm-field that belonged to our brother, Elimelek." If wives could not inherit land, how can he say this? Scholars have suggested several answers to the question. Some have proposed that Naomi could still act as "agent" of her deceased husband's land, even though she could not inherit it herself.[47] Other have hypothesized that she could receive the proceeds of a land sale, there being no male heir to receive it.[48] I propose that Jer 32:6–15 offers a simple solution. In Jeremiah 32, the prophet was invited to redeem land on behalf of his cousin Hanamel. Verse 9 reads, "So I bought the field at Anatoth *from Hanamel*, son of my uncle. I weighed out the silver to him, seventeen shekels of silver." Hanamel received money to pay his debts from Jeremiah, equivalent to the value of his ancestral land. Once the debt was paid, Hanamel's land would belong to the redeemer. So, Hanamel's land became Jeremiah's to dispose of as he saw fit until the Jubilee. On the Jubilee, Hanamel would repossess it. The essential point is that, despite an unnamed person having purchased the land, Jer 25:9 still describes the land as Hanamel's. I suggest that Ruth 4:3 is similar. Even though Naomi does not own Elimelek's land and cannot, and even though another party has possession of it, Boaz still describes it as if it were hers. He does this presumably because Naomi is the last living member of Elimelek's household. By this reading, the clause "Naomi is selling the allotment" is a convenient turn-of-phrase, not a legal assertion. The legal realities were more complex.

"Redemption" of Ruth

At the threshing floor, Boaz promises Ruth "even if he [Nobody] will redeem *you*, good; he will redeem. If he is not willing to redeem *you*, then I will redeem *you*" (3:13). As we have seen, *levirate* marriage is not referred to as an act of redemption, nor is any kind of marriage in the Hebrew Bible. Still, Boaz claims that marrying Ruth would be a redemption. This claim remains unclear to us. Scholars have proposed many solutions, but all of them are hypothetical. For example, Sasson translates "redeem *for* you."

---

46. Berlin, "Legal Fiction," 17–18.
47. Westbrook, *Property*, 79–80. Westbrook compares Ruth 4:3 with Prov 31:16.
48. See, for example, the argument by Daube, *Ancient Jewish Law*, 37.

Adding the word "for" makes the problem disappear. Schipper, citing 2:20 as supporting evidence, sees 3:13 as a reference to a type of kindred redemption unknown from elsewhere in the Hebrew Bible.[49] Eskenazi and Frymer-Kensky propose that Ruth, in asking Boaz to act as redeemer (3:9), was asking him to support the women, to provide for his needy relatives. Her request was not a legal act of redemption. Rather, it was a request in the *spirit* of the land-redemption law.[50] Though I have adopted the interpretation of Eskenazi and Frymer-Kensky, in truth, we lack sufficient information from the Hebrew Bible or ancient Near Eastern literature to answer the question with certainty.

Conclusion

Land redemption in the Book of Ruth corresponds with what we know from Leviticus 25 and Jeremiah 32. Ruth's and Boaz's marriage, though, is not a *levirate* marriage, unless it is a type of *levirate* practice unknown to us. It does not correspond to Deut 25:5–10, the only law on the subject in the Hebrew Bible. Boaz's offer to redeem Ruth (3:13 [3:9]) does not seem to have been an offer of marriage, though he wants that too. It was an offer to support Ruth and Naomi forever. His vow to "perpetuate the name of the dead man over his inheritance" sounds like *levirate* law too, but it appears to be a gracious gesture by Boaz, made for the sake of his dead relative Elimelek but not required by the law.

Excursus 14. Act 1 ‖ Act 4

The relationship of Act 1 to Act 4 is quite different from the relationship of Act 2 to Act 3. Acts 2 and 3 were bound by many complementary story-elements: characters, events, and settings. Even the contours of the conversations were similar (proposals, agreements, inquiries, instructions, and

49. Sasson, *Ruth*, 90–92; Schipper, *Ruth*, 151; Eskenazi and Frymer-Kensky, *Ruth*, 44, 64. Schipper's solution was also proposed by Ibn Ezra and Naḥmanides in the Middle Ages.

50. For a sustained argument that "the author of Ruth entertained a meta-legal attitude" that "his purpose was to extol the spirit rather than the letter of Israelite law," see Levine, "In Praise of the Israelite *Mišpaḥâ*," 95–106, quote at 97. Compare, Barmash, "Achieving Justice through Narrative," 181–99; Berlin, "Legal Fiction," 3–18.

so on). The relationship of Act 1 to Act 4 cannot be mapped in a similar way. Though the two Acts share some complementary events, the settings are different; the characters are different, and the conversations are different. The correspondences that exist are mostly antithetical to each other, or reversals. For example, all the characters in Act 1 are woman, but the characters in Act 4 are (almost) all men. Yhwh is accused in Act 1, but he is blessed in Act 4. Naomi is empty in Act 1 but full in Act 4. The other thing that binds the two Acts, making them cohere with one another, is a set of keywords and clever wordplay on those keywords. The keywords are essential to recognizing one of the arguments of the Book of Ruth.

The elements that are complementary, or antithetical, or reversed in Act 4 serve as signals that the story is reaching conclusion. The reversal of Naomi's situation, for example, signals that her problems have been resolved. That God is accused in Act 1 and blessed in Act 4 signals a reversal in Naomi's attitude and situation. Most of the correspondences, like the presence of the chorus at the end of each Act and the divine gifts in each Act, work like bookends around the story, ringing it in or closing it off. Most of these enclosing elements are clustered at the very beginning of Act 1 and at the very end of Act 4.

Act 1	Act 4
• Naomi's ill fortune (1:3–5, 13, 20–21)	• Naomi's good fortune (4:14–17)
• Three deaths (1:3–5)	• Three births (4:17)
• Naomi childless (1:5)	• Naomi given a child (4:17)
• Ruth widowed (1:5)	• Ruth married (4:13)
• God accused (1:20–21)	• God blessed (4:14)
• Fertility: God gifts his people with food (1:6)	• Fertility: God gifts Ruth with a pregnancy (4:13)
• Chorus appears (1:19)	• Chorus appears (4:14)
• All actors are women	• All actors are men (excepting chorus)

The keywords shared by the two Acts coalesce around a common theme: *returning home*. It is not immediately obvious how they all contribute to this theme, but once we see it, it alters our perspective on the book's purpose.

Act 4 ~ Ruth 4:1-22

The principal keywords, to which all the others are subordinate, are the Hebrew word *šwb*, "return," and its sound-alike *yšb*, "live" or "sit." "Return" appears a remarkable fourteen times in the book, especially in Act 1 (1:6, 7, 8, 10, 11 [twice], 13, 16, 21, 22 [twice]; 3:13; 4:1, 4). "Live/sit" appears eleven times, most densely in Act 4 (1:4; 2:7, 14, 23; 3:18; 4:1 [three times], 2 [twice], 4). It is not accidental that the two words are puns of one another, nor is it accidental that the two words, when combined, sum up the main action of the book: "return to live."[51] On three occasions, *šwb* is employed in an unexpected way that indicates its importance. The first two appear in Act 1, at its beginning and at its end:

> She started out with her daughters-in-law to return (*šwb*) from the fields of Moab (1:6)
>
> Naomi returned (*šwb*), and Ruth the Moabite her daughter-in-law with her (1:22)

These two verses are a bit less remarkable in English than in Hebrew. In Hebrew it is clear that it is not just Naomi who is "returning" to Israel but Ruth too. Ruth did not leave Israel. At the beginning of Act 1, Ruth had never been in Israel, and Ruth is not an Israelite. Nonetheless, the writers describe her as a returnee. The writers grant her the status of an Israelite who was exiled from the land of Israel and subsequently returned. The third unexpected use of *šwb* speaks of Naomi and her return. Speaking of Obed, the chorus says,

> He will restore (*šwb*) your life and sustain your old age. (4:15)

When Ruth conceives and gives birth to a son, she gifts Naomi with the child who will "return" ("restore") Naomi's life. Naomi's return to her people and her land is incomplete without him. Even in Israel, she had no security. When Ruth gifted her with Obed, Naomi finally achieved her return. Only then was she home.

The second set of keywords that bind Act 1 to Act 4 are also puns of one another, and they complement the themes of "return" and "living." They are the words "name," *šēm*, and "there," *šām*. "Name" occurs five times in Act 1 (1:2 [three times], 4 [twice]) and another seven times in Act 4 (4:5,

---

51. The word *yšb* must be translated as "sit" rather than "live," on several occasions, including most all the occurrences in Act 4. Nonetheless, I am persuaded that it serves as a pun on *šwb* and a complement to it.

10 [twice], 11, 14, 17 [twice]).⁵² "There" appears six times in total (1:2, 4, 7, 17; 3:4; 4:1). The importance of the two words and their linkage is most evident in two verses that do not even use the term "place."

> Boaz said, "On the day that you acquire the field from the hand of Naomi and from Ruth the Moabite, I acquire the wife of the dead man, in order to perpetuate the name (*šēm*) of the dead over his inheritance" (4:5).

> And also Ruth the Moabite, the wife of Maḥlon, I am acquiring as my wife, to perpetuate the name (*šēm*) of the dead man over his inheritance, that the name (*šēm*) of the dead man may not be cut off from among his kinsmen and from the gate of his place. (4:10)

"Name," in these two verses, is used in a special way. It refers to the line of the dead man, which has been terminated because he had no sons. It refers to his household, which has come to an end. In the Hebrew Bible, people are closely tied to places, to the land of their inheritance. In the Book of Joshua, the land of Canaan was distributed to all the tribes, clans, and families of Israel. It is that original land allotment that belongs irrevocably to a particular family. Even if sold, as Elimelek did with his land, it is restored to its original owners in the year of Jubilee. A name and a place. The two are intertwined, bound together forever in biblical law. (For further explanation see discussion in *Excursus 13*.)

Without a man to carry on Elimelek's name, Naomi has no place. She had no land and no household. Boaz persuaded Nobody to allow him to redeem Elimelek's land (4:3–9), but then he gifted it back to the terminated house of Elimelek (4:10). Unexpectedly, the line of Elimelek was restored, the land and household of Elimelek reconstituted. As was discussed in the comments on 4:7–10, Boaz was under no legal obligation to do this. It was a grand gesture and a costly one. Elimelek's land could have been joined to his estate. Nonetheless, he ceded his first child to the "dead man," Elimelek, so that his "name" would not be forgotten, and his inheritance would not be dissolved into another's.⁵³

---

52. Otherwise, "name" only appears in 2:1, 19. One of the unique stylistic features of Ruth is that when specific names appear in Acts 1 and 4 they usually appear in pairs: Elimelek and Naomi (1:2a), Maḥlon and Kilyon (1:2b), Elimelek and Naomi (1:3a), Orpah and Ruth (1:4), Maḥlon and Kilyon (1:5), Elimelek and Naomi (4:3), Naomi and Ruth (4:5), Naomi and Elimelek (4:9), Kilyon and Maḥlon (4:9), Ruth and Maḥlon (4:10), Rachel and Leah (4:11), Boaz and Ruth (4:13).

53. This may add another layer to Elimelek's (inappropriate) name. It is not the man

Act 4 ~ Ruth 4:1–22

The connection between these four keywords is obvious enough. Naomi and Ruth *returned* to Israel without a *name*, without a *place*, in search of a *living* and hoping for restoration and redemption. I am not suggesting that these keywords create meaning that is otherwise invisible. I am suggesting that they underline topics that otherwise *could* appear unimportant. They confirm our readerly suspicions, and they force us to recalibrate, to reconsider the importance of the topics thematized by these keywords. If we had considered Ruth to be a modest domestic story, or just a preamble to David's story, the intertwined themes of *returning, living, place,* and *name* force us reorient our understanding. They have been enduring themes of Israel's story from deep antiquity to the present. Ruth and Naomi are not just individuals seeking security for themselves. Ruth and Boaz are not just the incidental progenitors of important children. Ruth and Naomi are *exemplars*. Their return is a microcosm of Israel's return. Their quest for a place to rest, new life, and a new name in the land of Israel is mirrored in the quest of many children of Abraham's who live in *diaspora*. More than this, their longing for place, for peace, for life are echoes of a cry that is not the exclusive inheritance of Abraham's children. It is the inheritance of anyone who is poor and isolated, far from home and alone. It is the cry of the refugee, the homeless, the bereaved, and the lonely. Ruth is a human story with a human face. Focused on desperate people in desperate circumstances, it teaches us the importance of compassion for all, even those who are embittered like Naomi. It teaches us the power of *ḥesed*, the choice to be loyal or kind, like Ruth, even when there is no obligation to do so. It teaches us to become the kindness of God in the lives of others, like Boaz, even when it comes at a cost.[54]

---

who left Israel for whom "God is my king." It is Boaz who gives new life to the name, especially through his heir David.

54. The keywords "bread/food," *leḥem*, and "home," *bayit*, which are combined in the name Bethlehem (*bēt-leḥem*), have similar effects on the story. They were described in the discussion of Act 1, but the themes of home and food run though all four Acts.

Concluding Postscript
Reading Biblical Literature

IF YOU HAVE MADE it this far, it will be obvious that this little book had more than one goal. In addition to the aim of explaining the Book of Ruth, it has been my intention to place the literary sophistication of Ruth in the center of the stage—its poetic features, contours, and textures. I have attempted to show that Ruth is neither easy nor simplistic. It is so dense with poetic features that appreciating and absorbing its artistry is a time-consuming process. Reading biblical narrative requires attention to a host of details, patience to see how they develop and intertwine, and trust in the writers' purposes. It is a process that requires reading and rereading, usually for many years. Ruth is not unique in this respect. The works of William Shakespeare, James Joyce, and Virginia Wolf make similar demands on readers. And yet, biblical narratives are, at least in one respect, more difficult than anything in the canon of Western literature. They are foreign to Western readers. They were written by people from a different time, place, and culture. The Bible has been so much a part of Western culture and religion that we sometimes forget it is foreign literature. And that is another thing that this book has been about: learning the ways that this literature operates, the conventions and habits of writers who work according to cultural customs of their own. I hope that you have found the return to be worth the work, that the process of painstaking reading and the careful construction of meaning has opened the book up in ways that are both useful and rewarding.

(Re)reading Ruth

Specifically, I have been at pains to show how narrative structure, literary allusion, and wordplay were used by the biblical writers to add depths of pleasure and meaning to our reading. Two of those devices, structure and allusion, are deployed by biblical writers to construct analogies. They invite us to compare and contrast events, characters, ideas, and objects. For example, in many interpretations Boaz is a flat character, a man who always does the right thing, at the right time, in the right way, simply because he is good. This is not false, but he is certainly not flat. We can appreciate how multifaceted Boaz's character is when we observe how the writers have invited us to compare him with other characters, like Naomi (Act 3), Ruth (Acts 2–3), Nobody (Act 4), Judah (*Excursus* 10), and the Strong Woman (*Excursus* 11). These comparisons are invited by the structure of the Acts (Naomi and Nobody), the structure of the book (Ruth), and the allusions to other books (Judah and the Strong Woman).

In an article exploring the Hebrew Bible's dependence on ancient Near Eastern literature, Peter Machinist speaks eloquently about the importance of literary influence and allusion for understanding biblical literature. Machinist does not mention literary structure (that is not his focus), but the same words could be applied to it:

> What emerges . . . with no little clarity is how intricate and far-reaching "influence" and "allusion" could be. They were not simply fun and games, the leisurely and ultimately pointless luxury of an excessively learned authorship, although in places they could partake of this—but much more, a device to promote, even to create meaning. They stand, in other words, as a demonstration that the messages of the biblical passages in question would not be nearly so variegated, so nuanced, and yet so forceful were they not in some way appropriations of and often reactions to another text, or tradition, or custom. If such "influence" and "allusion" are a foundational feature of all human communication, they had a particular visibility in the ancient Near East and the Hebrew Bible that belonged to it, where writing was not only restricted, but also traditional: the point even in innovation was not to break, at least openly, with the works of the past, but to find some continuity with them. "Influence" and "allusion" in this context thus become not a possibility, but a necessity.[1]

I certainly could not have put the point better.

---

1. Machinist, "To Refer or to not Refer," 222.

APPENDIX

Ruth in the Jewish and Christian Bibles

THE FIRST AND MOST obvious thing that needs saying here is that the Jewish Bible and the Christian Bible are not the same. More than this, there are different Christian Bibles: the Protestant Bible, the Catholic Bible, and the Orthodox Bible. When I say that they are different, what I mean to say is that they each include a different list of books and present them in a different order. This appendix compares the contents and arrangement of books that make up the Jewish Bible and three of the Christian Bibles.

Ruth in the Jewish Bible

Every Jewish Bible is divided into the same three parts: *Torah*, *Nevi'im*, and *Ketuvim*, or (in English) Law, Prophets, and Writings. Based on the first letter of the names for each of the three parts, the Jewish Bible is also referred to as the TaNaK (or *Tanak*). Twenty-four books make up the Jewish Bible. This number has been largely fixed since the dawn of the fifth century CE.[1]

---

1. St. Jerome, in the late fourth century, asserted that only a minority of Jews held that the *Tanak* contained twenty-four books. He claimed that Ruth was considered by most to be part of Judges and Lamentations to be part of Jeremiah, but many scholars are suspicious of this assertion. Whatever the case, Jerome's calculation brings the count of biblical books to twenty-two, or one book for each letter of the Hebrew alphabet. See Gallagher and Meade, *Biblical Canon Lists from Early Christianity*, 197–216.

Appendix

The following is the most common table of contents for a *Tanak*, the one you would find at the beginning of almost any printed Hebrew Bible:

Torah	*Nevi'im*	*Ketuvim*
Genesis	Joshua	Psalms
Exodus	Judges	Job
Leviticus	Samuel	Proverbs
Numbers	Kings	**Ruth**
Deuteronomy	Isaiah	Song of Songs
	Jeremiah	Kohelet (Ecclesiastes)
	Ezekiel	Lamentations
	Book of the Twelve*	Esther
		Daniel
		Ezra-Nehemiah
		Chronicles

* The so-called "Minor Prophets"

To someone who is only familiar with the Christian Bible, the most obvious difference other than the arrangement of books, is that some books are divided differently. Samuel and Kings are each one book not two. The minor prophets are a single book called The Twelve, and Ezra-Nehemiah is one book not two. With respect to Ruth, though, it is the order of books that is more interesting. Though the order of books in the Torah is invariable and the Prophets nearly so, there is some variety in the order of the *Ketuvim*. Most often, Ruth appears after the Song of Songs or the book of Proverbs.

The five books from the *Ketuvim* that are read aloud in their entirety in the synagogue liturgy—Song of Songs, Ruth, Lamentations, Kohelet, and Esther—are called the *Megillot*, that is, the "scrolls." They are always grouped together in the Jewish Bible, as they are in the list provided above. In the list above, Ruth is first in the *Megillot*, immediately after Proverbs. This arrangement puts the *Megillot* in chronological order. Ruth is set in the days of the Judges. Song of Songs and Kohelet are attributed to Solomon. Lamentations mourns the fall of Jerusalem to the Babylonians, and Esther is set during the Persian period.[2] Those editions that placed Ruth between

---

2. This is the order that is the most common in manuscripts of the Hebrew Bible and was usually found in printed editions of the Hebrew Bible before 1937.

Song of Songs and Lamentations do so for a liturgical reason. They are in the order in which they are read during the year, from Spring to Winter: Song of Songs for Passover, Ruth for Shavuot, Lamentations for Tisha B'Av, Kohelet for Sukkot, and Esther for Purim.

In *Excursus 11*, I detailed the similarities between Ruth and the Strong Woman of Proverbs 31. It must be admitted that those similarities could be overlooked by many readers. When Ruth is located immediately after Proverbs in the canon, it is juxtaposed with Proverbs 31. This makes it more likely that readers will observe the relationships between them. This is one of the things the different arrangements of books can accomplish. They make different sets of connections and allusions more evident, underscoring some of the ways that biblical books have been coordinated with one another. The same is true if one reads Ruth immediately after Judges, as it appears in Christian Bibles.

Ruth in Christian Bibles

The three great traditions of Christianity—Orthodox, Catholic, and Protestant—have different Bibles. The Old Testament books that they share appear in a similar order, but they each include a slightly different list of books. The Protestant Bible is the shortest, and the Orthodox Bible is the longest. The following chart represents the arrangement that is typical for each tradition:

Orthodox[3]	*Catholic*	*Protestant*
Genesis	Genesis	Genesis
Exodus	Exodus	Exodus
Leviticus	Leviticus	Leviticus
Numbers	Numbers	Numbers
Deuteronomy	Deuteronomy	Deuteronomy
Joshua	Joshua	Joshua
Judges	Judges	Judges

3. There is no way to generalize about the canons of the Orthodox churches, because they have never collectively committed themselves to one list of canonical books. For a historical review of the issue, see Pentiuc, *Eastern Orthodox Tradition*, 101–34. The list provided here is essentially that of the Synod of Jerusalem in 1672.

Appendix

Orthodox[3]	Catholic	Protestant
Ruth	Ruth	Ruth
1 Kingdoms (1 Samuel)	1 Samuel	1 Samuel
2 Kingdoms (2 Samuel)	2 Samuel	2 Samuel
3 Kingdoms (1 Kings)	1 Kings	1 Kings
4 Kingdoms (2 Kings)	2 Kings	2 Kings
1 Paraleipomenon (1 Chronicles)	1 Chronicles	1 Chronicles
2 Paraleipomenon (2 Chronicles)[4]	2 Chronicles	2 Chronicles
1 Ezra (2 Esdras)	Ezra	Ezra
2 Ezra (Ezra)	Nehemiah	Nehemiah
Nehemiah	Tobit	Esther
Tobit	Judith	Job
Judith	Esther	Psalms
Esther	1 Maccabees	Proverbs
1 Maccabees	2 Maccabees	Ecclesiastes (Kohelet)
2 Maccabees	Job	Song of Songs
3 Maccabees	Psalms	Isaiah
Psalms[5]	Proverbs	Jeremiah
Job	Ecclesiastes (Kohelet)	Lamentations
Proverbs of Solomon	Song of Songs	Ezekiel
Ecclesiastes (Kohelet)	Wisdom of Solomon	Daniel
Song of Songs	Ecclesiasticus (Sirach)	Hosea
Wisdom of Solomon	Isaiah	Joel
Wisdom of Sirach	Jeremiah	Amos
Hosea	Lamentations	Obadiah
Amos	Baruch	Jonah

4. Includes Prayer of Manasseh.
5. Includes Psalm 151.

Ruth in the Jewish and Christian Bibles

Orthodox[3]	Catholic	Protestant
Micah	Ezekiel	Micah
Joel	Daniel	Nahum
Obadiah	Hosea	Habakkuk
Jonah	Joel	Zephaniah
Nahum	Amos	Haggai
Habakkuk	Obadiah	Zechariah
Zephaniah	Jonah	Malachi
Haggai	Micah	
Zechariah	Nahum	
Malachi	Habakkuk	
Isaiah	Zephaniah	
Jeremiah	Haggai	
Baruch	Zechariah	
Lamentations of Jeremiah	Malachi	
Epistle of Jeremiah		
Ezekiel		
Daniel[6]		

In all three of the Christian traditions, Ruth follows Judges. This abides by the order in the Septuagint, the pre-Christian Jewish translation of the Hebrew Bible into Greek.[7] Locating Ruth after Judges and before Samuel could be dismissed as nothing more than an attempt to place the historical books in chronological order. They are in chronological order (more or less), but that is not the *only* reason for this placement of Ruth. As we saw in *Excurses* 5 and 7, Ruth is bound in an intertextual relationship with Judges 19–21 and 1 Samuel 1–2. When Ruth is placed after Judges and before Samuel, the relationships between the books are more easily perceived.[8]

---

6. Includes Susanna, Bel and the Dragon, and the Song of the Three.
7. Köhlmoos, "Textual History of Ruth."
8. See also Jobling, "Home," 125–39.

Bibliography

Adelman, Rachel. "Seduction and Recognition in the Story of Judah and Tamar and the Book of Ruth." *Nashim: A Journal of Jewish Women's Studies & Gender Issues* 23 (2012) 87–109.

Alter, Robert. *The Art of Biblical Narrative.* New York: Basic, 1981.

Anderson, Francis I. "Israelite Kinship Terminology and Social Structure." *BT* 20 (1969) 29–39.

Auerbach, Eric. *Mimesis: The Representation of Reality in Western Literature.* Translated by W. R. Trask. Princeton, NJ: Princeton University Press, 1953.

Bal, Mieke. *Lethal Love: Feminist Literary Readings of Biblical Love Stories.* Bloomington, IN: Indiana University Press, 1987.

Barmash, Pamela. "Achieving Justicet through Narrative in the Hebrew Bible: The Limitations of Law in the Legal Potential of Literature." *ZABR* 20 (214) 181–99.

Beattie, D. R. G. *Jewish Exegesis of the book of Ruth.* JSOTSup 2. Sheffield, UK: Sheffield Academic Press, 1977.

———. "Ruth III." *JSOT* 5 (1978) 39–51.

Belkin, Samuel. "Levirate and Agnate Marriage in Rabbinic and Cognate Literature." *JQR* 60 (1969) 275–329.

Ben-Porat, Ziva. "The Poetics of Literary Allusion." *PTL: A Journal of Descriptive Poetics and Theory of Literature* 1 (1976) 105–28.

Berlin, Adele. *The JPS Bible Commentary: Esther.* Philadelphia: Jewish Publication Society, 2001.

———. "Legal Fiction: Levirate *cum* Land Redemption in Ruth." *JAJ* 1 (2010) 3–18.

———. "On the Bible as Literature." *Prooftexts* 2/3 (1982) 323–37.

———. *Poetics and Interpretation of Biblical Narrative.* Winona Lake, IN: Eisenbrauns, 1994.

Berman, Joshua. *Narrative Analogy in the Hebrew Bible: Battle Stories and Their Equivalent Non-Battle Narratives.* Leiden: Brill: 2004.

Bernstein, Moshe J. "Two Multivalent Readings in the Ruth Narrative." *JSOT* 50 (1991) 15–26.

Bibliography

Bertman, Stephen. "Symmetrical Design in the Book of Ruth." *JBL* 84 (1965) 165–68.
Beyer, Andrea. *Hoffnung in Bethlehem: Innerbiblische Querbezüge als Deutungshorizonte im Ruthbuch*. BZAW 463. Berlin: de Gruyter, 2010.
Black, Armstrong. *Ruth, a Hebrew Idyl*. London: Hodder Stoughton, 1906.
Bledstein, Adrien J. "Female Companionships: If the Book of Ruth Were Written by a Woman...." In *Feminist Companion to Ruth and Esther*, edited by Athalya Brenner, 116–33. Sheffield, UK: Sheffield Academic Press, 1993.
Blenkinsopp, Joseph. "The Family in First Temple Israel." In *Families in Ancient Israel*, edited by Leo Perdue et al., 48–103. Louisville, KY: Westminster/John Knox, 1997.
Bohlen, Reinhold. "Die Rutrolle: Ein aktuelles Beispiel narrativer Ethik des Alten Testament." *Trierer Theologische Zeitschrift* 101 (1992) 1–19.
Bos, Johanna. "Out of the Shadows: Genesis 38; Judges 4:17–22; Ruth 3." *Semeia* 42 (1988) 37–67.
Braulik, Georg. "The Book of Ruth as Intra-Biblical Critique on the Deuteronomic Law." *AT* 19 (1999) 1–20.
Brichto, Herbert Chanan. "Kin, Cult, Land, and Afterlife—A Biblical Complex." *HUCA* 44 (1973) 9–24.
Bridge, Edward. "Self-Abasement as an Expression of Thanks in the Hebrew Bible." *Biblica* 92 (2011) 255–73.
Burrows, Millar. "The Marriage of Boaz and Ruth." *JBL* 59 (1940) 445–54.
Bush, Frederic W. *Ruth, Esther*. WBC 9. Dallas, TX: Word, 1996.
Campbell, Edward F. Jr. *Ruth: A New Translation with Introduction, Notes, and Commentary*. AB 7. New York: Doubleday, 1975.
Carmichael, Calum M. *Sex and Religion in the Bible*. New Haven, CT: Yale University Press, 2010.
———. *Women, Law, and the Genesis Traditions*. Edinburgh: Edinburgh University Press, 1979.
Chapman, Cynthia. *The House of the Mother: The Social Roles of Maternal Kin in Biblical Hebrew Narrative and Poetry*. ABRL. New Haven, CT: Yale University Press, 2017.
Claassens, L. Juliana M. "Resisting Dehumanization: Ruth, Tamar, and the Quest for Human Dignity." *Catholic Biblical Quarterly* 74/4 (2012) 659–74.
Cohen, Mordechai. "*Ḥesed*: Divine or Human? The Syntactic Ambiguity of Ruth 2:20." In *Ḥazon Naḥum: Essays in Honour of Dr. Norman Lamm*, edited by Yaakov Elman and Jeffery Gurock, 11–38. New York: Yeshiva University Press, 1997.
Cohen, Shaye J. D. *The Beginnings of Jewishness: Boundaries, Varieties, Uncertainties*. Berkley: University of California Press, 1999.
Corbett, George, and Heather Webb. "Introduction." In *Vertical Readings in Dante's Comedy*, vol. 1, edited by George Corbett and Heather Webb, 1–11. Cambridge: Open Book, 2015.
Daube, David. *Ancient Jewish Law, Three Inaugural Lectures*. Leiden: Brill, 1981.
———. "Consortium in Roman and Hebrew Law." *JR* 62 (1950) 71–91.
Davies, Eryl. "Inheritance Rights and the Hebrew Levirate Marriage, Part 1." *VT* 31 (1981) 138–44.
———. "Inheritance Rights and the Hebrew Levirate Marriage, Part 2." *VT* 31 (1981) 257–68.
Dell, Katharine. "Didactic Intertextuality: Proverbial Wisdom as Illustrated in Ruth." In *Reading Proverbs Intertextually*, edited by Katharine Dell and Will Kynes, 103–14. LHBOTS 629. London: Bloomsbury T. & T. Clark, 2019.

Bibliography

Demsky, Aaron. "Names and No-Names in Ruth." In *These are the Names: Studies in Jewish Onomastics*, vol. 1, edited by Aaron Demsky and Joseph R. J. Tabory, 27–37. Ramat-Gan, Israel: Bar Ilan University Press, 1997.

Dommershausen, Werner. "Leitwortstil in der Ruthrolle." In *Theologie im Wandel: Festschrift zum 150 jährigen Bestehen der Katholisch-Theologischen Fakultät Tübingen 1817–1967*, 394–407. Herausgegeben von der Katholische-theologischen Fakultät and der Universität Tübingen. Munich: Wewel, 1967.

Doniger, Wendy. *The Bedtrick: Tales of Sex and Masquerade*. Chicago: University of Chicago Press, 2000.

Douglas, Mary. *Thinking in Circles: An Essay on Ring Composition*. New Haven, CT: Yale University Press, 2007.

Ebach, Jürgen. "Fremde in Moab—Fremde aus Moab: Das Buch Ruth als politische Literatur." In *Bibel und Literatur*, edited by Jürgen Ebach and Richard Faber, 277–304. Munich: Fink, 1995.

Ellingworth, Paul, and Amoo Mojola. "Translating Euphemisms in the Bible." *BT* 37 (1986) 139–43.

Eskanazi, Tamara, and Tikva Frymer-Kensky. *The JPS Bible Commentary: Ruth*. Philadelphia: Jewish Publication Society, 2011.

Feldmann, Louis. "Conversion to Judaism in Classical Antiquity." *HUCA* (2003) 115–56.

Fewell, Danna Nolan, and David M. Gunn. *Compromising Redemption: Relating Characters in the Book of Ruth*. Louisville, KY: Westminster-John Knox, 1990.

Fisch, Harold. "Ruth and the Structure of Covenant History." *VT* 3 (1982) 425–37.

Fischer, Irmtraud. *Rut*. HTKAT. Freiburg: Herder, 2001.

———. "Von der Vorgeschichte zur Nachgeschichte: Schriftauslegung in der Schrift—Intertextualität—Rezeption." *ZAW* 125 (2013) 143–60.

Fishbane, Michael. *Biblical Text and Texture: A Literary Reading of Selected Texts*. Oxford: OneWorld, 1998.

Fowler, Jeaneane. *Theophoric Personal Names in Ancient Hebrew: A Comparative Study*. JSOTSup. Sheffield, UK: Sheffield Academic Press, 1988.

Fox, Michael. *Proverbs 10–31: A New Translation with Introduction and Commentary*. AB 18B. New Haven, CT: Yale University Press, 2009.

Frevel, Christian. *Das Buch Rut*. NSKAT. Stuttgart: Verlag Kath. Bibelwerk: 1992.

Gage, Warren. "Ruth upon the Threshing Floor and the Sin of Gibeah: A Biblical-Theological Study." *WTJ* 51 (1989) 369–75.

Gallagher, Edmon, and John Meade. *The Biblical Canon Lists from Early Christianity: Texts and Analysis*. Oxford: Oxford University Press, 2017.

Garsiel, Moshe. *Biblical Names: A Literary Study of Midrashic Derivations and Puns*. Ramat Gan, Israel: Bar Ilan University Press, 1991.

———. *The First Book of Samuel: A Literary Study of Comparative Structures, Analogies and Parallels*. Ramat Gan, Israel: Revivim, 1985.

Gerleman, Gillis. *Rut—Das Hohelied*. BKAT 18. Neukirchen: Neukirchen-Vluyn, 1965.

Glanzman, George S. "The Origin and Date of the Book of Ruth." *CBQ* 21 (1959) 201–7.

Glover, Neil. "'Your People, My People': An Exploration of Ethnicity in Ruth." *JSOT* 33 (2009) 293–313.

Gnilka, Joachim. *Das Evangelium nach Markus*. 3nd ed. EKKNT II/2. Zurich: Benzinger and Neukirchener, 1989.

Goitein, Shlomo D. "Women as Creators of Biblical Genres." *Prooftexts* 8/1 (1988) 1–33.

Bibliography

Goh, Samuel. "Ruth as a Superior Woman of חיל: A Comparison between Ruth and the 'Capable' Woman in Proverbs 31:10–31." *JSOT* 38 (2014) 487–500.

Goodman, Martin. *Mission and Conversion: Proselytizing in the Religious History of the Roman Empire*. Oxford: Clarendon, 1994.

Gordon, R. P. "David's Rise and Saul's Demise: Narrative Analogy in 1 Samuel 24–26." *TB* 31 (1979) 37–64.

———. "Simplicity of the Highest Cunning: Narrative Art in the Old Testament." *SBET* 6/2 (1988) 69–80.

Gow, Murray D. *The Book of Ruth: Its Structure, Theme, and Purpose*. Leicester, UK: Apollo, 1992.

Green, Barbara. "The Plot of the Biblical Story of Ruth." *JSOT* 7 (1982) 55–68.

———. "A Study of Field and Seed Symbolism the Biblical Story of Ruth," PhD diss. Graduate Theological Union, 1980.

Greengus, Samuel. *Laws in the Bible and in Early Rabbinic Collections: The Legal Legacy of the Ancient Near East*. Eugene, OR: Cascade, 2011.

Greenstein, Frederick. *When Brothers Dwell Together*. New York: Oxford University Press, 1994.

Grossman, Jonathan. "'Dynamic Analogies' in the Book of Esther." *VT* 59 (2009) 394–414.

Hals, Ronald M. *The Theology of the Book of Ruth*. FBBS 23. Philadelphia: Fortress, 1969.

Harm, Harry J. "The Function of Double Entendre in Ruth Three." *JTT* 7 (1995) 19–27.

Hayes, Christine. *Gentile Impurities and Jewish Identities: Intermarriage and Conversion from the Bible to the Talmud*. Oxford: Oxford University Press, 2002.

Holmstead, Robert. *Ruth: A Handbook on the Hebrew Text*. Waco, TX: Baylor University Press, 2010.

Hubbard, Robert Jr. *The Book of Ruth*. NICOT. Grand Rapids: Eerdmans, 1988.

Hyman, Ronald T. "Questions and Changing Identity in the Book of Ruth." *USQR* 39/3 (1984) 189–201.

Jackson, Bernard. "Ruth's Conversion: Then and Now." *JLA* 19 (2011) 53–61.

———. "Ruth, the Pentateuch and the Nature of Biblical Law: In Conversation with Jean-Louis Ska." In *The Post-Priestly Pentateuch. New Perspectives on its Redactional Development and Theological Profiles*, edited by Konrad Schmid and Federico Giuntoli, 75–111. Tübingen: Mohr Siebeck, 2015.

Jackson, Melissa. *Comedy and Feminist Interpretation of the Hebrew Bible: A Subversive Collaboration*. Oxford: Oxford University Press, 2012.

Jakobson, Roman. "Closing Statements: Linguistics and Poetics." In *Style in Language*, edited by Thomas A. Sebeok, 350–377. Cambridge: MIT Press, 1960.

Japhet, Sara. "The Expulsion of the Foreign Women (Ezra 9–10). The Legal Basis, Precedents, and Consequences for the Definition of Jewish Identity." In *"Sieben Augen auf einem Stein" (Sach 3,9)—Studien zur Literatur des Zweiten Tempels; Festschrift für Ina Willi-Plein zum 65. Geburtstag*, edited by Friedhelm Hartenstein and Michael Pietsch, 141–61. Neukirchen-Vluyn: Neukirchener Verlag, 2007.

Jobling, David. "Ruth Finds a Home: Canon, Politics, Method." In *The New Literary Criticism and the Hebrew Bible*, edited by Cheryl Exum and David J. A. Clines, 125–39. JSOTSup 143. Sheffield, UK: JSOT, 1993.

Jones III, Edward Allen. *Reading Ruth in the Restoration Period: A Call for Inclusion*. LHBOTS 605. London: Bloomsbury, 2016.

Joüon, Paul. *Ruth. Commentaire philologique et exégétique*. SB 9. Rome: Pontifical Institute Press, 1986.

Bibliography

Kahn, Geoffrey. "Ketiv and Qere." In *Encyclopedia of Hebrew Language and Linguistics Online*, edited by Geoffrey Khan et al. Leiden: Brill, 2016. http://dx.doi.org/10.1163/2212-4241_ehll_EHLL_COM_00000455

Kellett, Ernst E. *Literary Quotation and Allusion*. Port Washington, NY: Kennikat, 1969.

Klagsbrun, Francine. "Ruth and Naomi, Rachel and Leah: Sisters under the Skin." In *Reading Ruth: Contemporary Women Reclaim a Sacred Story*, edited by Judith Kates and Gail Reimer, 261–72. New York: Ballentine, 1994.

Köhlmoos, Melanie. "Textual History of Ruth." In *Text History of the Bible*, edited by Armin Lange. 6 vols. Leiden: Brill, 2016–20.

Koosed, Jennifer. *Gleaning Ruth: A Biblical Heroine and Her Afterlives*. Columbia: University of South Carolina Press, 2011.

Kosmala, Hans. "גבר." In *TDOT*, vol. 2, 367–82.

Kruger, Paul A. "The Hem of the Garment in Marriage: The Meaning of the Symbolic Gesture in Ruth 3:9 and Ezek 16:8." *JNSL* 12 (1984) 79–86.

Kugel, James. "On the Bible and Literary Criticism." *Prooftexts* 1/3 (1981) 217–36.

Kukharenko, Valeria "Some Considerations about the Properties of the Text." In *Text vs Sentence: Basic Questions of Text Linguistics, First Part*, edited by János Petöfi, 235–44. Hamburg: Helmut Buske, 1979.

LaCocque, André. *Ruth*. Translated by K. C. Hanson. CC. Minneapolis: Fortress, 2004.

Levine, Baruch. "In Praise of the Israelite Mišpaḥa: Legal Themes in the Book of Ruth." In *The Quest for the Kingdom of God*, edited by Baruch Levine and George Mendenhall, 95–106. Winona Lake, IN: Eisenbrauns, 1983.

Linafelt, Tod. *Ruth*. Collegeville, MN: Liturgical, 1999.

Lunn, Nicholas P. "The Deliverance of Rahab (Joshua 2,6) as the Gentile Exodus." *TB* 65/1 (2014) 11–19.

Luz, Ulrich. *Matthew 21–28: A Commentary*. Hermeneia. Philadelphia: Fortress, 2005.

Machinist, Peter. "To Refer or to Not Refer: That Is the Question." In *Subtle Citation, Allusion, and Translation in the Hebrew Bible*, edited by Ziony Zevit, 182–227. Sheffield, UK: Equinox, 2017.

Malamat, Abraham. "The Danite Migration and the Pan-Israelite Exodus-Conquest: A Biblical Narrative Pattern." *Biblica* 51 (1970) 1–16.

Markus, Joel. *Mark 8–16: A New Translation with Introduction and Commentary*. AB 27A. New Haven, CT: Yale University Press, 2009.

McCreesh, Thomas. "Wisdom as Wife: Proverbs 31:10–31." *RB* 95 (1985) 25–46.

Meyers, Carol. "In the Household and Beyond: The Social World of Israelite Women." *Studia Theologica* 63 (2009) 19–41.

———. "'To Her Mother's House': Considering a Counterpart to the Israelite Bêt-aḇ." In *The Bible and the Politics of Exegesis*, edited by David Jobling et al., 39–51. Cleveland, OH: Pilgrim, 1991.

———. "Women in Ancient Israel—An Overview." In *The Torah: A Women's Commentary*, edited by Tamara C. Eskenazi and Rabbi Andrea Weiss, xli–xliii. New York: Union for Reform Judaism Press, 2008.

Michael, Matthew. "The Achan/Achor Traditions: The Parody of Saul as 'Achan' in 1 Samuel 14:24—15:35." *OTE* 26/3 (2013) 730–60.

Morgenstern, Julian. "The Book of the Covenant II." *HUCA* 7 (1930) 19–258.

Niehr, Herbert, and Gert Steins. "שדי." In *TDOT*, vol. 14: 418–46.

Nielsen, Kirsten. *Ruth: A Commentary*. OTL. Louisville, KY: Westminster/John Knox, 1997.

Bibliography

Noble, Paul R. "Esau, Tamar, and Joseph: Criteria for Identifying Inner-Biblical Allusions." *VT* 52 (2002) 219–52.

Novick, Tzvi. "Liturgy and the First Person in Narrative of the Second Temple Period." *Prooftexts* 32 (2012) 269–91.

———. "Wages from God: The Dynamics of the Biblical Metaphor." *CBQ* 73 (2011) 708–22.

O'Connell, Robert H. *The Rhetoric of the Book of Judges.* VTSup 63. Leiden: Brill, 1996.

Osgood, S. Joy. "Women and the Inheritance of Land in Early Israel." In *Women in the* Mellen, 1992.

Ostriker, Alicia. "Ruth and the Love of the Land." *BI* 10/4 (2002) 343–59.

Pentiuc, Eugen J. *The Old Testament in Eastern Orthodox Tradition.* Oxford: Oxford University Press, 2014.

Péter-Contesse, René. "Main, pied, paume? Les noms des extrémités des membres (כף, יד, רגל,), en hébreu et en araméen biblique." *RB* 105 (1998) 481–91.

Plum, Karin Friis. "Genealogy as Theology." *SJOT* 1 (1989) 66–92.

Porten, Bezalel. "The Scroll of Ruth: A Rhetorical Study." *Gratz College Annual of Jewish Studies* 7 (1978) 23–49.

———. "Structure, Style, and Theme of the Scroll of Ruth." *AJSN* 17 (1976) 15–16.

———. "Theme and Historiographic Background of the Book of Ruth." *GCAJS* 6 (1977) 69–78.

Prager, Yossi. "Megillat Ruth: A Unique Story of Torat Ḥesed." *Tradition* 34/4 (2001) 15–22.

Quick, Laura. "The Book of Ruth and the Limits of Proverbial Wisdom." *JBL* 139 (2020) 47–66.

Raskas, Jennifer. "The Book of Ruth: A Contrast to the End of the Book of Judges." *JBQ* 43 (2015) 223–32.

Rauber, D. F. "Literary Values in the Bible: The Book of Ruth." *JBL* 89 (1970) 27–37.

Rendsburg, Gary. "Hebrew Philological Notes (2)." *HS* 40 (1999) 27–32.

Riffaterre, Michel. "Intertextual Representation: On Mimesis as Interpretive Discourse." *CI* 11 (1984) 141–62.

Rofé, Alexander. *Introduction to the Literature of the Hebrew Bible.* Translated by Harvey N. Bock and Judith H. Seeligmann. Jerusalem: Simor, 2009.

Sakenfeld, Katharine Doob. *Faithfulness in Action: Loyalty in Biblical Perspective.* OBT 16. Philadelphia: Fortress, 1985.

Sasson, Jack. *Ruth: A New Translation with a Philological Commentary and a Formalist-Folklorist Interpretation.* Atlanta: Scholars, 1979.

Saxegaard, Kristin Moen. *Character Complexity in the Book of Ruth.* FAT II/ 47. Tübingen: Mohr Siebeck, 2010.

———. "'More Than Seven Sons': Ruth as Example of the Good Son." *SJOT* 15 (2001) 257–75.

Schept, Susan. "Ḥesed: Feminist Ethics in Jewish Tradition." *Conservative Judaism* 57/1 (2004) 21–29.

Schipper, Jeremy. *Ruth: A New Translation with Introduction and Commentary.* AB 7D. New Haven, CT: Yale University Press, 2016.

———. "The Use of *blṭ* in Ruth 3:7." *VT* 66 (2016) 595–602.

Shepherd, David. "Ruth in the Days of the Judges: Women, Foreignness, and Violence." *BI* 26 (2018) 528–43.

Bibliography

Siquans, Agnethe. "Foreignness and Poverty in the Book of Ruth: A Legal Way for a Poor Foreign Woman to be Integrated into Israel." *JBL* 128/3 (2009) 443–52.

———. "Israel braucht starke Männer und Frauen. Rut als Antwort auf spr 31,10–31." *BZ* 56 (2012) 20–38.

Smith, Mark. "'Your People Will Be My People': Family and Covenant in Ruth 1:16–17." *CBQ* 69/2 (2007) 242–58.

Stendebach, F. J. "רגל." In *TDOT*, vol. 13, 309–24.

Sternberg, Meir. *The Poetics of Biblical Narrative: Ideological Literature and the Drama of Reading.* Bloomington, IN: Indiana University Press, 1987.

Stone, Timothy J. "Six Measures of Barley: Seed Symbolism in Ruth." *JSOT* 38 (2013) 189–99.

Sutskover, Talia. "The Themes of Land and Fertility in the Book of Ruth." *JSOT* 34 (2010) 283–94.

Thompson, Thomas, and Dorothy Thompson. "Some Legal Problems in the Book of Ruth." *VT* 19 (1968) 79–99.

Tooman, William A. *The Torah Unabridged: The Evolution and Deployment of Intermarriage Law in the Hebrew Bible.* University Park, PA: Pennsylvania State University Press, forthcoming.

Trible, Phyllis. *God and the Rhetoric of Sexuality.* OBT. Philadelphia: Fortress, 1978.

Trudgill, Peter. *On Dialect: Social and Geographical Perspectives.* Chichester, UK: Wiley-Blackwell, 1983.

Tsevat, Matitiahu. "חלקII." In *TDOT*, vol. 4, 447–48.

Unterman, Jeremiah. "The Literary Influence of the 'Binding of Isaac' (Genesis 22) on 'The Outrage at Gibeah' (Judges 19)." *HAR* 4 (1980) 161–66.

von Wolde, Ellen. "Texts in Dialogue with Texts: Intertextuality in the Ruth and Tamar Narratives." *BI* 5 (1997) 1–28.

Walsh, Jerome. *Style & Structure in Biblical Hebrew Narrative.* Collegeville, MN: Liturgical, 2001.

Weisberg, Dvora E. *Levirate Marriage and the Family in Ancient Judaism.* Waltham, MA: Brandeis University Press, 2009.

———. "The Widow of Our Discontent: Levirate Marriage in the Bible and Ancient Israel." *JSOT* 28 (2004) 403–29.

Wenin André. "La Stratégie Déjouée de Noemi en Rt 3." *EstBib* 56 (1998) 179–99.

Westbrook, Raymond. *Property and the Family in Biblical Law.* JSOTSup 113. Sheffield, UK: Sheffield Academic Press, 1991.

———. "Redemption of Land." *ILR* 6 (1971) 367–75.

Wetter, Anne-Mareike. *"On Her Account": Reconfiguring Israel in Ruth, Esther, and Judith.* LHBOTS 623. London: Bloomsbury, 2015.

Wojcik, Jan. "Improvising Rules in the Book of Ruth." *PMLA* 100 (1985) 145–53.

Wünch, Hans-Georg. *Das Buch Rut.* Neuhausen: Hänssler, 1998.

———. "Ruth, a Proselyte Par Excellence—Exegetical and Structural Observations." *JS* 24 (2015) 36–64.

Zakovitch, Yair. "Intermarriage and Halakhic Creativity: The Book of Ruth." *MFS* 19 (2013) 56–69.

———. *Ruth: Introduction and Commentary.* Mikra Leyisra'el: A Bible Commentary for Israel. Tel Aviv and Jerusalem: Am Oved and Magnes, 1990 (Hebrew).

———. "The Threshing Floor Scene in Ruth." *Shnaton* 3 (1979) 29–33 (Hebrew).

———. "Through the Looking Glass: Reflections/Inversions of Genesis Stories in the Bible." *BI* 1/2 (1993) 139–52.

———. "'A Woman of Valor, *'Eshet Ḥayil'* (Proverbs 31:10–31): A Conservative Response to the Song of Songs." In *A Critical Engagement: Essays on the Hebrew Bible in Honour of J. Cheryl Exum*, edited by David Clines and Ellen van Wolde, 401–13. Sheffield, UK: Phoenix, 2011.

———. *"And You Shall Tell Your Son": The Concept of the Exodus in the Bible.* Jerusalem: Magnes, 1991.

Zenger, Erich. *Das Buch Ruth.* ZBK. 2nd ed. Zürich: Theologischer Verlag Zürich, 1992.

Zevit, Ziony. "Dating Ruth: Legal, Linguistic, and Historical Observations." *ZAW* 117 (2005) 574–600.

Ziegler, Yael. *Ruth: From Alienation to Monarchy.* Jerusalem: Koren, 2015.

———. "'So Shall God Do . . .': Variations of an Oath Formula and Its Literary Meaning." *JBL* 126 (2007) 59–81.

Author Index

Adelman, Rachel, 103n32, 106n37
Alter, Robert, 67n21, 81n45, 82n45, 85n48
Anderson, Francis I., 57n2
Arend, Walther, 81n45
Auerbach, Eric, 2n4, 2n5

Bal, Mieke, 30n27
Barmash, Pamela, 139n50
Beattie, D. R. G., 80n44, 96n18
Belkin, Samuel, 132n32
Ben-Porat, Ziva, 8n15
Berlin, Adele, xvi n2, 10n16, 22n2, 46n68, 138n46, 139n50
Berman, Joshua, 7n13
Bernstein, Moshe, 108n40
Bertman, Stephen, 19n24, 117n58
Beyer, Andrea, 7n13, 54n88, 67n20, 85n50, 101n30, 103n32, 109n43, 121n2
Black, Armstrong, 1n1
Bledstein, Adrien J., 94n13
Blenkinsopp, Joseph, 57n2
Bohlen, Reinhold, 36n42
Bos, Johanna, 103n32
Braulik, Georg, 58n5, 88, 134
Brichto, Herbert Chanan, 54n89, 55n89
Bridge, Edward, 62n14
Burrows, Millar, 133n35
Bush, Frederic W., xvii, 57n3, 59n7, 71n30, 80n44

Braulik, Georg, 58n5, 88n57, 134n38

Campbell, Edward F. Jr., xviii n6, 29n23, 73n33, 77n37, 91n4, 92n4
Carmichael, Calum M., 94n13, 97n19, 103n32
Chapman, Cynthia, 24n10
Claassens, L. Juliana M., 103n32
Cohen, Mordechai, 35n41, 78n39
Cohen, Shaye J. D., 45n63, 45n64, 45n65, 46n66, 47, 48, 88n55, 88n56
Corbett, George, 20n26

Daube, David, 92n5, 96n18, 137n45, 138n48
Davies, Eryl, 133n37
Dell, Katharine, 109n43
Demsky, Aaron, 27n19, 121n1
Dommershausen, Werner, xix n8
Doniger, Wendy, 97n21, 98n22, 103n32, 108n40, 132n29
Douglas, Mary, 5n9

Ebach, Jürgen, 101n30
Ellingworth, Paul, 94n11
Eskenazi, Tamara, xx n12, 36n42, 47n73, 48n74, 61n12, 85n48, 92n5, 97n20, 101n29, 130n23, 130n26, 139n49

Author Index

Feldmann, Louis, 46n66
Fewell, Danna Nolan, 60n11, 96n18
Fishbane, Michael, 2n5
Fisch, Harold, 101n28, 103n32
Fischer, Irmtraud, xxi n14, 19n24, 27n18, 52n81, 54n88, 64n17, 73n33, 101n30, 103n32, 110n43
Fox, Michael, 113n52, 114n53
Fowler, Jeaneane, 28n21
Frevel, Christian, xviii, xix n8
Frymer-Kensky, Tikva, xx n12, 36n42, 47n73, 61n12, 85n48, 92n5, 97n20, 101n29, 130n23, 130n26, 139n49

Gage, Warren, 101n30
Gallagher, Edmon, 147n1
Garsiel, Moshe, 7n13, 24n11, 30n27, 32n32, 67n22, 126n15
Gerleman, Gillis, 29n24, 130n23
Glover, Neil, 48n74
Gnilka, Joachim, 70n27
Goitein, Shlomo D., xvii
Goh, Samuel, 110n43
Goodman, Martin, 45n64
Gordon, R. P., 7n13, 10n17
Gow, Murray D., xviii n7, 130n23
Green, Barbara, 24n9, 109n41, 132
Greengus, Samuel, 24n8, 133n34
Greenstein, Frederick, 132n30
Grossman, Jonathan, 7n13
Gunn, David M., 60n11, 96n18

Hals, Ronald M., 1n2
Harm, Harry J., 106n38
Hawk, L. Daniel, 124n13, 129n22
Hayes, Christine, 87n54
Holmstedt, Robert, xviii n6, 28n21, 35n41, 59n6, 94n12, 126n16
Hubbard, Robert Jr., xviii n6, 46n70, 60n11
Hyman, Ronald T., 48n73

Jackson, Bernard, 47n71, 121n3, 134n38
Jackson, Melissa, 96n15
Jakobson, Roman, 39n49
Japhet, Sara, 47n71

Jobling, David, 63n15, 64n17, 151n8
Jones, Edward Allen, III, 82n47, 101n30, 116n57, 137n44
Joüon, Paul, 99n24

Kahn, Geoffrey, 123n8
Kellett, Ernst E., 6, 6n12
Klagsbrun, Francine, 127n17
Köhlmoos, Melanie, 151n7
Koosed, Jennifer, 60n11, 115n56
Kosmala, Hans, 57n3
Kruger, Paul A., 96n18
Kugel, James, xvi n2
Kukharenko, Valeria, 34n38

LaCocque, André, 115n56
Levine, Baruch, 139n50
Linafelt, Tod, 99n25

Machinist, Peter, 146
Malamat, Abraham, 7n13
Markus, Joel, 69n26
McCreesh, Thomas, 110n43
Meade, John, 147n1
Meyers, Carol, 31n29, 31n30, 32n31
Michael, Matthew, 7n13
Mojola, Amoo, 94n11
Morgenstern, Julian, 106n36

Niehr, Herbert, xxii n15
Nielsen, Kirsten, 109n41, 131n27
Novick, Tzvi, 15n22, 67

O'Connell, Robert H., 73n32
Osgood, S. Joy, 135n39
Ostriker, Alicia, 22n2

Paine, Thomas, 1
Pentiuc, Eugen J., 149n3
Péter-Contesse, René, 94n11
Plum, Karin Friis, 130n25
Porten, Bezalel, 19n23, 27n18, 32n31, 67n22, 82n47, 101n29, 109n41, 117n58
Prager, Yossi, 33n35

Quick, Laura, 110n43

Author Index

Raskas, Jennifer, 61n13, 64n17, 73n33, 74n35
Rauber, D. F., 49n76
Rendsburg, Gary, 29n23
Riffaterre, Michel, 82n46
Rofé, Alexander, xviii n6

Sakenfeld, Katharine Doob, 35n40
Sasson, Jack, xviii n6, xviii n7, 1n3, 30n28, 50n77, 60n11, 122n6, 124n13, 138n49, 139
Saxegaard, Kristin Moen, 29n25, 128n19
Schept, Susan, 36n43
Schipper, Jeremy, 59n7, 99n25, 101n29, 101n30, 139n49
Shepherd, David, 60n11
Siquans, Agnethe, 23n5, 88n57, 110n43, 111n44, 112n48, 112n49
Smith, Mark, 40n52, 67n20
Steins, Gert, xxii n15
Stendebach, F. J., 94n13
Sternberg, Meir, 6n11
Stone, Timothy J., 109n41
Sutskover, Talia, 24n9, 109n41

Thompson, Dorothy, 134n38
Thompson, Thomas, 134n38

Tooman, William A., 87n54
Trible, Phyllis, 44n62, 107n39
Trudgill, Peter, 15n21
Tsevat, Matitiahu, 122n3

Walsh, Jerome, 19n25
Webb, Heather, 20n26
Weisberg, Dvora E., 38n45, 132n29, 132n31
Wenin André, 101n30
Westbrook, Raymond, 24n6, 24n8, 134n38, 135n40, 136n42, 138n47
Westermark, Edward, 132n29
Wetter, Anne-Mareike, 48n75
Wojcik, Jan, 124n13, 127n17
Wolde, Ellen von, 101n30, 103n32
Wünch, Hans-Georg, 47n73, 48

Zakovitch, Yair, xxi n14, 7n13, 8n14, 52n80, 52n81, 64n17, 73n33, 85, 100n26, 101n30, 106n38, 110n43, 112n47, 113n52, 114n54
Zevit, Ziony, xviii n6
Ziegler, Yael, 22n2, 27n18, 40n51, 47n72, 55n90, 64n17, 73n33, 85n51, 101n30, 103n32, 117n48

Ancient Document Index

OLD TESTAMENT/ HEBREW BIBLE

Genesis

1:22	131
2:4	131n27
2:15	32n33
2:23	54n87
2:24	54, 55n91
4:1–16	26
4:1	4n6
4:2	133
4:17	4n6
4:25	4n6
5:25–29	26
6:9	131n27
8:9	32n33
9:21	93
12	26, 67
12:1–4	100
12:1	66
12:2–3	66
12:3	58n5
12:7	100
12:10–20	26n17
13–19	98
13	100
13:5–15	100
13:8–11	99
13:8	133
13:9	101
13:11	101
14:16	133
14:25	122n3
15:1	66
15:2	133
16	26n17
16:7–14	82
17:7	44
18:2–3	62
19	72, 101
19:14	99
19:19	33n36, 34
19:30–38	29, 90, 98, 99, 101
19:30	99n25, 99
19:31–32	99
19:33	4n6, 99
19:34	99
19:35	4n6, 99
19:36–38	99
19:36	99n25, 99
19:37	29
20	98
20:1–18	26n17
20:4	106n38

Genesis (*cont.*)

Reference	Page
20:6	60n11
20:13	34
21	26n17
21:10	96n16
21:12	96n16
24–25	85
24	xix, 32n31, 81, 82, 85n48
24:2–3	85, 86
24:4	83
24:5	84
24:7	83
24:8	84
24:10	83
24:11–20	83
24:12	33n36, 83
24:14	33n36, 83, 84
24:15	83
24:16	4n6, 84
24:21–17	83
24:22–24	35
24:22	84
24:23–24	83
24:23	59, 59n9
24:24	101
24:27	33n36, 83
24:28	32n31
24:31–33	83
24:31	83
24:34–51	84
24:37–38	85, 86
24:39	84
24:49	83
24:53	84
24:54	83, 84
24:58	84
24:60	84
24:61	60n10, 84
24:67	83, 84
25:1–6	72n31
25:21	84
25:25	27
25:26	27
25:27–34	42
26–28	xix
26	26
26:29	60n11
27:1—28:5	42
27:1–29	90
27:1	116
27:4	116
27:6–17	116
27:10	116
27:12	116
27:17–18	116
27:18	116
27:19	116
27:28	116
27:36	27
28	79
28:1–5	86
29	81, 82, 85, 86
29:1–3	85
29:4–6	85
29:4	133
29:9	85
29:10	85, 101
29:11–12	85
29:11	86
29:13–14	85
29:14	54n87
29:15–35	90n1
29:15–30	98
29:15	133
29:31–35	127
30:14–21	90n1
30:15	4n6
30:25–43	41
31	41, 43, 44
31:1–3	41
31:22–30	41
31:42—32:1	41–42
31:43	42
31:43–50	7
31:53	42
31:55	42n55
32:1	42n55
32:25	60n11, 94n11
32:32	94n11
33:3	62
33:19	121n3
34	26n17
34:3	68

Ancient Document Index

36:1	131n27	2:5	60n10
36:8	27	2:7–9	128–29
36:9	131n27	2:10	27
37:2	131n27	2:15	86
37:4	133	2:16–23	86
37:27–28	122n7	2:16–17	86
37:35	68	2:17	27, 86
37:36	122n7	2:18–22	86
38	98, 102, 132n31, 133, 137	2:22	86
		3:7	50
38:1–30	90	3:17	50
38:1	103	4:25	94n10
38:2	103	4:31	50
38:6	103, 104	5:3	60n11
38:7–10	103	6:6	78
38:7	104	6:7	44
38:8	104	10:3	50
38:11	31, 102, 103, 104	12:19	46
38:12–14	92n5	12:43–45	46
38:12–13	104	15:13	78
38:12	104	16	56n1
38:13	104	20:2	44n60
38:14–19	29	20:6	33n36, 35
38:14	104	20:10	96n16
38:15–19	104	20:17	96n16
38:15	104	20:23	93
38:16	104, 104n34	20:26	93
38:20	104	21:7	93n16
38:22	104	21:7–8	122n7
38:23	104	21:16	122n7
38:24	104	21:20	93n16
38:26	4n6, 104, 104n34	21:26–27	93n16
38:27–29	104	21:32	93n16
38:29	104	21:35	122n7
39:12	76n36	22:2	122n7
39:21	33n36	22:15	4n6
41–46	26	22:21	31
42:35–38	106	22:26–27	108n40
43:8–10	106	29:46	44n60
43:9	106	34	xix
43:30–34	106	34:6–7	33n36
45:4	122n7	34:7	35
50:21	68		
		Leviticus	
Exodus		11:44	44n60
2	81, 82, 85	15:33	4n6
2:3	128n21	17:8	46

Leviticus (cont.)

18:2	44n60
18:4	44n60
18:6–18	38n45
18:6	106n38
18:7	93
18:9	93
18:10	93
18:11	93
18:14	106n38
18:15	93, 105n35
18:17	93
18:18	93
18:19	93, 106n38
18:21	44n60
18:29	105n35
19	58
19:9–10	57, 58
19:10	58
19:12	44n60
20:10–21	38n45
20:17	93
20:18	93
20:21	131
21:12	44n60
22:13	31
22:18	46
23:22	57
25:6	96n16
25:8–22	134
25:23–28	134–36
25:23	80n43
25:25–28	78, 80
25:27	135
25:29–34	134
25:29	78
25:35–38	134
25:39–54	134
25:39–43	78n41, 80n43
25:47–55	78
25:47	122n7
26:1	44n60

Numbers

3:13	44n60
3:41	44n60
6:24–26	59n7
12	xix
12:1	86n52
27:5–11	24
27:8–11	24n6
27:8–10	133n33, 135
31:17	4n6
31:18	4n6
35:16–29	78n40
36:5–9	24

Deuteronomy

2:9	101n27
2:19	101n27
4:20	44
4:37–38	105
5:14	96n16
5:21	96n16
7	xix
7:9	33n36, 35
7:25–26	87n53
9:10	87
10:4	87
10:14–17	105
10:18	31
12:12	96n16
12:18	96n16
12:31	87n53
15:17	96n16
16:11	88n58
18:16	87
18:18	122n3
19:4–13	78n40
21:10–14	108n40
21:19	109n42
22:13–14	108n40
22:13	96n16
22:14	106n38
22:22	4n6
22:23–24	103n31, 108n40
22:28–29	108n40
23	62, 88
23:1	97n19
23:4	61
23:3–8	61–62, 87
23:4–7	61–62

Ancient Document Index

23:4-9	25n12, 61, 87, 88, 89, 89n59	11:39	4n6
24	58	13-16	71
24:1-4	108n40	15:12	60n11
24:19-22	57, 58	17-18	71
24:22	58	17:6	75
25	137	18:1	75
25:5-10	79, 106, 121, 131-34, 139	18:7	60n11
		18:20	95
25:5-6	37, 37n44	18:25	60n11
25:6	123n10	19-21	71, 72, 72n32, 151
25:9-10	106, 136	19-20	72, 75
25:9	125	19	75
25:10	106	19:1-2	31, 73
26:11	88n58	19:1	27, 75
28:57	4n7, 93	19:2	76
28:65	32n33	19:3	68, 74, 76
29:10-11	88n58	19:6	73, 76
33:8	34	19:9	73, 76
		19:11	76
		19:12	72, 75
Joshua		19:21-22	73
1:14	57	19:22	4n6, 75, 76
2	9	19:25-28	75
2:12	33n36	19:25	4n6, 76
6	9	19:27	74, 76
6:24-25	88n58	19:29-30	72n32
7	9	19:29	76
9:19	60n11	21	75
15:18	4n6	21:3	74
23	xix	21:6	74
23:12	88n56	21:17	74
24:32	121n3	21:11	4n6
		21:15-24	75
Judges		21:25	27, 75
1:14	62	**Ruth**	
1:24	33n36	1	40, 44n61, 64, 73
2	xix	1:1-22	21
3	23	1:1-5	11, 12, 16, 18, 21, 22, 23n4, 25n12, 61, 122, 126n15
3:12-30	25n13		
3:24	4n7, 93		
4:16-23	90n1	1:1	50, 63, 73, 98n23, 99, 103
4:21	99		
6:12	57	1:2	73, 98n23, 99, 103, 141, 142, 142n52
8:21	60n11		
9:18	133	1:3-5	140
11	23		

Ruth (*cont.*)

1:3	25n12, 38n46, 50, 57, 142n52
1:4	29n26, 64, 85, 103, 141, 142, 142n52
1:5	21, 38n46, 50, 99, 103, 140, 142n52
1:6—4:17	12
1:6–22	12, 16, 22, 30, 53n86
1:6–7	5n10, 14, 18, 21
1:6	xix n8, 14, 23, 29n26, 42, 76, 140, 141
1:7	xix n8, 29n26, 42, 43n58, 141, 142
1:8–19	18, 21
1:8–9	31, 36, 37, 83
1:8	xix n8, 29n26, 33, 35, 36, 42, 43, 54, 57n2, 73, 76, 103, 141
1:9	32n33, 42, 54, 61, 67, 86, 91, 91n3, 94
1:10–14	28, 37, 79, 102
1:10	xix n8, 42, 141
1:11–13	36, 54, 63, 100, 103, 136
1:11–12	xix n9, 38n47
1:11	xix n8, 29n26, 42, 50, 61, 91n2, 141
1:12	xix n8, 29n26, 38n47, 42, 91n2, 92
1:13	29n26, 61, 119, 140, 141
1:14–19	99
1:14–18	76
2:14–16	126
1:14	29n26, 54, 61, 86
1:15–19	39
1:15	xix n8, 42, 54, 124n12
1:16–18	7, 104
1:16–17	53, 70, 85, 88
1:16	xix n8, 29, 29n26, 42, 141
1:17	42, 47, 100, 101, 142
1:18	44
1:19–22	18
1:19–21	21, 48–49
1:19	16, 59, 140
1:20–21	xxii, 14, 16, 50, 52, 53, 119, 137, 140
1:20	28
1:21	xix n8, 42, 127, 141
1:22	xix n8, 5n10, 21, 29n26, 29n26, 42, 53, 56, 61n13, 68, 83, 87, 98n23, 101n29, 141
2:1–23	12, 16, 56
2:1–3	18, 56, 117, 118, 119
2:1–2	12
2:1	21, 30, 56, 105, 108n40, 111, 142n52
2:2	13, 29n26, 29n26, 58, 62, 67, 87, 91n2, 98n23
2:3	56, 83, 111, 119, 121n3
2:4–17	18, 117
2:4–7	58–59, 118
2:4	42, 83, 107
2:5–6	83
2:5	29n26, 96
2:6	29n26, 87, 98n23
2:7	71, 110, 141
2:8–13	60, 109, 118
2:8–9	60, 71, 108n40
2:8	29n26, 55n91, 76, 91n2, 107, 110
2:9	60n11, 61, 71, 75, 76, 77n37, 77n38, 81, 83, 86, 91n4, 98
2:10	29n26, 43n58, 62, 63, 67, 68, 77n38, 87, 114
2:11–12	7, 12, 66, 77n38, 83, 87, 104, 107, 108n40
2:11	55n91, 67n22, 83
2:12	96, 107
2:13—3:8	xix n9,

Ancient Document Index

2:13	29n26, 63, 64, 67, 73, 76, 96, 107, 110	3:7–9	104
2:14–16	83	3:7–8	99
2:14	62, 64, 68, 70, 71, 73, 109, 118, 141	3:7	73, 73n34, 76, 84, 94, 96, 98, 104, 106n38
2:15	60n11, 76	3:8–9	95
2:15–19	111	3:8	76, 94, 106n38
2:15–17	71, 118	3:9–15	109
2:15–16	71, 75, 86, 108n40	3:9–13	75
2:16	17, 55n91, 109, 112	3:9–11	84
2:17	110	3:9–10	115, 116
2:18–23	18, 77, 91, 117, 118, 121	3:9	29n26, 107, 108, 116, 119, 139
2:19–20	84	3:10–14	118
2:19	15, 16, 42, 142n52	3:10–13	85, 100, 106–7
2:20–22	91	3:10–11	30, 108n40, 110
2:20	29n26, 33, 35, 42, 55n91, 64, 67n22, 78, 79, 80, 83, 97, 108n40, 117, 119, 128	3:10	15, 16, 29n26, 33, 36, 42, 64, 83, 84, 91n2, 110, 112, 116, 117, 126
		3:11–15	74–75, 126–27
2:21	29n26, 55n91, 87, 98n23	3:11	29n26, 91n2, 105, 109, 111
2:22–23	12	3:12	111, 128
2:22	29n26, 29n26, 76, 77n37, 92n4, 112	3:13–15	84
		3:13	104, 119, 125, 138, 139, 141
2:23	13, 13n19, 55n91, 91, 104, 141	3:14–15	3, 4, 108, 108n40, 118
3	4, 90, 98, 102	3:14	3, 74, 76, 92, 94, 104, 104n34, 106n38
3:1–18	12, 13, 16, 90		
3:1–6	18		
3:1–5	91, 97n19	3:15	17, 84, 106n38, 111, 116, 126
3:1–4	91, 99, 116, 117, 118, 128		
3:1–2	13, 91	3:15–18	117, 118
3:1	13, 13n20, 29n26, 91n2, 94, 112	3:16–18	13, 18, 114–15, 117
		3:16	29n26, 91n2
3:2	13, 13n19, 104, 116	3:17	126
3:3–4	104	3:18	13n20, 29n26, 85, 91n2, 121, 141
3:3	104, 104n34, 106n38		
		4:1–22	120
3:4	94, 95, 106n38, 110, 116, 142	4:1–17	12, 13, 16
		4:1–6	128
3:5	93, 116	4:1–3	14
3:6–15	117	4:1–2	18, 111, 120
3:6–9	118	4:1	24n8, 30, 79, 141, 141, 142
3:6–7	95, 104		
3:7–15	18	4:2	109n42, 141

Ancient Document Index

Ruth (cont.)

4:3–12	18
4:3–9	142
4:3–4	121–22
4:3	14, 98n23, 138, 138n47, 142n52
4:4	138, 141
4:5–6	137n43
4:5	29n26, 74, 87, 98n23, 111, 141, 142n52
4:6–10	74n35
4:6	121, 125
4:7–10	28n22, 125, 136, 142
4:7	136
4:9–10	103, 104
4:9	142n52
4:10	28n22, 29n26, 74, 87, 98n23, 125, 128m 129, 137, 137n43, 142, 142n52
4:11–17	127n18
4:11–15	110
4:11–13	99
4:11–12	8, 84
4:11	29n26, 111, 142, 142n52
4:12	29n26, 63, 104, 109
4:13–17	16, 18
4:13	29n26, 47, 64, 65, 84, 103, 127, 140, 142n52
4:14–17	21, 22, 140
4:14–15	14, 16, 53, 112
4:14	140
4:15	22, 29n26, 52, 63, 110, 112, 141
4:16–22	xviii
4:16–17	128
4:16	129
4:17–22	75, 104
4:17	27, 64, 129, 137, 140, 142
4:18–22	11, 12, 16, 18, 63, 129
4:22	27, 119

1 Samuel

1–2	63, 129, 151
1	63
1:2	64
1:4–5	64
1:8	63
1:11	96n16
1:12–18	64
1:17	63, 64
1:18	63, 64
1:19–20	64
1:19	4n6
2:1–10	65n18
2:7–10	130
2:19	63
2:22	4n6
6:9	60n11
8	28
8:4–5	26
8:7	28
8:11–18	28
9:11–26	82
10:5	60n11
14	9
15:6	33n36
16:19	130
18:22	99
19:11–18	9
20:1—22:1	90n1
20:8	33n36, 34
20:14	33n36
20:41	62
20:42—21:1	133
20:42	41
21:3	121
22:8	93
22:17–18	60n11
24:4	4n7, 93
24:5	99
25:23	62
25:25	26
25:28	96n16
25:31	96n16
25:41	96n16
25:42	60n10
27:3	43
29	43
30:26	29

2 Samuel

1:26	133
2:5	33n36
3:8	34
5:1–5	75
5:1	54n87
7:8	130
7:15	33n36
9:1–12	133
9:7	33n36
11	98
11–12	xix, 9, 90n1
12:7–8	130
13:14	4n6
13:23–33	43
13:28	73n34, 95
14:1–20	90n1
14:10	60n11
14:21–22	62
14:30–31	122n3
15	41, 44
15:13–16	43
15:19–20	43
15:21	43
16:4	62
16:21	4n6
20:3	4n6
23:11	121n3
25:7	60n11
25:15	60n11

1 Kings

1:4	4n6
1:11	130
2:25	60n11
2:31–32	60n11
3:6	33n36
8:65	87
9:13	133
11	xix
11:1–3	88n56
11:3	72n31
11:28	57
14:31	130
16:31	130
17:10–16	31
20:31	33n36, 34
21:7	95
22	43, 44
22:4	40

2 Kings

3	43, 44
3:1–3	130
3:7	40
6:8	121
9:22	130
9:25–26	122n3
15:20	57
18:27	4n7, 93
24:14	57

1 Chronicles

12:9	57
17:7	130

2 Chronicles

3:17	30n27
7:8	87
20:5	87
20:14	87
32:32	33n36
35:26	33n36

Nehemiah

3:5–6	76n36
5:13	87
13:1–3	88
13:14	33n36

Esther

1:10–12	95
1:10	73n34
1:11	95n14
2:9	33n36
2:17	33n36
5:9	73n34, 95
8:17	46

Ancient Document Index

Job

1–2	52n81
1:13–19	51
1:21	53
2:12–13	51
3:5	78
7:11	52n83
10:1	52n83
13:26	52n83
24:21	31
27:2	52
31:7	94n11
42	52n81
42:7–10	53
42:12–13	52
42:13	52n79

Psalms

5:8	33n36
13:5	33n36
22:23	87
22:26	87
23:6	33n36
31:7	33n36
40:10	69n27
52:8	33n36
78:70	130
86:16	96n16
89:19–21	65n18
89:49–52	105
94:6	31
107:32	87
132:1	105
132:5	105
136:1–26	35
136:10	35
136:15	35
136:17–20	35
151	150n5

Proverbs

1:20–33	113
2:16–29	113
2:16	114
5:1–23	113
5:10	114
5:15–20	114
5:20	114
6:20–35	113
6:25	113
6:24	114
6:29	60n11
7:1–27	113
7:5	114
7:11–27	113
7:19–20	113
8:1–36	113
9:1–12	113
9:13–18	113
12:4	109, 111
20:6	33n36
20:16	114
20:28	33n36
22:14	113n51
23:27	113n51, 114
27:2	114
27:13	114
30:1–33	110
31	109–14, 149
31:1–31	110
31:3	110
31:10–31	108, 110, 127
31:10	109, 110
31:11	112, 113
31:12	110
31:15	60n10, 110
31:16	111, 138n47
31:17	29, 111
31:18	110
31:20	111
31:23	109n42, 110, 111, 113
31:26	35, 110
31:27	110
31:29	110
31:30–31	110
31:30	113
31:31	110

Ecclesiastes/Kohelet

11:2	122n3

Ancient Document Index

Canticles/Song of Songs
3:4	32n31
5:5	94n11
8:2	32n31

Isaiah
1:12–17	31
6:2	94n10
7:20	4n7, 93
8:3	106n38
10:2	31
14:7	13n20
22:13	73n34, 95
26:5	60n11
36:12	93
40:1–2	68n24
40:6	33n36
47:3	93
54:8	33n36
54:10	33n36
55:3	33n36
56–66	65
57:1	33n36
58:8	94n11
58:10	94n11
63:7	33n36

Jeremiah
2:2	33n36, 60n11
6:15	31
7:6	31
13:22	76n36
29	xix
30:22	44
31:3	33n36
31:33	44
32:6–15	135–36, 138
32:9–12	135–36
32:9	135, 138
33:14–26	xviii

Lamentations
1:3	32n33

Ezekiel
13:14	93
14:11	44
16:8	96
16:25	4n7, 93
16:36–37	93
18:6	106n38
23:10	93
34:23–31	xviii
36:28	44

Daniel
1:9	33n36
9:4	35
10:6	94

Hos
2:21	33n36
4:1	33n36
9:1–17	90n1
12:4	27
12:6	33n36

Amos
4:7	122n3
5:12	109n42
9:7	66n19

Jonah
1:14–16	46

Micah
6:8	33n36
7:18	35
7:20	33n36

Zechariah
8:8	44
8:23	44n60
12:7–14	xviii

Malachi
2	xix

Ancient Document Index

NEW TESTAMENT

Matthew
10:4	69
24:23	69n27
26:14	69, 70
26:16	69, 70
26:25	69
26:21–23	69
27:3	69

Mark
3:19	69
14:10–11	69
14:10	70
14:18–20	69

Luke
6:16	69
22:6	69
22:21	69n25
22:48	69

John
4:4–42	82
6:71	69
12:6	70
13:2	69, 70
13:21–30	70
13:29	70
18:2	69
18:5	69

ANCIENT AND MEDIEVAL JEWISH DOCUMENTS (NON-BIBLICAL)

2QRutha	xix n10
4QRutha	xix n10

Florilegium
1:4	88n55

Judith
14:10	45n65

Midrash Lekaḥ Tov	114n54
Midrash Ruth Rabba	29, 33, 33n35, 47, 92n9, 101n30, 103n32, 111n46, 121n1
Midrash Ruth Zuta	92n9, 103n32
Mishnah	88n56
Pesharim	xv n1
Pesiqta Rabbati	64n17

Talmud	88n56
T. Megillah 14a	65
T. Megillah 14b	88n58

Temple Scroll
39:5	88n55
40:6	88n55

Tobit	xvi, 90n1
4–8	82

Zohar	47n71

ANCIENT AND MEDIEVAL CHRISTIAN DOCUMENTS (NON-BIBLICAL)

Dante, *Divine Comedy*	20n26
Hugh of St Chair, *Postils*	46n70
Isadore of Seville, *On Ruth*	46n69